the plays of Bruce Mason

the plays of Bruce Mason

a survey · John Smythe

Playmarket
and
Victoria University Press

VICTORIA UNIVERSITY PRESS
Victoria University of Wellington
PO Box 600 Wellington
vup.victoria.ac.nz

PLAYMARKET
PO Box 9767
Wellington 6141
www.playmarket.org.nz

First published in 2015 by Victoria University Press in association with Playmarket

A catalogue record for this book is available from the National Library of New Zealand.
The Plays of Bruce Mason: a survey / John Smythe
Includes bibliographic references and index
ISBN 9781776560554

Playmarket receives major funding from

creative nz
Arts Council of New Zealand Toi Aotearoa

Every effort has been made to ensure the information in this book is accurate. The authors/publishers will be happy to rectify any errors at the earliest opportunity. Unless otherwise credited, all images are property of the Mason family estate.

Cover: Rena Owen in *The Pohutukawa Tree*, directed by Colin McColl, Auckland Theatre Company; photograph by Michael Smith

Design by Cansino & Co
Foreword by Belinda Robinson
Editing, indexing and production by Whitireia Publishing
Printed and bound by Ligare, Auckland

This book was taken from manuscript to bookshelf by students of the Whitireia New Zealand publishing programme, who worked on editing, production and design For more information about our editing and publishing training, visit www.whitireiapublishing.co.nz

To persistent playwrights everywhere

CONTENTS

FOREWORD

When my father Bruce Mason finally succumbed to a rare type of cancer on New Year's Eve 1982, he was at the peak of his creative powers. He had recently completed four television dramas, was working on a screenplay for *The End of the Golden Weather* with Ian Mune and gestating a novel which, had it been written, might have exploded onto the New Zealand literary scene with a force similar to that of Nabokov's *Lolita,* a work that he (Bruce) greatly admired.

He may have hoped that this extension of his artistic reach (beyond writing for the stage) would make his work more relevant to his contemporaries. But sadly, he was never to achieve the recognition that was his due during his lifetime. Although it was studied in secondary schools for many years, it was not until the second professional production, by Auckland Theatre Company in 2009, that *The Pohutukawa Tree* achieved its status as one of New Zealand's finest plays. Others of similar merit have not yet been seen on stage, even in amateur productions.

Perversities of fate have also stymied all the family's attempts to initiate a biography of Bruce. My mother was determined that Michael King was the only worthy biographer; but he died tragically in a road accident just at the point when he might have had the time to take it on. Then, after my mother's death in 2008, I commissioned another biographer, who later had to abandon the project due to ill health.

Meanwhile, in 2005, theatre critic, playwright and friend John Smythe began to plan a book covering fifty years of New Zealand theatre, with the working title *NZ On Stage*. He decided to limit the scope of this book to full-length plays that had been professionally produced, beginning with *The Pohutukawa Tree*. However, he told me, as he read Bruce's other plays and contemplated how to write them up, he realised the only way to do his work justice was to devote a whole book to it.[1]

After years of painstaking research and juggling the demands of the book with his other commitments, John has completed what I consider to be a definitive critique of my father's work, with just enough background on his life to contextualise the plays, but not enough to deter a future biographer. Quite the reverse: I hope that John's book will create renewed interest in what was a remarkable life, lived in vivid 3D and documented in exquisite detail.

In late 2014, when he had almost finished writing his book, John sent me the manuscript and gallantly accepted all my comments. In constant communication over the following months, we both went on a journey of discovery at the Victoria University library, poring over a significant portion of Bruce's voluminous correspondence.

Amongst other revelations, a previously undiscovered play came to light. An allegorical, therapeutic piece, it was clearly not intended for performance or publication at the time. Nevertheless, John and I agreed that this play and the circumstances that provoked it needed to be included in the book; so John had to write a whole new chapter at the last minute.

Working through this process with John has been enlightening for me, and my appreciation of my father's plays, especially the lesser-known ones, has grown enormously. I paraphrase John's conclusion: if Bruce Mason and his plays had been fully appreciated in his lifetime, who knows where New Zealand theatre would be now.

And my addition to that is: if John Smythe's appraisal of Bruce Mason's plays is fully appreciated now, New Zealand theatre will be greatly enriched by their future production.

Belinda Robinson

PROLOGUE

Being a playwright in post-WWII New Zealand was a triumph of the imagination over the obstacles of our limited self-awareness, low self-esteem and rampant cultural cringe. Although many playwrights had preceded Bruce Mason, few pursued the cause with such dogged persistence in the face of almost insuperable odds. In 1973 Mason wrote: 'I once heard a West Indian writer asked what it was like to be a writer in her archipelago, [and] she replied: "Like being a shoemaker where everyone goes barefoot." So it has sometimes seemed to me as a playwright, and doubtless also to my colleagues, of whom there are now many.'[1]

The modern era of the professional New Zealand playwright began in 1955 with Bruce Mason's *The Pohutukawa Tree* which emerged from a decade of writing that included semi-autobiographical prose pieces destined for solo performance and short plays and sketches. In 1959 with *The End of the Golden Weather*, Mason cracked the conundrum of how to turn his vocation into a profession: by being the play's sole actor as well as its playwright. Many of the larger-cast plays that followed were premiered by amateur theatre societies and never made it onto the professional stage.

After returning from war service in the Navy, an experience that 'afforded a good deal of time for random reflection' and in the wake of seeing a variety of theatre in London, Mason would articulate—in his 'Theatre in Danger' correspondence with Dr John Pocock (a political science lecturer at the University of Otago)—the three conditions he believed were crucial for the development of a creative theatre. Fully discussed in chapter two, they emphasise the primary importance of written plays, continuity of purpose and a love of theatre (the true meaning of amateur) as the driving force.[2]

Many amateur groups would strive to meet these conditions in the 1950s and 'a love of theatre' remained the primary driving force in the evolution of professional theatre practice. As a family man, albeit married to a fully employed doctor, Mason had 'day jobs' and other paying work while pursuing his true vocation, and this remains common to all but one or two playwrights. The enduring difficulties of maintaining a fulltime career in professional theatre within New Zealand have also led experienced actors and other theatre practitioners to work in non-paying or low-paying co-operative productions because they love the project and want to keep working to maintain 'match fitness'. A large proportion of new home-grown works continues to be created by passionate practitioners in circumstances where payment, if any, falls well below the minimum, let alone average, wage.

That said, much more could be done by the better-resourced theatre companies to support and sustain New Zealand playwrights. It is a sad fact of history that during Bruce Mason's lifetime (he died on the last day of December 1982, aged sixty-one) and for more than a quarter of a century following, most of New Zealand's professional theatres wilfully disregarded his plays while paying regular homage to Russian, Norwegian, British and American playwrights whose skills he matched. This failure was in part remedied by the Auckland Theatre Company's productions of *The Pohutukawa Tree* (2009), an ensemble version of *The End of the Golden Weather* (2011) and *Awatea* (2012), all of which proved highly successful both critically and at the box office. In 2015, many more of his plays remain in limbo.

The major objective with this book is to critically survey the extraordinary body of work Bruce Mason left us. Chapter one aims to sketch in the 'state of play' in New Zealand theatre practice over the century before Mason came on the scene. Chapter two covers biographical details that are relevant to Mason's evolution as a playwright, and chapter three develops that theme by examining the semi-autobiographical prose works he would later bring into solo performance. The remaining chapters pay individual attention, in chronological order, to the works the playwright wrought until his premature death.

The personal is clearly political in all Mason's sketches and plays. The instantly recognisable and sometimes idiosyncratic characters he has created, and their intimate, familial and social relationships within a wide range of given circumstances, give us invaluable access to an extraordinary depth and breadth of New Zealand culture, distilling the particular in ways that make it universal and timeless. His lifelong enquiry into what it is to be a man in New Zealand permeates most of his work. Likewise, the distinctions of being Māori or Pākehā, Kiwi or not, male or female, single or married, domesticated or itinerant, accepted or rejected, recur as abiding themes. Mason also explores lesbian relationships in two of his final scripts. However, apart from a passing reference by a pregnant Miranda to two male flatmates who were 'busy . . . with each other' (in *The Light Enlarging / Virtuous Circle*) gay male characters and relationships are conspicuous by their absence. This is a poignant omission because as well as being a husband and father, Mason was secretly gay. The illegal status of male homosexuality meant its existence was either absent or coded in the works of such playwrights as Oscar Wilde, Noel Coward and Tennessee Williams. There are few hints in the plays of Bruce Mason apart, perhaps, from the adolescent incident with Ginger Finucane, recalled in *Not Christmas, but Guy Fawkes*. We can only wonder what else he might have written in a parallel universe or a more accepting era.

CHAPTER ONE

THE STATE OF THE HOME-GROWN PLAY PRE-1953

Theatre has enlivened the landscape of Aotearoa New Zealand for centuries. There is an inherent theatricality in many aspects of Māori culture. It was with the rise of British immigration soon after the Treaty of Waitangi was signed that theatre in its European mode began to grace stages in the new colony. The following overview of early New Zealand playwriting is underpinned by the scholarship of Howard McNaughton, Peter Downes, Peter Harcourt, John Thomson, Adrian Kiernander, Sebastian Black, and Sue Dunlop. Bruce Mason also passed critical judgement on some of his predecessors while finding his own voice and establishing his career as a playwright. The century of theatre practice from 1850 to 1950 saw big stage spectacles give way to more realistic and intimate conventions and styles. In the process of considering these works, it is interesting to note how topics and themes were treated that Mason would go on to address in his plays.

19th-century Melodrama and Spectacle

In *The Oxford History of New Zealand Literature in English*, Howard McNaughton identifies the first original New Zealand play as *Marcilina, or The Maid of Urnidorpt*, a two-act play written by James Marriott, manager of Wellington's Britannia Saloon. It premiered in July 1848, and was followed by a 'Shakespearean festival' and a return to English melodrama, with acting assistance from members of a locally stationed regiment.[1] In 1863 the twenty-eight-year-old co-founder/owner and editor of the *Otago Daily Times*, Julius Vogel (who was also a local councillor and destined to become prime minister of New Zealand), dramatised English writer Mary Elizabeth Braddon's new best-selling novel *Lady Audley's Secret*. It was produced to great acclaim although, as theatre historian Peter Downes notes, the adaptation was mysteriously attributed to 'a gentleman resident in Dunedin'.[2]

McNaughton cites 1870–1871 as a time when an exceptionally large number of local scripts were performed in Auckland: 'though they comprised only a fraction of the total output of Auckland theatres'.[3] He describes *Philo Maori, or New Zealand As It Is* (1870) by A Western, as raising 'complex issues to do with the consciousness of New Zealand audiences.' The 'central action of lust, massacre and betrayal' is balanced with 'the portrayal of the Pakeha Maori and a situation of intermarriage.' The ignorance most Pākehā shared about traditional Māori culture was revealed by the critic for the *New Zealand Herald*:

> Had it not been for the novelty of several 'real Maoris', who played the parts of savages, the piece would have been a complete failure, but these gentlemen kept the audience in a pretty good humour by their dance—the first of which by-the-way, was anything but a pleasing exhibition—and general movements.

With a little more cultural awareness, the *Daily Southern Cross* critic took issue with:

> Its simplistic portrayal of drunken Maori, cowardly constabulary, and lustful Europeans, arguing that these were neither typical nor the cause of wars, that the reality of such massacres was too recent a memory for them to be burlesqued, and that the whole work amounted to a 'libel upon Maoris'.

The critic described the final tableau as 'representing a young and very pretty Britannia very triumphant, amidst flags and crimson fire, with Maoris sticking their heads into the dust in token of subjection'.[4]

While three of the four acts of Laurence Booth's *Crime in the Clouds* (1871) are set in England, a clandestine marriage and romantic intrigue bring the key characters to New Zealand where they become involved in the Land Wars, and experience torture and burning at the stake. 'The New Zealand act included specific historical allusions,' writes McNaughton, 'with Booth himself playing the part of von Tempsky, whose actual death and Hauhau cremation in 1868 may have formed the basis of the tribal torture scene. Since the action recalled such a recent past, the use of Maori actors (remarkable in itself at the time) must have contributed to an atmosphere of topicality.' The final act of retribution involved 'a knife attack by a jealous rival, ending with the victim being hurled from a balloon hovering twelve feet above the stage.' Booth's satirical farce *Guided by the Auckland Public, or The Fortunes of a New Chum* followed a few months later. McNaughton describes it as 'sufficient to antagonise part of the Auckland public'. Other home-grown entertainments included an anonymous satire of local politicians, entitled *The Tomahawk, or Auckland and its Insolvent Laws* (1870) and FL Davey's topical farce *Potagold's Deep* (1871) which, according to McNaughton, was 'ostensibly about the courtship of a sailor's supposed widow . . . but also accommodating observations on [as the *New Zealand Herald* put it], "the City Board, the railway, the scrip mania, Queen Street sewer, and other subjects that possess special interest to an Aucklander".'[5]

McNaughton records that in 1879, under the pseudonym 'Grif', Mr Griffen of Wanganui wrote the first local play to be published in New Zealand. Described as a 'New Grand Semi-Maori Christmas Pantomime', the extravaganza's full title was *Kainga of the Ladye Birds, or Harlequin Prince Tumanako, the Fair Ataahua, and the Demon of Colonial Finance.*[6] Wellington's Academy of Music presented it in December 1879 and according to Peter Harcourt, in *Fantasy and Folly—The Lost World of New Zealand Musicals 1880–1940*, it was adapted from an English original based on the 'Ladybird, Ladybird' nursery rhyme. 'In style and content *Kainga* matched all the conventions of burlesque,' writes Harcourt. 'Its strange amalgam of topical allusions, pantomime characters and New Zealand settings strongly suggests an effort to reconcile thoughts of "home" with the reality of a new life in the antipodes.' He sums up the plot from the *Evening Post* review:

> How Prince Tuamanako* chose his bride Princess Ataahua, daughter of Rangatira, Queen of the Kainga and mother of the Ladye Birds—Papanoa, Tupare, Kanapa, Reka and Kua.* Their love was nearly thwarted by the

> tactics of Koura te Kino, the Demon of Colonial Finance, who ordered Whiro, a fiery spirit from Taupo, to set fire to Rangatira's whare. In a spectacular finale the blaze was doused by the Wellington cadets, led by 'a dear little boy, four years old.' This airy fantasy was heavily larded with topical gags and political allusions, as in a song 'Zealandia the Free', sung to the air 'Erin my Country.'
>
> *The names were all carefully chosen: for instance Tumanako means hope, Ataahua beauty, Rangatira chief, Kanapa gleaming, Tupare a garland, Reka sweetness, and Koura te Kino may be translated as 'the bad crayfish.'[7]

Koura also means gold, so 'bad gold' is equally valid for the Demon of Colonial Finance.

Harcourt records that Wellington journalist HB Bridge,[8] born in New Zealand and educated in England, wrote a number of plays, including *Gareth and Lynette*, *The Very Witty Diggings* (making a pun of 'Terawhiti') and *Women's Parliament*. Most notable was *The Monarch of Utopia*, with music by FW Jones, which premiered at the Wellington Opera House in 1893. Described by Harcourt as 'written in a style strongly reminiscent of WS Gilbert [and] chockfull with puns and brash satire', it questioned the colony's attachment to monarchs, knights of the realm, and their ladies, and lampooned politicians. However, although the *Evening Post* championed it as 'a clever local work, locally produced, locally mounted and locally interpreted . . .', it made a significant loss, prompting the *Otago Witness* critic P Rompter to observe (15 September 1893):

> Truly, Messrs Jones and Bridge have found, even in their humble efforts, that the lot of the prophet in his own country is a hard one . . . There is decided evidence of talent in *The Monarch of Utopia* but playgoers, who like their opinions second-hand 'from the other side', exclaim, "Can anything good come out of our own city? Never!" And they stay away . . .

Harcourt (writing in the 1990s) saw this as 'convincing proof of the "cultural cringe" which became a lasting legacy of the colonial era and persists to this day.'[9]

Englishman George Darrell worked as a reporter on the West Coast before moving to Christchurch, becoming an actor and writing his first play, *Transported for Life* (1876). He then moved to Australia (where it was set) to become an Australasian actor, manager and playwright. His play *The Pakeha* (1890), derived from his West Coast experiences, was wholly set in New Zealand, with the role of 'a cavalier stage journalist' written for himself. McNaughton records that the play's qualities were advertised as being 'of the sensational order, replete with exciting scenes and incidents, the most notable being the sticking up of the gold escort on the route between Christchurch and Hokitika. In this scene a coach and horse will be driven on stage, with mounted troopers.'[10] Sensational spectacle, it seems, was the antidote to cultural cringe.

London-born actor, playwright and theatre manager George Leitch gained quite a reputation in Australia and New Zealand. In 1883 he accepted an engagement as a 'low comedian' with the theatrical firm Williamson, Garner and Musgrove before going on to adapt and produce Marcus Clarke's novel *For the Term of His Natural Life*. After much financial and logistical struggle, Leitch's sensational five-act melodrama, *The Land of the Moa*, finally opened at the Wellington Opera House in July 1895. It went on to enjoy the most extensive tour to date of any locally set melodrama. Adrian Kiernander, who resurrected, edited and introduced a surviving text for Victoria University Press (1990), suggests the script owes something to a novella called *Over the Sea with a Sailor* by Walter Besat, with whom Leitch had previously collaborated, although *Over the Sea* went to the east coast of the United States' deep south before pitching its villain from a bridge into Niagara Falls.[11]

McNaughton describes *The Land of the Moa* thus:

> The action takes place in New Zealand in the period of the Land Wars, and involves a complex structure of intrigue, revenge, and romance . . . Historical Maori characters . . . were fictionalised, presumably to allow more narrative freedom, but the resultant characterisation is close to the stereotypes of stock company melodrama. Leitch's concern for immediacy is reflected in the way the first scene was always set in the town in which the company was playing, with completely repainted

> scenery. The final two acts involve the dispensation of natural justice as the characters converge on the boiling mud-pools of Rotorua and then happen to be present at the Tarawera eruption . . . Its main impact was as a scenic spectacular, with an impressive reconstruction of the famous Pink and White Terraces (destroyed in the 1866 eruption), the lowest of which were strong enough to support actors and horses. There were three 'practical' thermal pools, but the geyser produced only a cascade of 'rice and spangles.' The eruption scene was not the only one to use pyrotechnical sensation: earlier [at the end of Act III] a bridge was blown up as the villain rode over it on his horse, in a scene which also used a real waterfall, a 'fount of fire', and an airborne flock of alarmed waterfowl.[12]

Kiernander asserts this handwritten scene 'is almost certainly a late addition to the play . . . and it was never performed; there is no reference to this scene in any reviews or publicity'. A different bridge scene advertised as 'The Leap for Life', and consisting of 'the escape of the Black Angel jumping a horse across a chasm 22 feet wide at a height from the stage of 15 feet', was devised for the Melbourne season.[13] Kiernander also observes that:

> The major Maori characters are treated sympathetically for the time, even perhaps romantically . . . The Maoris are portrayed as having sincere and apparently justified grievances over the questions of land and their treatment at the hands of the Pakeha. They are intelligent and compassionate in their handling of the English characters who fall into their control, and it is a Maori character, and a woman at that, who is given the honour of dispatching the white, male (American) villain.

Few of the colonists, Kiernander observes, would have shared the notion that reconciliation between Māori and the settlers was only possible through the restoration of lands to their original owners.[14]

Other stage entertainment through the Land Wars, gold rushes and further settlement by colonisers into the new century was largely characterised by melodramas (mostly from Britain, America and Australia), burlesque, music hall and vaudeville (which sometimes included locally written sketches and songs), operettas and operatic recitals. Gilbert and Sullivan, and Oscar Wilde were popular and so was Shakespeare, or excerpts from his plays, at least, which were usually mounted to showcase the talents of famous performers. This was the age of the entrepreneurial actor-managers and showbiz family dynasties, where names such as Buckingham and Foley were followed by Caradini, Simonsen, Rickards, Fuller, (JC) Williamson, Holt and Pollard.[15] While stars and their egos were doubtless key drivers, commercial imperatives would have largely determined the productions they programmed.

Early 20th-century Drama: Between the Wars

Theatre historian John Thomson agrees that the small amount of drama written in New Zealand before 1920 'followed the popular recipes for melodrama and spectacle, though there was also a lively line in satirical burlesque which lived on into [university] capping concerts.' Here is how he marks the transition into more realistic theatre following WWI:

> The start of the new drama is marked by Alan Mulgan's book with the carefully phrased title, *Three Plays of New Zealand* (1922); in the preface James Shelley expressed the hope that these plays might 'presage the development of an adequate means of expressing the growth of our national consciousness.'[16]

But McNaughton takes issue with the parallels Shelley draws between Mulgan and the Australian realist Louis Esson[17] who, with his amateur Pioneer Players, had come to be seen as a keystone in building a distinctively Australian theatre:

> Compared with Esson's whole-hearted commitment to an Australian drama, Mulgan's gesture towards national identity is at best tentative. *For Love of Appin* depicts a Cockney migrant in backblocks New Zealand cushioning a feud between her homesick Scottish husband and a Stranger who turns out to be his boyhood enemy. New Zealand is a land of egalitarian opportunity where the old world social hierarchy is neutralised or inverted: the Stranger comes from Highland gentry,

> but is now reduced to a drunken beggar. Interestingly, it is uncertain whether it is in the name of Scottish or New Zealand hospitality that the men retreat to the whisky bottle; there is no strong affirmation of a new society welding itself together. In *The Daughter*, the educated wife of a dairy farmer is visited by an old university friend whom she almost married; the drama pivots on the disillusionment of impoverished rural life for a woman. References to farming and to the universities indicate that the play is located in New Zealand, but its main impact is in its brutal undercutting of glamourised images of colonial country life. In *The Voice of the People* a reactionary New Zealand member of parliament proposes marriage to a woman who is about to blackmail him before standing as a Labour member herself. The satirical thrust is mainly against the man, whose discourse locates him firmly in the world of English politics, but again there is little suggestion of a more relevant local alternative emerging.[18]

Nevertheless, Mulgan's depictions and critiques of New Zealand life raise valid questions and offer relevant challenges to audiences as they attempt to mature their nationhood. As such, the comparison with Australia's Louis Esson seems fair.[19]

Before considering further the relatively modest-in-scale home-grown works presaged by Mulgan's early sortie, mention must be made of a major play by Gisborne-born-and-raised Merton Hodge. Having become a stage-struck frequenter of JC Williamson shows when his family moved to Auckland during WWI, Hodge studied medicine in Otago and was a locum at Wellington Hospital when he felt the fringe of the Napier earthquake. This precipitated his first attempt to write a play for English actress and Noel Coward favourite Gertrude Lawrence. Peter Harcourt writes:

> Read today, *Earthquake* seems like a somewhat fevered combination of Noel Coward's decadent Mayfair and Drury Lane's epic melodramas. It starts in a sophisticated London drawing room . . . and continues on the deck of an ocean liner bound for New Zealand. Bridget, the neglected wife of a 'something-in-the-City' type, has a shipboard romance with Peter, a 'younger-son-off-to-the-colonies-to-make-good' type. The scene then changes to the living room of a prosperous sheep farmer's home in

Hawkes Bay, described in great detail by Hodge. Act III opens in the lounge of the Masonic Hotel in Napier, where Bridget and Peter have spent the night of 2–3 February 1931. Had the play been produced (apparently Gertrude Lawrence was interested but it came to nothing), and had the earthquake scene been realised in the way Hodge describes it, the spectacle would probably have had more impact than its moral resolution, whereby Peter is killed and Bridget survives to be reunited with her husband in a 'romantic corner at Claridge's.'[20]

Undeterred, Hodge sailed to Britain as a ship's doctor and, stuck in a cold and cheerless Edinburgh, began writing a play called *As It Was in the Beginning* which, after a trial run at London's Arts Theatre (thanks to his influential friends), was renamed *The Wind and the Rain*. Harcourt argues it was a New Zealand play in all but setting:

The New Zealand play that got away: Celia Johnston and Robert Harris in *The Wind and the Rain*, St Martin's Theatre, London, 1933. ALEXANDER TURNBULL LIBRARY

> The play dealt with the maturing of a young medical student during his university years [in Edinburgh], and his affaire with a sculptress living in the same city. This girl, Anne Hargreaves, says of herself, 'I'm that awful thing—a colonial . . . from New Zealand. My father is a doctor there. I don't expect you've ever heard of it outside a butter advertisement! But we're not all "in butter", you know!'
>
> That is one of the play's few direct references to New Zealand, but its whole spirit of student camaraderie and ebullience can only have come from Merton's own days at Otago [University].[21]

The Wind and the Rain opened in Manchester in October 1933, transferred to London's St Martin's Theatre to both critical and popular acclaim, and established a new record with its thousand-performance run. It played six months in Berlin, four months in Paris and then enjoyed further success on Broadway. Harcourt reports that the New York *Evening Post* critic claimed, 'Mr Hodge has written some of the best scenes of undergraduate pleasure and worry that have been set upon the New York stage . . . it is these scenes which are the most winning feature of Mr Hodge's script.' Given Harcourt's description of *The Wind and the Rain* as the New Zealand play that got away, and the relative lack of success suffered by Hodge's later London plays—which, according to McNaughton, were somewhat Noel Cowardesque in their pretensions ('prurience compounded with a well-made morality'), or unfashionably 'grandiose in scale' by London standards—one could argue they suffered from his cultural dislocation.[22]

Drama Post-WWII

Remaining resident in New Zealand did not necessarily make playwrights less susceptible to Anglocentricity. The first four plays of Claude Evans, for example, privately produced in Christchurch from 1946 to 1949, were neither about nor set in New Zealand. Bruce Mason took issue with this in a 1956 *Landfall* review, having by that time written three short plays and a playful operetta, and the first draft of *The Pohutukawa Tree*, all set in New Zealand:

> [Claude Evans' plays] are set in Hertford, London, near London, and China, with excursions to Buckinghamshire. This interests me, because the plays I wrote in my teens also had the *mise-en-scene* in London, or within thirty miles of the metropolis. I should like to say that certainly neither I nor, no doubt, Mr Evans wrote our plays with our eyes firmly set on the London market. We may have had our dreams of sudden and dazzling success, but I think in our hearts we knew that if our plays were produced, they would be on the amateur stages of large New Zealand towns . . . If I may speak here for Mr Evans too, we clearly felt when we began writing for the theatre that there was not sufficient resonance in the raw themes provided in our own land to make any sort of play about them. One must, after all, be sure of whom one is writing for: paradoxically, it seemed easier for us to write about England, a consciousness of which was the one area of common experience we could assume in our audience, than about say, Christchurch, which could easily be esoteric in Wellington . . . [and] there simply cannot be in one century of continuous occupation a sufficient body of raw experience which might be shaped into art. So I argued, so I take it, did Mr Evans. And yet we were hamstrung by this situation. For what would one imagine the plays of a young man to be like who had never been to England, yet wrote pieces purporting to say something of life in it, in entirely the same terms as English dramatists? One would expect them to be awful hokum. Mine were and I was advised to destroy them. I did . . . [but] what I am trying to point out is that for the purposes of communication in this country, Mr Evans, and I too, were forced to write our first plays in an English convention, because this was the only way we could convey what we had to say in dramatic form.[23]

Claude Evans' first play set in New Zealand, *That Man Harlington*, was about an immoral solicitor. It was produced in 1952 by the Canterbury Repertory Society, which went on to premiere his *Overtime*, voted their 'best play' for 1954 in an audience survey.[24] Having noted Evans' 'surprising lack of interest in people' in his comments on *Harlington*, John Thomson rated *Overtime* 'much the best of his plays':

> Ted is a 70-year-old cabinetmaker whose handcrafted furniture is greatly appreciated by those who value his skills. But even they are not prepared to pay for it at its true price. In the machine room next door, cheap chairs can be run up at a fraction of Ted's cost. Evans avoids the risk of one kind of sentimentality: Ted's heart is not all gold. He is cantankerous, stubborn, soured. It is the play's attitude to Ted's work which is sentimental: his efforts to preserve his way of life in an unnoticed backwater are implicitly approved, while the foreman and workers of the new factory age are unashamed caricatures.[25]

In an essay on New Zealand history in New Zealand plays for *Australasian Drama Studies*, Sebastian Black opines that Terence Rattigan's apocryphal Aunt Edna (his target audience) would have been just as much at home with *Overtime*, set in Christchurch, as with Evans' earlier plays set 'among English gentlefolk'[26], noting that Ted's knowledge of timber is so vast that it is said: 'If you ever want a history lesson bring in a piece of old oak and he'll take you back to the battle of Hastings.'[27]

> Kauri is not allowed to sully the stage and a reference to the battle of Ruapekapeka would be deemed incomprehensible. The same diffidence about native timber can be seen in Stella Jones's *The Tree* (1957). In this autumnal drama, set in an unspecified South Island town, the unnamed tree that dominates the stage sheds exotic leaves.[28]

(For the record, Black's assertion that *The Tree* is set in a South Island town is questionable. There is no mention of it in the published text, and a character who took a morning car ride from Auckland arrives at the house before lunch.)[29]

Despite their Anglocentric preferences, the role of the amateur societies in fostering home-grown plays is important. Thomson credits the Great Depression with encouraging communities to create their own cultural activities and entertainment opportunities by forming amateur dramatic societies. Commentators also acknowledge the importance of the British Drama League (BDL) in encouraging local writing through the playwriting competitions that were part of their area, regional and national one-act play festivals. Although New Zealand settings and themes were not required in original scripts, they were encouraged with special awards. The criteria for judging were 'dramatic construction, characterisation, quality of dialogue, idea, pace, climax and actability.'[30]

A wealth of aspiring playwrights was revealed when seventy scripts were entered in the first year (1932) and nearly a hundred in the second. Aware that the availability of texts was crucial to their being produced, the BDL (with Radio Publishing) also published selected plays, and built a library of five volumes containing thirty-one one-act plays by 1936. 'But within a few years,' McNaughton observes, 'it became apparent that the bulk of such scripts scarcely merited such publicity, and only a couple were revived after the war.'[31]

An important exemplar of playwrights who emerged through the competitions was Violet Targuse. Her plays are well documented in Sue Dunlop's unpublished MA thesis, *The Role of Women in the Culture and Context of a Developing New Zealand Theatre, 1920–1950*. Targuse's play *Rabbits* won the first South Canterbury Drama League playwriting competition in 1930, and then *Fear* and *The Touchstone* were placed first equal in the BDL's inaugural original playwriting competition in 1932. In 1933 a production of *Rabbits* won the BDL's Central Taranaki Area Festival while *The Touchstone* won the South Taranaki Area Festival. *Rabbits* and *The Touchstone* were also the only New Zealand plays among the eleven presented at the first BDL National Final Festival (Wellington, 1933), where they placed first equal.[32]

Dunlop describes *Rabbits* as 'a wonderful example [of the plays] written about the kinds of lives real New Zealand women were living (with dramatic licence of course).' Keeping house for ten years at an isolated railway siding in the Canterbury Plains has left Maggie Blake severely depressed. Her husband Joe works for the Railways, and her son Stodger, who is away at school during the day, keeps a pet rabbit in a cage. Hearing unofficially that Joe is to be transferred back to Christchurch, Maggie frees the rabbit. But Joe, oblivious to Maggie's concerns, has opted to stay for an extra quid a week. Stodger finds his rabbit's paws damaged from trying to climb out of a gravel pit, and gleefully brings him home. The play ends as Joe reflects Maggie's entrapment by patting the rabbit affectionately: 'What's the sense in tearing your claws to pieces trying to escape when you know fate's against you? You silly little creature!'[33]

Other BDL trail-blazers who proved we had stories to tell and the skills to do so in drama included the prolific Isobel Andrews, whose plays won many BDL awards for script and production in the 1940s. She is probably best known for *The Willing Horse*, a comedy built around a group of women preparing the supper for a dance in a rural hall. This was one of six one-act plays selected by Dunlop to be presented as rehearsed playreadings under the title *Backblocks and Beyond* by professional actors and directors at Wellington's Circa Theatre in October 2000. The full list reads as an honour roll of women playwrights up to 1950: *Rabbits* by Violet Targuse (1930), *Fear* by Violet Targuse (1932), *Interlude* by Constance Merritt (1931), *Local Colour* by Mary Scott (1931), *The Willing Horse* by Isobel Andrews (1941), *The Trap* by Kathleen Ross (1949). Radio New Zealand recorded the playreadings and presented three of them (*Local Colour*, *The Willing Horse* and *The Trap*) on National Radio on Waitangi Day (6 February) 2001, along with a brief documentary on the background to these plays and their writers.[34]

Verse Plays

In the post-WWII period, as an alternative to the growing preference for social realism in writing style and naturalism in performance, a number of poets were drawn to writing verse plays, possibly inspired by the likes of Britain's TS Eliot and Christopher Fry.

Douglas Stewart had moved to Australia in 1938 and wrote verse plays about Scott's doomed expedition to the Antarctic (*The Fire on the Snow*, 1941) and Australia's most infamous bush ranger (*Ned Kelly*, 1942). He also found inspiration in Māori mythology for *The Golden Lover* (1943). It draws on the legend of the fair-skinned, red-haired, blue-eyed patupaiarehe, the 'fairy people' who aroused fear and awe among darker-skinned Māori. All three plays enjoyed early success as Australian Broadcasting Corporation radio plays and eventually found their way onto the stage: *Ned Kelly* on tour with the New Zealand Players in 1953; *The Golden Lover* with Downstage Theatre in 1967 (both directed by Richard Campion) and *The Fire on the Snow* with Sydney's Old Tote Theatre Company in 1968.

Charles Brasch, the founding editor of *Landfall*, ventured into drama with *The Quest* (1946), a verse script to accompany a mimed performance. *Life Sentence* (1949) by Howard Wadham, editor of *The Year Book of the Arts in New Zealand*, is described by McNaughton as 'a mountaineering drama with a romantic sub-plot, contained in a taut, poetic mode.' Around the same time, Allen Curnow made a little more impact with *The Axe* (1948), which grew from Sir Peter Buck's account of the Christianising of Mangaia in the Cook Islands, in *Anthropology and Religion*. According to his preface in the published version, Curnow saw it as a metaphor for New Zealand. McNaughton summarises it thus:

> [It] concerns tribal conflicts in 1824 associated with the introduction of Christianity and Western technology, symbolized in the axe itself. Within this social context Curnow introduced a sub-plot about two young natives whose love is destroyed by the axe, and a chorus of two masked ancestral figures from the island who, with more allusive poetry, explore themes such as time, the island, the seas, and mutability. The complexity of thought contained in the choric passages contrasts with the simplicity and occasional banality of the human action, where rudimentary motivation and general incomprehension of wider issues generates a great deal of poignancy but little that approaches tragedy.[35]

Thomson comments, 'The themes were new to the stage but not to poetry. Despite the dramatic material of tribal conflict under the influence of Western innovation, the best parts of the play were the choruses, which were really only so many new poems to add to Curnow's already well-established poetic meditations on islands and time.'

D'Arcy Cresswell's *The Forest* (1952) also draws comment from both McNaughton and Thomson. McNaughton notes its 'erudite verse form' in its dealing with 'the love of nature and the threat of commercial exploitation . . . with appearances from Lucifer and the Archangel Gabriel.'[36] Thomson describes its themes as 'the baleful effects upon civilisation of science since Copernicus, and the virtues of male homosexuality. It is a comedy not without life and wit, so it is presumably its doctrine which has kept it almost entirely off the stage.'[37]

It was in the following year that Bruce Mason began to make his mark as a playwright. But before we look at his plays, it is relevant to consider what, in his early life, contributed to his discovering and embracing his vocation.

CHAPTER TWO

EMERGING FROM THE FLAXBUSH

It is a truism that the particular is universal; that good plays rooted in particular times and places are best able to connect with humanity anywhere in any age. While the purpose of this book is to survey Bruce Mason's plays—to appraise 'the works of' rather than 'the life of'—a bit of biographical background will help to position him and his works in their historical, cultural and socio-political contexts.

Mason's mother, Anne March, the third of five children, was born in Bethnal Green, East London, and worked first in a corset factory then in a toothpaste factory until she joined the Royal Flying Corps in WWI, rising to the rank of sergeant. His father, Howard Mason, was a New Zealand-born bank clerk who had planned to study law until WWI saw him enlist as a private. They were married in their respective uniforms at St Mary's Church, Letchworth, in 1919 (by Gerard Kerr Olivier, father of yet-to-be-famous Laurence) and departed three weeks later, on a troop ship, for New Zealand where Howard would become general manager of W D & H O Wills (NZ) Ltd. In 1977 Bruce Mason would note in a letter to author Claire Tomalin that his 'Ma' and her two sisters had produced 'one University Professor, Felix Leakey, Professor of French at Bedford College and a world expert on Baudelaire; a doctor of science in Dr James Lovelock (*The Quest for Gaia*) and a doctor of literature, in me'.[1]

Bruce Edward George Mason was born in Wellington on 28 September 1921, and moved with his family to the seaside suburb of Takapuna, Auckland, when he was five.[2] 'That huge panorama has formed a backdrop to my life,' he wrote in 'Narcissus Observed', the first variation in his semi-autobiographical solo work *Not Christmas, But Guy Fawkes*. 'No anguish but was not subtly redeemed by it: no joy not deepened by it.'[3] Aged seven or eight, his secret writing place was a cubby-hole he had scooped out in a flaxbush by a lawn where his parents and their friends often gathered. Writing 'at no other time but in the flaxbush and only when there were adults in front, unaware I was there' he had sensed that being artistic was 'something arcane: if not precisely forbidden, then heavy with the possibility of discovery and guilt. Like masturbation, then . . . a secret and guilty joy'. Music was his other passion: 'I still hold it as the most exciting day of my life when, after an agonising delay, a piano at last arrived in our house'. He was a late starter at age thirteen and soon learnt, when he began to show off his talent, 'that this prowess secured for me not the awed respect I had hoped for, but the most withering contempt. "Classical music? You bloody queen . . ."' Regardless, he credits this attitude with bringing him out of the flaxbush and setting him on the path that would take him to the stage as a solo performer twenty-five years later.[4]

Educated initially at Belmont School, where he became dux in 1934, Mason went on to attend Takapuna Grammar School, where he suffered an ignominious soaking with water by way of initiation (the school took both boys and girls, but classes and grounds were segregated). He spent his final year of secondary school at Wellington College after the family moved back to the capital city. The question of what it is to be a man in New Zealand was ever-present for Mason and would permeate most of his plays. His childhood 'reverberated with the manly exhortation: "Be a little man, be a brave boy, chin up, chest out, shoulder back, stiff upper lip, don't cry, don't give in, try try again, be strong, be British!"—yes, even this!' His father was exasperated by a fifteen-year-old son who hadn't 'one single manly pursuit', unlike his younger brother, who would go on to become an All Black. Throughout his education Mason had resisted rugby and all it stood for: 'I knew it was The Test, our puberty rite, our induction in manly ways: I failed spectacularly'. As a sixth-former he was caned, 'six of the best', for insolence when his answer to a public demand at assembly to explain why he had not been to rugby practice was, 'Because it bores me!' However, while serving with the Navy, Mason's perspective shifted. He found that 'uncompelled or coerced' he could be 'a quite serviceable wing three-quarter'. The essay he wrote about these experiences, called 'Manifesto for the Unmanly', was rejected by the editor of *Landfall*, Charles Brasch, who suggested Mason should nevertheless hold onto it in case it came in useful. Later revised as 'Beginnings', the essay was published in June 1966 and went on to become the first variation in *Not Christmas, But Guy Fawkes*.[5]

Recalling his final paragraph as 'bad; intolerably lofty and holier-than-thou' Mason nevertheless quotes it in 'Narcissus Observed', to expose his young self at his 'highest-flown':

> And now, men of my country, I address myself to you. Persist, if you must, in fashioning us from your own botched, perverted image; crush the mind, extinguish the spirit—I hold you enemies. And you, women of my country, doxies of politicians and cartoonists, who teach us at your knees that we are dirty and unclean: accept, if you please, my hatred. Together, in your fear of the flesh and scorn of the spirit, you will ruin us. And yet, there are grounds for hope. We still have our boobs and ninnies, those who will not accept your empty shibboleths, will not equate the rules of the game with Holy Writ, and there is more truth in their fumbling search for grace than you will ever know. Boobs and ninnies, accept my homage, and this manifesto ends with an invocation to you, authentic voices of my country.[6]

Left: Bruce Mason with his mother, Anne, at Takapuna (c.1937). Right: Bruce Mason, toy soldier, aged seven or eight.

'Well, that was telling them,' Mason quips in retrospect. But judgemental polemics were not destined to curb his style as a playwright; a vocation he had not yet claimed, although he did credit the world he lived in as giving him the neurosis that compelled him towards it. 'I in my flaxbush and the people on the lawn, form a context: if I could not communicate with them, it was because they refused communication with me, or the likes of me. And the reasons for this refusal have become the mainspring of my work.' An anecdote about how he resolved a problem as a five-year-old at school, when a boy was stealing his lunch, reveals he rejected his parents' advice to fight the boy and instead offered him half. While accepting that some may see the act as cowardice, Mason gave thanks thirty years later, 'that, at a time when self-regard was rudimentary, insight and self-criticism nil, I had recognised another's need—there were many hungry children in 1927—and made my first social commitment'. Although 'The Conch Shell' story in *Not Christmas, But Guy Fawkes* reveals something other than compassion in his dealings with those less fortunate, this trait does manifest strongly in the twelve-year-old boy's response to both the Depression riots and Firpo in *The End of the Golden Weather*, the semi-autobiographical play that also celebrates his father's talents as 'a figure of wild, outrageous comedy.' Mason would thus conclude that his work was at its best when the three separate elements he had identified in retrospect—'the prodigious over-reaching, the compassionate and the comic'—were deployed in a 'beneficent tension'.[7]

Despite being derided as a 'bloody queen' for his prowess at the piano, Mason persisted with it, and it was that prowess and his language skills that drew him towards theatre. While working as a law clerk, Mason offered his services as a piano accompanist to the French club and went on to perform in the French version of Terence Rattigan's *French Without Tears*. The following year he performed in *La Nuit d'Auberge* by Gabriel Nigond. As a student at Wellington Training College he became involved with the drama club, which he described as the most enterprising group in Wellington, 'under the intelligent direction of Walter Scott'. Their major productions introduced him to plays by Robert Ardrey, George Bernard Shaw, WH Auden and Christopher Isherwood. The 'autobiographical cruise' that opened his *Theatre in Danger* correspondence with Dr John Pocock, then a political science lecturer at the University of Otago, reveals that Mason acted in a variety of roles at Wellington Training College and wrote 'half a dozen one-act plays, several of which were produced by university groups and in which there may have been a little merit'. David Dowling records that *Focus*, a one-act play Mason wrote when he was nineteen, was presented at Wellington Training College in 1941, but no copy of this script appears to have survived. Mason also admits to attempting 'a three-act drama (about which the least said the better)'.[8]

In Mason's *Landfall* review of Claude Evans' plays, he confessed that his own early attempts at playwriting had conformed to the default setting of 'in London, or within thirty miles of the metropolis'. It is tempting to conclude that this is the basis of the fictionalised account he offers in his prose work *Courting Blackbird: A Theme and Variations in the Baroque Style*, of co-writing his first play with the improbably named Boris Godunov (Bo) Baron, a larger-than-life Marxist who had been exiled from England to cousins in the colonies by his industrious refugee parents. Mason already had a plot in mind:

> The play was set in England in the eighteen-nineties. Two sisters, Maud and Clara. Maud, twenty-eight, plain and unmarried, Clara twenty-three, unmarried but ferociously nubile. Maud is furiously jealous of her beautiful sister, but compensates by becoming a New Woman in Shavian style, reading Ibsen, Shaw, Marx and Freud, and playing the solo sonatas of Bach very loudly on the violin at three o'clock in the morning. Enter a young man with whom both sisters fall instantly in love. He chooses Clara, but the night before the wedding, Maud sets fire to the inn where he is staying, incinerating him, but—shattering irony!—winning the Royal Humane Society's gold medal for bravery for rescuing Clara, who was paying her lover an illicit visit, from the flames. The play was called *All Is Not Gold*. No. No, indeed. All was not even silver. All was, as it proved, lead, lead, lead.
>
> We warred from the beginning. Maud certainly needed to be interested in theology, politics, psychoanalysis, but the poor creature was forced to deliver speeches on these themes lasting for three pages at a time. When I demurred that a country girl, however well-read, could

> hardly have mastered *The Psychopathology of Everyday Life* twenty-five years before Freud wrote it, he [Bo Baron] simply said, 'dramatic licence, comrade,' and on she prattled for another two pages.
>
> Bo's chief contribution, apart from the wads and gobbets and three-tiered buns of talk our characters were weighed down with, were some execrable wisecracks which he called—optimism!—'groundling bait.'

Mason also credited Bo with supplying authentic English touches, admitting that 'neither of us suspected there was any drama to be dredged up in our own provincial backwater'.[9]

Those in the know say Bo Baron was based on Lindsay Nathan, who lived next door to the Masons in Karori, Wellington. He was shipped to the colonies by his wealthy, London-based, Jewish-born and now Anglican parents, after a series of disruptions including attempts to debate religion with the officiating clergy at Westminster Abbey, exhibiting socialist tendencies at a private school and being expelled from a Swiss university. His European émigré relations in Wellington included the Chief Justice, Sir Michael Myers, and Joseph Nathan, who had founded the firm that invented the dried milk product Glaxo in the early twentieth century. Lindsay worked for his uncle Charles Nathan and lived in Karori with an aunt in an early colonial house that had been converted into two flats. The Masons lived in the front flat. When Bruce was aged about eighteen or nineteen, he and Lindsay, who was nearly two years older, appeared together in the 1941 *Extravaganza*, Victoria University of Wellington's annual capping revue. Mason wrote original music for, and sang in, a Noel Coward parody called 'Knowall Coward', and Nathan appeared as the Ghost of Hairy Skolland, evoking the late Harry Holland, first leader of the New Zealand Labour Party.[10]

In 1942 Mason was active with Wellington Repertory Theatre, performing in JM Barrie's *Rosalind,* AA Milne's *Mr Pim Passes By*, and with the drama club at Victoria University College where he continued to study while serving with the New Zealand Scottish Regiment and then the Divisional Signals. In 1943 he joined the Royal New Zealand Navy and saw active service in the North Sea, on the Murmansk convoys and during the Allied invasion of continental Europe, becoming a sub-lieutenant in 1944.[11]

As 'Ordinary Seaman Mason, a neat figure in his bell-bottoms, twenty-one and very young for his age, striking off from his native shores in the service of his King', he took every shore-leave opportunity to go to the theatre. His quest—shared and debated with Pocock in 1955—was for a relevant and authentic theatre that represented the contemporary world. In his opening salvo, Pocock had claimed the New Zealand Players (set up by Richard and Edith Campion and now entering its third year of operation) were 'avoiding the real stuff of theatre by concentrating on effects and gimmickry', which he termed 'decadent theatre'. In response Mason recalled the first professional production he had seen, in New York, and his shock at finding the admired film actress Elisabeth Bergner starring in a 'pretentious thriller'. While her 'florid, showy part' allowed her to give a brilliant performance, 'the actors with her, several well known in films, gave performances which Wellington

Bruce Mason serving with either the New Zealand Scottish Regiment or Divisional Signals (1942).

Repertory could equal and often had'. He also found it 'ridiculous [that] although this was a New York Theatre, every actor spoke as if he had been bred in London, SW7, with the exception of Bergner, whose intonation was Viennese'. The play involves an Englishman who, hoping to rediscover his artistic muse, meets an exotic 'other woman' while his wife slowly dies. 'If the New Zealand theatre in its social aspect (by which I mean the large and prosperous metropolitan repertories, not the small adventurous groups) was removed from life and intellectually worthless,' Mason wrote, 'I was to observe that a highly praised New York production could exemplify all these faults, the difference being merely one of magnitude.'[12]

Hoping to have his faith restored in London, Mason was instead further dismayed to see husband-and-wife team Alfred Lunt and Lynn Fontanne in a cynically relocated production of Robert E Sherwood's Pulitzer Prize-winning *There Shall Be No Night.* Originally set in Finland with Russia as the tyrant, it now depicted Greeks in the shadow of the swastika.

> I saw and admired the incomparably subtle playing of the Lunts, for which they are justly famous, but the performances around them ranged from the merely adequate to the excruciating, and all this in a thin play of no real eloquence or conviction. And as, on my leaves I moved around London theatres, I found nothing to change my original impression that the professional theatre was merely marking time, that its actors performed no more than a set of routine, conventional gestures, and that its playwrights were a collection of not over-competent theatrical journalists.[13]

Admitting to youthful arrogance, Mason described how, while based in Portsmouth in the spring of 1944, he set out to 'remedy this deficiency' by writing a play in four hour-long acts called *The Secret People* (after GK Chesterton's poem), that 'purported to be a tribute to that portion of the English who have not yet found their voices, the majority in other words'. Given the premise that the only time a nation finds a creative myth to live by is when it is at war, the play asked 'how to preserve this after the Armistice . . . [and] offered the solution of spiritual values accruing from collective living, as if the whole of England were some vast, hearty holiday camp.' Mason wrote to JB Priestley, whom he saw as 'a triton among minnows at this time, with several plays running at once', asking for his advice. He was surprised when Priestley broke his rule 'never to read plays in manuscript' and offered to read it because Mason was a serviceman a long way from home. The result was a summons to meet him in his Piccadilly *pied-à-terre*, an apartment once occupied by Oscar Wilde. 'He received me courteously, and equally courteously told me that my play was impossible, and if it were ever produced no one would sit through it, not even me. He admitted, however, that the dialogue was good and that two scenes were effective. So the bleakness of the London wartime theatre had to remain unredeemed by me.' Elements of *The Secret People*, particularly the premise of 'values accruing from collective living', may well have been resurrected fourteen years later when Mason wrote *Birds in the Wilderness* in a rush to meet a deadline.[14]

The Old Vic Theatre's production of *Richard III* with Laurence Olivier in the title role redeemed English theatre in Mason's eyes. 'I cannot describe to you the intensity of feeling in the theatre on that first night, to which as a serviceman I had a free ticket: the splendid presence and dazzling brilliance of Olivier, the feeling at every moment of a great personality in wonderful eruption; never have I seen an audience so frenzied after the final curtain. We shouted, we cheered, we jumped up and down: our faces shone, our eyes glistened.'[15] Mason realised 'that the Old Vic triumph in the West End was no isolated phenomenon, but the logical result of many years of planning and training.' He reflected that the Old Vic Theatre had been set up 'on the wrong side of the river, in Waterloo Road [by] two cranky old tartars, Emma Cons and her niece Lilian Baylis, both distinguished by sound business sense and an implacable love of the theatre', and that it had been 'sustained by the modest offerings of the poor . . . because they liked the theatre and for no other reason' and that the likes of Gielgud, Olivier and Richardson had learned their trade there before the war.[16]

Back in Wellington after the war, Mason married Diana Shaw, a general practitioner who specialised in obstetrics. They had met when she was seventeen and he eighteen, and he 'slowly bewitched her by his quicksilver mind, and outpouring of words and his stunning piano playing.'[17] He graduated with a BA from Victoria University College, became a research assistant with the Department of Internal Affairs War History Branch and was then appointed assistant curator of manuscripts at the Alexander Turnbull Library. His short story 'The Glass Wig' was published in *Landfall* in 1947, and two years later *Landfall* also published 'Summer's End', which was later revised as 'The Made Man' in *The End of the Golden Weather*. The same year he joined Unity Theatre where, as president, he called on members to write their own plays.[18]

Mason then returned to London with Diana and their newborn daughter, Belinda, where they shared a house with Richard and Edith Campion. Having, as David Dowling puts it, 'rejected a career as a concert pianist after auditioning with Albert Ferber,' and failed to find a place in theatre, journalism or music, Mason ended up teaching children involved in screen and stage work while Diana furthered her studies in obstetrics. They returned to New Zealand in 1951, where Mason managed Diana's parents' orchard in Tauranga (an experience that would feed into *The Pohutukawa Tree*) before the family settled back in Wellington, where their son Julian was born later that year. Their third child, Rebecca, was born early in 1954, while Mason was a public relations officer for the New Zealand Forest Service. In 1957 Mason became a senior journalist with the Tourist and Publicity Department.[19]

It was in Wellington, as a public servant, husband of a doctor and father of two with the third yet to come, that Mason revived his vocation as a playwright and returned to Unity Theatre. Early in 1953 he played Flamineo in Webster's *The White Devil*. Later that year Unity produced his two short plays *The Bonds of Love* and *The Evening Paper*, then *The Verdict* in 1955 and *A Case in Point* in 1957. In an interview ten years later, Mason credited Unity with getting him 'properly' interested in theatre, noting it had a very young membership when he joined. 'Men outnumbered women, which is pretty unusual. Because of this the society had a very strong

Diana Mason in London on Red Cross Day, while completing her post-graduate studies at Great Ormond Street Hospital for Sick Children (c.1950).

masculine bias which is a very good thing in a country which regards most artistic aspiration or exploration as effete.'[20]

When Richard Campion, also back in Wellington, needed a local playwright to write linking pieces and sketches for the 'potted plays' programmes the New Zealand Players Drama Quartet toured to schools, Bruce Mason was the obvious choice.[21] But while he was happy to oblige those immediate needs, Mason was also working on something bigger. In the first two months of 1955 he wrote the first draft of *The Pohutukawa Tree*, destined to become his best-known and most studied work. It would, however, be two-and-a-half years before the New Zealand Players Theatre Workshop gave it a trial run of four performances in Wellington, jointly directed by Campion and Mason.

Mason entered into his *Theatre in Danger* correspondence with Pocock soon after completing that first draft, 'much of

Bruce Mason (seated, in black) plays Flamineo in *The White Devil* by Webster. Unity Theatre (March 1953).

which was written under the influence of ideas thrown up in this correspondence'.[22] Having shared his perception of the Old Vic's post-war emergence, Mason set out the only conditions under which he believed a creative theatre could develop. There were three:

> First, that the primary preoccupation of a group shall be plays, and that acting, producing, design and so on shall be subordinate both separately and together to this overriding preoccupation. The idea of choosing plays merely as vehicles for this or that talented performer should be cast out as if it were the devil.
>
> Second, there must be continuity of purpose and activity. No group should be surprised if it takes them ten years to produce a really first-rate theatrical season.
>
> Third, the group shall consist only of amateurs, in the strict sense of those who love theatre. Payment does not matter so much; it is the attitude to what the actors are doing which is important. This, of course, is the most difficult of the three.
>
> When these three conditions are complied with, something may happen—I say may, because even with all the conditions present, there are still imponderables to consider: the times, for example, the emotional and political temper of audiences, their sophistication and receptivity and so on. The theatre is, and always has been, a damnably chancy business.[23]

The first condition is especially interesting in light of Mason's admiration of Laurence Olivier's *Richard III*. The following year Olivier's insistence on double billing Sheridan's *The Critic* and Sophocles' *Oedipus Rex*, in which he would star as both Mr Puff and Oedipus, provoked his co-artistic director Tyrone Guthrie to resign from the Old Vic because he saw it as a totally inappropriate pairing, designed solely to show off the egotistical Olivier's talent.[24] As for 'love of theatre' being the driving force, the enduring difficulties of maintaining a fulltime career in professional theatre in New Zealand has often, in the decades that have followed, led seasoned practitioners to work in non-paying or low-paying co-operative productions because they love the project and want to keep working to maintain 'match fitness'. Indeed the most innovative productions of new home-grown work have invariably been created by passionate practitioners in circumstances where payment, if any, falls well below the minimum wage.

In his 'Impressions of the Theatre in the Soviet Union', written following his visit to Moscow in 1958, Mason responded to the apparent dismissal, by the Theatrical Conference of the USSR, of B Laverenev's view that 'in art, there are no little themes; there are only superficial treatments of themes'. Mason argued that 'an artist, of whatever nature, is an explorer into the yet unknown territory of reality; he makes us more ourselves, and thus justifies his function as what the English poet Shelley once described as "the unacknowledged legislator of mankind." I repeat . . . it is the artist's task to explore reality, rather than actuality; reality as a whole.' He then asserted that the Moscow Art Theatre's treatment of actuality 'often seems to be falsely equated with reality' and cited an example from the last act of Chekhov's *The Three Sisters*, where—seated in the third row—he saw an actual tear spring to the eye of the actress playing Masha as she embraced the departing Vershinin.

> Here was a piece of imaginative acting so intensely realised that the actress was completely identified with her part. But what were my own reactions? Was I moved by the force with which Chekhov saw and felt this classic scene of parting? Not at all. All I thought, was, 'Tears! Real tears! How does she do it?' I was reminded as forcibly as possible, not of actuality but of artifice. Art and actuality are surely completely opposed.

Mason compared this with the same moment in a London production where Margaret Leighton, playing Masha, 'turned right away from us, and one saw only her back; her grief was implied and here it was inexpressibly moving. Too much actuality, I repeat, leaves you with only the appearance of reality: with fiction, and not with fact.'[25]

This thinking reflects the battle British playwright Dennis Potter and his contemporaries waged in the 1960s and 1970s against the phoniness of 'kitchen sink' naturalism, arguing that 'reality' was better accessed through more artful means, described as 'realism and non-naturalism'.[26] The 'real tears' versus 'implied grief' incident also speaks to what practitioners have variously called the 'get it' moment;

the 'moment of nothing' where everything happens; the space that we are drawn into by empathy rather than objective observation. Given Mason's valuing of subtext, it is important his plays are read and performed with an awareness of what is not being said too: of what is being thought and felt by his characters. That said, Mason's strong suit is the quality of the spoken text in his plays. He displays a superb ear for dialogue, clearly delineating the different cultures and classes within what we like to think of as our egalitarian society. A lot of the dialogue in his plays is richly articulate. He explained why in an interview with Helen Paske for Television New Zealand's *Kaleidoscope* programme (recorded in 1982, the last year of his life):

> I'm interested in eloquence. And you know, the tradition inaugurated by Frank Sargeson—with every possible respect to a great man and a great writer—was of a nation of dumb oxen who, in his most characteristic work, spoke in monosyllables and very few of those. Eloquence is something I feel very strongly about—hence my attraction to Dmitri Alexeyvitch in *To Russia, with Love* because if the Russians are not eloquent, nobody is. The Māori people are eloquent also, they've got this enormous richness of language . . . Against the bleats of 'the numbed ones', which is how I look at us Pākehās, there's still this enormous eloquence of the Māori people, which I can only admire and revere.[27]

As the husband of a medical practitioner, Mason was more of a hands-on father and 'house husband' than most men of the time. However, while pursuing his true vocation where possible throughout the 1960s and beyond, he did find other paid employment. He was editor of *Te Ao Hou*, a magazine about Māori issues produced by the Department of Maori Affairs, from 1960 to 1961, and wrote for the *New Zealand Listener* as record critic (1961–1962) and music critic (1964–1969). He was a senior copywriter for Wood and Mitchell Advertising Limited (1969–1971). Wellingtonians knew him best, however, as a theatre critic and commentator who elevated that craft to an art form with the knowledge and intelligence he brought to the discourse. He reviewed for *The Dominion* from 1958 to 1960, *Act* magazine (a Downstage initiative for which he was founding editor) from 1967 to 1970, *The Dominion* again from 1973 to 1978, and

The Evening Post from 1980 to 1982.[28] In his 1967 interview with *New Zealand Stage* magazine, Mason recalled his response to Emlyn Williams' judgemental surprise that, in attempting to make a living as a solo performer, he had written his own script (*The End of the Golden Weather*). 'It may be gross audacity,' Mason replied, 'but there is no-one here to say no and I've got to do it, otherwise I might just as well cut my throat or go and sit in a government office!' Mason also disagreed with those who said New Zealand was a cultural desert:

> Our difficulty is not that we haven't got the opportunities; we've got immense opportunities. Our difficulty is that although there's no-one to say *no*, at the same time there's no-one to say *yes*. We haven't sufficient velocity of imagination generated in our community to make it certain that once you get onto the bottom rung of the ladder you then ascend, if you're worthy of it, to the next one. Eventually, again if you're worthy, you might get to the top, but unfortunately we have no top; we have no ladder, let alone rungs. So I've no patience with people complaining that there is no possibility for creation in New Zealand. There's every possibility for creation in New Zealand. There's every possibility to call out of this country the most extraordinary creative exploits . . . I don't think I've ever fully understood why the word 'culture' and all it implies is so suspect in this country. I believe it's because it is regarded as being excrement from the culture we took all that energy to leave a hundred years ago; it's looked on as 'father substance' that we want to get rid of, because in relation to Europe we are a community of sons who have left the father. That's why I think we've got this great suspicion of the overseas expert.[29]

This interview took place, it must be noted, the year after the New Zealand Theatre Centre had imported a Royal Shakespeare Company production of *The Comedy of Errors,* along with directors and lead actors. This was also the year (1966) in which the Canterbury Theatre Company imported its professional company from Britain to 'set the standard' in Christchurch, and Wellington's Downstage Theatre was discovering its error in appointing a Canadian, Sandy Black, as its artistic director.[30] Mason had by this time concluded that Richard Campion's now defunct New Zealand Players model of touring large-scale productions of classics or modern plays from overseas was unworkable. Theatre's challenge, as he saw it, was 'to make an intimate dialogue with our community'.[31]

The question of whether or not New Zealand has a unique culture had arisen some years earlier when, as the newly appointed editor of *Te Ao Hou* in 1960, Mason attended a Young Leaders' Conference in Marton. On witnessing a young and passionate Māori hurling at the Pākehā delegates, 'How can you talk to us of art? You who have no culture of your own!', Mason wanted to reply, 'What about pubs, TABs, gambling, cities, railways, airplanes?'[32] Mason had, by that time, begun to create a significant body of plays that provocatively defined, explored and distinguished New Zealand culture in its Pākehā, Māori, urban, suburban and rural manifestations.

CHAPTER THREE

Self-reflection from Page to Stage

Not Christmas, but Guy Fawkes; Courting Blackbird

Just as some visual artists are drawn to self-portraiture, Mason sought to discover himself and exercise his writing muscles with a number of semi-autobiographical prose pieces. While *Not Christmas, but Guy Fawkes* and *Courting Blackbird* mostly relate to the years before he became a playwright, they add to our understanding of how he gravitated towards his true vocation. Years later he would, for various reasons, develop these writings for solo performance.

Not Christmas, but Guy Fawkes

Most of the material that makes up *Not Christmas, but Guy Fawkes*, first performed as a solo show in 1976, was published much earlier in *Landfall*, in an order that differed from how it would play in performance. 'Et in Arcadia Ego', which would come second in the solo show compilation, was published in December 1955; 'The Conch Shell' (fourth) appeared in December 1958; 'Narcissus Observed' (first) was based on Mason's essay 'Beginnings', published in June 1966. 'Limp Bananas' (third) began as 'A Caprice for Radio' and was broadcast twice in 1973. [1] From his mid-thirties, Mason was able to send himself up mercilessly, thereby earning an extra right to satirise others and the world he shared with them. In his author's note he describes *Not Christmas, but Guy Fawkes* as 'a set of variations on over-reaching, on getting too big for your breeches, with the comic disasters that accrue from overweening aims.' The title comes from the school playground put-down, 'He thinks he's Christmas, but he's only Guy Fawkes.' Although, at first glance, they may seem to support the 'tall poppy syndrome', the stories may also be read as confronting it.

'Narcissus Observed'

Mason jokingly opens the performed version of 'Narcissus Observed' with the by then famous words 'Consider, if you will, Te Parenga . . .', which introduce *The End of the Golden Weather* (first performed in 1959). However, 'Narcissus Observed' offers a more factual account of his childhood. The aspects of his nature and the experiences that influenced his becoming a playwright and generated the three elements he aimed to deploy in his work, 'the prodigious or over-reaching, the compassionate and the comic', are covered in chapter one. This variation ends not with the advent of puberty but with what may be seen as the premature end of his youth when, on 3 September 1939, a few weeks short of his eighteenth birthday, he interrupts his late night translating of *Le Crapaud*—a poem by Victor Hugo—to sit in the dark on his parents' bed as they hear 'London calling'. His readers and audiences did not need reminding this is the announcement that Britain and its allies are now at war with Germany following the invasion of Poland two days before. 'My mother wept, rocking with anguish,' Mason writes. 'I went back to my room without a word, and continued with *Le Crapaud*.'[2] Is this ignorance, insensitivity or a resistance to facing the responsibilities of adulthood as a new war looms? He leaves us to empathise or judge as we will.

'Et in Arcadia Ego . . .'

The stated theme of 'Et in Arcadia Ego' is snobbery. Mason reveals how his 'stupid anti-American prejudice, underpinned by shyness' was subverted one Sunday afternoon when he strayed into a concert in the Albert Hall. An airman with a 'vintage south' accent recognises his New Zealand shoulder flashes, enthuses over Katherine Mansfield and invites him to the Churchill Club, 'which a devoted band of titled and distinguished ladies had started with the aim of introducing servicemen from overseas to the best in British culture'.

Here, the mythical greats of art, literature, music and ballet become physically real. An impromptu piano lesson from pianist Myra Hess is a highlight. 'After a week or two of this sort of thing,' he writes, 'I was no longer living in the real world—this was Arcadia.' On the other hand, agog at finding himself at a table for four with novelist EM Forster, sculptor Henry Moore and poet Stephen Spender, he is disappointed that they offer no pearls or gems but talk 'in a homely way on two themes only—cooking and railways.' In sharing his anecdotes Mason counterpoints his shameless name-dropping by bringing some of his idols down to human size and characterising himself as the gauche innocent abroad.[3]

A vivid account of a poetry recital by the bizarre and eccentric Edith Sitwell and her bothers, Osbert and Sacheverell, is offset by Mason's powerfully understated and sobering evocation of a London beset by air raids—'the flying bombs were giving everyone the tom tits'—which in turn allows him to epitomise, through Edith, the formidable British capacity for keeping calm and carrying on. Calling it all 'my glittering snob's pageant', he recognises that the 'coinage of snobbery . . . buys nothing at all' and claims his 'four weeks in Arcadia . . . was just long enough.' Only when he returns to England five years later, in civilian dress, does he realise how 'fantastically over-privileged' he has been as a serviceman. Doors that had flown open at the sight of his uniform now remain 'obdurately shut', and to friends he had made five years before, he is as dead 'and about as appetising as New Zealand mutton.'[4]

'Limp Bananas: An Occult Farce'

Limp bananas are what Mason feels his fingers become when he attempts to sight-read music. Having summarised his early passion for the piano, which only arrived in their house when he was thirteen, and at which he fanatically practised early each morning, he describes the awful experience of volunteering to accompany a celebrated, if now aging but unstoppable, singer of lieder at a post-concert party held in her honour. His vividly entertaining descriptions include an encounter where he is confronted by a musical challenge and utterly humiliated when she plucks his 'limp bananas' from the keyboard and presses them to her ample bosom in order to complete her song unencumbered.[5]

The 'occult farce' dimension arises from Mason's attempts to rectify his inadequacies by following the late Luigi Bonpensiere's *New Pathways to Piano Technique*. To say, as he does, that he is 'away with the pixies' while attempting to liberate his 'Eternal Poet' through 'Ideo-Kinetics' (the study of the relationship between mind and body) is an understatement. Given there is no suggestion elsewhere in the historical record that Mason went temporarily insane, this variation must be read as rich in hyperbole. It must also be assumed the musician and society hostess he satirises so wickedly are fictionalised (although doubtless there were those in the know who exchanged winks and nods on reading it or seeing it performed). But Mason mocks no one more mercilessly than himself as he describes how his ego inflates with mastery of the mystical art only to be ignominiously deflated at yet another post-concert soirée. This experience most likely occurred in 1969, because he identifies himself as working in an office with a typing pool and as a music critic whose credibility has expired as a result of the fiasco.

'The Conch Shell'

'The Conch Shell' was first published in December 1958, nine years after 'Summer's End' appeared in *Landfall* and the year before *The End of the Golden Weather* was created. It is surprising that for his solo presentation, at least, Mason did not replace fictional Te Parenga with actual Takapuna, given the emphasis he places on setting 'Narcissus Observed' in the relatively real world. On the other hand, 'Limp Bananas' suggests a fictionalised and heightened reality, therefore his reverting to Te Parenga here may be intended as evidence that the same is true of 'The Conch Shell'. In *The End of the Golden Weather*, the first-person narrator recalls and explores the emotional complexities of late childhood throughout most of the story, but in 'The Conch Shell' (as with 'The Night of the Riots') the past-tense prose mode diminishes its theatrical impact in performance.

'The Conch Shell' is a heartfelt and often comical story about his changing view of, and relationship with, Ginger Finucane (who also gets a mention in 'The Night of the Riots'). At the outset they are eleven and Ginger is 'the ugliest boy in the class . . . I hated his ugliness and I hated his dignity.' A portrait emerges of the youngest of three sons whose Irish father gets blind drunk every Friday night, sings his way home, beats his wife, and assaults his sons. Ginger's unfriendly response to the offer of blackberries, freshly picked by Mason and his mates, leads to one of the boys crowning him with a handful. When Ginger's mother makes all the boys scrub him clean, dislike becomes hatred. Heading home one day around the rocks, Mason, alone, encounters Ginger dressed in a new suit and, having 'cast my lot in with the herd', pushes him into the water. Instantly contrite and to avoid being reported, he agrees to become Ginger's slave. At Mason's home, while waiting for Ginger's clothes to dry, he has to give up half his shell collection, which includes a conch shell. He obeys an order to dress up in his mother's clothes, and when Ginger does the same, they suddenly become friends and share stolen cigarettes. But his mother comes home and there is trouble.[6]

Rather than paint himself as a victim, Mason offers a compelling psychological portrait of how he and Ginger create 'a myth between us, with pasteboard ogres like parents, judges, police, all ready to pounce at the first disclosure of my perfidity.' To buy Ginger's continued silence, he maximises the pleasure of the pain he feels giving Ginger half his lawn-mowing and birthday money, and half his books, including 'the *Grimm's Fairy Tales* I loved, rather than the back-slapping, empire-building, flag-waving *Chums* I hated.' When they both get sick of it, Ginger gives most of the books and shells back but not the conch, saying he's lost it. While Mason has become 'the modest penitent on the road to integrity', Ginger has come to see his hard and cruel life as 'a comedy, and thus take possession of, or command, any situation that involved his dignity. And where he had been dour, now he was light, witty, detached and quickly, very popular. In my last year at Te Parenga, he was captain of the school.'[7] Given Mason was a sixth-former when his family moved back to Wellington, it's fair to assume this is at Takapuna Grammar School.

If the final sequence in London after the war is not based on real experience, Mason may have fashioned it to confront his own hubris in thinking he could make it as an actor in Britain. His fictional self discovers, by chance, Fergus Finucane playing the Shakespearean clown Costard in an out-of-town tryout of *Love's Labour's Lost.* This leads not to a happy backstage reunion but an awkward scene where Ginger—who is looking forward to a season at the Old Vic followed by a year at Stratford and whose vowels are now 'purest Kensington'—has only a vague recollection of his visitor. Although the titular conch shell is on the bench, and he says he's 'had it for years. I keep it for luck,' he can't remember how he came by it. While his narrator could 'hang no shred of meaning' on it all, Mason leaves us to consider whether Ginger's transformation is a triumph of personal reinvention or a tragedy of lost identity.[8]

Mason's papers include an undated draft screenplay adaptation of 'The Conch Shell', 'for film or television'. The same story now plays out in present action, and the character who previously narrated it (i.e. Mason) is now called Ross Stone. Ginger is more loquacious, which makes his post-war metamorphosis as a Shakespearean actor rather less surprising. The most notable difference is that Ross becomes an actors' agent. With a rather sardonic secretary, he drives some distance to see an actress perform in a Cremorne Players production of *Love's Labour's Lost.* The references to Cremorne and a *Spotlight* casting magazine suggest he has relocated this sequence to Sydney (although the night-driving scenes and theatre interiors would not need to be shot there). As in the prose version, Ross is surprised to see Fergus (Ginger) playing Costard. Fergus is an impressive actor just out of drama school, however he only vaguely recalls his childhood enemy-turned-friend, Ross, who offers to represent him. While the script is typed in the prevailing format for a television drama, albeit rather badly and without proper scene headings, it has a quality of heightened reality that could have been developed in ways similar to Dennis Potter's ground-breaking teleplays (such as *Blue Remembered Hills*, 1979).

Overall, *Not Christmas, but Guy Fawkes* reads as a series of cautionary tales in which Mason keeps bringing himself down to size while demonstrating his undoubted artistic talents and revealing exotic elements of his life to date. His psychological profiling sets a standard for revealing human nature and experience in its 'warts and all' glory, which his audience is free to engage with through empathy, judgement or both.

It was a commission to present something at the South Pacific Festival of the Arts in 1976 that saw Mason bring the pieces together for solo performance. His script maintains the past-tense reportage rather than giving it the present-tense dynamic most of *The End of the Golden Weather* enjoys. Following its premiere at the Rotorua Town Hall's Concert Chamber in March, he took *Not Christmas, but Guy Fawkes* to the Christchurch Festival of the Arts and subsequently presented it at Palmerston North's Centrepoint Theatre, Whanganui's Four Seasons, Wellington's Downstage (twice), Auckland's Maidment, Hamilton's Playbox, Tauranga's Gateway, Dunedin's Fortune and Nelson's Garrick Theatre.[9]

Courting Blackbird: A Theme and Variations in the Baroque Style

After writing two variations and a coda of *Courting Blackbird: A Theme and Variations in the Baroque Style*, Mason set it aside in 1952. He waits until the coda to explain that, as a child, he misheard and mispronounced the words of 'Sing a Song of Sixpence', replacing the four and twenty blackbirds with 'courting, courting blackbird', and was given to asking, 'When am I going to see the courting blackbird?' By the time amused adults explained his error, he had vividly imagined 'a fabulous, heraldic beast, like the unicorn or the gryphon.' His repeated question was not answered until Mason created the character of Boris Godunov (Bo) Baron: 'A short, slim, elegant young man with fine Semitic features, full mouth, high-bridged nose and glossy black hair . . . a creature compound of mystery and candour, slyness and charm', in the character and lineaments of an English Jew. And so Courting Blackbird shall stand forever as his blazon.'[10]

In charting the fortunes of Bo Baron, a largely fictionalised version of Lindsay Nathan, Bruce Mason also maps his own initiation into student life and Marxist dogma, and reviews it against a Soviet history he would return to with *To Russia with Love*. Although artistic licence is undoubtedly taken, we may take Mason's experience and vivid portrait of Bo Baron as a dramatically heightened autobiography, at least until the dramatic finale. It becomes apparent that *Courting Blackbird* embodies a significant awakening of Mason's socio-political consciousness. We must take the 'I' of his narrator as Mason himself, both as witness to the realities and inventor of the fictions. In order to distinguish their voices, however, the narrator within the work is referred to as Bruce while the writer of the work is Mason. Again, the past tense is maintained in the performance script.

Theme: Progenitors

'Bo Baron was dead' is the stark opening phrase that provokes Bruce's enquiry into his friend's 'strange life and tragic, labyrinthine end'. Having traced Bo's parentage—his mother, Micaela, was brought to England in 1898 by a father fleeing a Tsarist pogrom; his eccentric father, Israel, was 'an English and very emancipated Jew'. Bruce reveals that Bo's birth and naming were accompanied by the roaring of an 'immense, bearded, barbaric . . . Tsar Boris' in a 1919 *Boris Godunov* at Covent Garden, presented by Russian émigrés escaping 'with the breaths of the Bolsheviki hot on their necks'. After being expelled from Charterhouse at the age of seventeen for publishing a clandestine newspaper with a lewd cover, Bo takes to his room for three days and reads *Das Kapital* and *The Communist Manifesto*. Later, at a French school near Menton, he reads Marxist literature for two full terms then spends the third 'devising a scheme for breaking the bank at the Menton Casino'. Finding himself 'richer by more than three hundred thousand francs . . . he simply vanished'. Discovered in a Belgrade hotel with an ex-WWI female spy, he is returned to his parents, who ship him off to a cousin in Wellington: Ezra Baumberg, and his wife Sophie. Bo sees a challenge in New Zealand's reputation as an unspoiled, green and pleasant land with 'noble savages'. Once there, he accepts a job in Ezra's textile firm.[11]

While undoubtedly heightened, it may be deduced that this fictionalises the arrival of Lindsay Nathan in Mason's life and, as we shall see, his avid pursuit of a Marxist agenda.

Variation I: Bo Baron and the Impressionable Young

In the story, young Bruce is instantly impressed with the 'vividness of Bo's conversation, the satisfying geometry of his speech'. However, Bo's support for the Bolsheviks in their abortive attempt (following the October Revolution) to overthrow the elected Finnish government, which Bo saw as 'fascist', disconcerts Bruce. Bo also declares manners to be the bourgeois habit of 'a dying society crystallising into formal decadence'.[12]

When Bo declares, 'All art is didactic. It must have a moral purpose, a function', and challenges his colonial friend to explain why he writes, Bruce replies that he dislikes morality because it reeks of the tribal taboos of his family's limited circle of friends. Bo is blunt: 'If you've got something to say, say it. If you haven't, shut up. There's far too much writing done as it is.' Bruce's worldview changes radically as Bo elucidates the principles of dialectical materialism, guides him through the venomous invective of Thomas A Jackson's *Dialectics,* and infuses him with such Marxist jargon as 'social-fascist reptile, deviationist jackal, opportunistic hyena', so that he comes to believe in 'capitalism as Original Sin'. His Marxist honeymoon lasts only six weeks, however.[13]

Finding himself 'inexplicably bereft of faith' but unwilling to lose their 'marriage of true minds', Bruce seeks to retain Bo's respects and to be sure of his company by suggesting they make their fortune by writing a play. Despite severe artistic differences (chapter one), they complete *All is Not Gold.* Bo then rejects Bruce's suggestion they submit this masterpiece to Wellington Repertory Theatre. Instead, they send it to American actress Katharine Cornell in New York after finding her in a *Theatre Arts* magazine. Signing themselves as Paul Quinault (Bruce) and Roger Saltzenthal (Bo), they enclose a tape recording which, despite Bruce's protestations, begins 'We in New Zealand, who believe in the historic ascendancy of the working class' and goes on to claim it would be an honour for her to play their heroine Maud, who exemplifies 'the contradictions of capitalist society'. It is not rejection they suffer fourteen weeks later but the ignominy of being dismissed by a secretary: 'Miss Cornell is not reading plays this year.' They get drunk and send an abusive letter to her, and then, in sober remorse, send her Frank Sargeson's *A Man and His Wife* as an appeasing gift. They repeat this pattern until she has 'amassed almost the entire corpus of New Zealand literature'. But to no avail. At this point, noting that Bo's ascendancy over him has begun to weaken, Bruce announces his withdrawal from the narrative as a participating character to become 'Chorus, to this history . . .'[14]

Given Wellington Repertory, *Theatre Arts* and Katharine Cornell were all real, it is tempting to think the rest of the story is too.

Variation II: Bo Baron and the Bourgeoisie

Bruce's political perspective becomes less impressionable and more critically aware as Bo continues with his activism. Turning the word 'bourgeoisie' on 'the ferris wheel of Marxist ideology', Bo's attempts to shock, wound and scare Wellington society out of its middle-class liking for 'comfort and squalidly respectable morality' alienates all but the childless Baumbergs, who suffer him as their lodger. As Ezra's accountant, Bo sets about undermining his fellow workers' loyalty to their 'foreign' boss. Ezra, a Jewish-born émigré from Austria, has married Sophie, born in New Zealand of German Jewish stock. Images of the British royal family inhabit their house 'as permanent, honoured guests'. Bo's 'Baumbaiting' includes subverting their loyalty to all things British Empire and bourgeois, not least with conspiracy theories, so they too will man the barricades come the revolution. Although Bo tires of the sport, the disillusioned Baumbergs never host another Empire Day dinner, 'guilt and shame their lot'. Bo is 'the Marxist serpent who has broken them down and expelled them, naked, from Eden.'[15]

This much plus the coda was all Mason had written when he laid it aside in 1952. It may never have seen the light of a reading lamp again, let alone a spotlight, had Mason not been invited by teacher and theatre director Ralph McAllister to address a session of the New Zealand Theatre Federation-sponsored Summer School of Drama in January 1976. In preparation for an informal chat about his life in New Zealand theatre, Mason exhumed his account of how he came to write his 'first and appallingly bad play'. It got such a good reception he completed the prose work and went on to use it as the text of his fourth solo performance piece for touring.[16] In marked contrast to Bo's preference for didactic propaganda, Mason continues to 'tell it like it was', albeit passed through his authorial prism with eloquent wit, and leave his readers and audiences free to judge as they choose.

In the next variation he contrasts Marxist idealism with social realism, allowing a new character to critique Bo's politics from a 'working-class' perspective, and testing our sympathies in the process.

Variation III: Bo Baron, Love and Marriage

Bo falls in love with Elsie Granger, a watersider's daughter. 'In the interests of the class struggle,' he insists, 'for my future and my present peace of mind, I must marry a proletarian'. A typist by day in 'a capitalist bog', Elsie spends her nights typing envelopes for *The People's Voice* though she would rather be reading *True Romances.* Despite Sophie's contemptuous dislike of Elsie and his parents' strong opposition by cable, the wedding goes ahead with Bruce as Bo's best man. But Bo's proletarian wife resists his attempt to wean her off *True Romances* and on to Marxist dialectics. After insisting she must give up her job because 'it's a man's job to keep his wife', Bo discovers she is 'a real sloven'. When Elsie throws him out after three weeks, Bo asks Bruce to go to her. He finds their tiny attic flat trashed and Elsie seething with hatred for his 'dialectical bullshit, Marxist bullshit' and his preference, in bed, for turning on the light to 'read jaw-breaking bullshit books' to her. Elsie goes home to her mother and Bo returns to the Baumbergs, never to flirt again with the proletariat.[17]

It is important to note that Elsie Granger bears no resemblance to Sonja Vile (later to achieve prominence as socialist activist Sonja Davies), whom Lindsay Nathan married in 1941 when she was a naïve seventeen-year-old nurse, although they too proved incompatible and parted.[18] According to Stephen Hamilton's *A Radical Tradition: A History of the Victoria University of Wellington Students' Association 1899–1999*, however, the people Mason fictionalises in the next variation, which begins in 1941, are based on real Marxists and radicals with whom Mason and Nathan mixed at Victoria College.[19] Victoria College was part of the University of New Zealand until the end of 1961; its independence as Victoria University of Wellington began in 1962. Here Mason fictionalises it as Queens College, Wellington.

Variation IV: Bo Baron and Higher Education

The 'notable personalities of the College' are identified by Hamilton as Jim Winchester ('The Portable Red Front'), Mike Mitchell ('The Portable Porn') and Ron Meek ('Clive Rogant'). They are in the cafeteria when Bruce introduces them to Bo:

> I pointed out to Bo a fierce little man who spoke very rapidly and walked very quickly, padding about in a well-articulated but not quite human fashion, as if he had stepped from an animated cartoon. His advocacy of bloody revolution was so adamant and so sustained that he was known as The Portable Red Front. Over by the window, a lean-faced, saturnine youth was recounting yet another bawdy story. His collection of obscene tales was so large, his performance of them so authoritative, he was known as The Portable Porn.
>
> At the table next to us, the centre of an admiring claque, sat Clive Rogant, brilliant in conversation, with a sardonic charm of manner which could crush an adversary but never quite make an enemy of him. From a head almost imperially grand, his physique fell away to a shrunken body and a leg withered from poliomyelitis. He carried a stick and, whenever moved to launch a profundity, would bang it loudly on the stone floor of the Caf as if he were the prompter in a French theatre, his 'deux coups' silencing his audience.[20]

Mason's love of eloquence gets full rein as he evokes the verbal skills of these precocious undergraduates while tracing the rise of Bo's star within the debating society and his fall as a trusted emissary of the Students' Association Executive. In the process he vividly summarises prevailing views on politics and religion.

Opposing the motion 'That this House believes the USSR has betrayed the working class', Bo's beautifully articulated passion raises the stock phrases of Marxist dogma 'to a higher power' and sees him judged best speaker. His popularity in the 'Caf' rivals that of Clive Rogant who, for the next debate, moves, 'That this house believes Christianity has no message for the modern world.' A 'delirium of surprise' greets the news that it is to be opposed by Mr B Baron. By invoking the Albigensian Crusade and the Spanish Inquisition, and ridiculing the Christian concept of turning the other cheek, Rogant seems to render himself unassailable. But Bo rejects Rogant's examples as token Christianity that take the Holy Word in vain to further the interests of established power. He argues that each of the dogmatic articles of the Christian faith has found their exact parallel in the Soviet Union, which he comprehensively enumerates. Again he wins, which Bruce sees as a triumph: 'Of skill. Of polemic. Of rhetoric . . . A brilliant performance. A display of the art of oratory'. But for Bo it is 'all quite literally, word for word, true.'[21]

When Hitler invades Russia (22 June 1941) the Executive of the Students' Association entrusts Bo with a telegram declaring their 'confidence in the power of the Soviet forces under Generalissimo Stalin'. But, with Bruce there to witness it, he tears it up and instead sends 'fraternal greetings to Comrade Stalin in his heroic stand against the Hitlerite hordes . . .' When Bruce objects because it is not the agreed message, Bo calls him bourgeois and claims it is 'the same in essence, only more colourful'. Its broadcast in English on Radio Moscow leads to Bo's expulsion from the Students' Association. Claiming it is a Rogant-led vendetta, he decides to 'write to Stalin! The Great Wise Teacher! He'll understand!' which leads Bruce to feel that 'Bo's bright star had suddenly plunged to its nadir.'[22]

Variation V: Bo Baron and the War for Civilisation

From late 1941 until 1945 Bruce is 'almost continuously engaged in defeating the King's enemies' (as was Mason). However, Ezra's business has been declared an essential industry and, because Bo is essential to him, it is not until mid-1943 that Bo is conscripted.

During basic training at Waiouru, he uses Sophie Baumberg's Cordon Bleu recipe book to radically reform the appalling cookhouse fare, and so is banned from the kitchens. After being arrested for attempting to stage a revolt against the privates' cramped conditions on the troop-ship, he joins the Fourth Armoured Brigade in Italy and lands a cushy driving job. On his return from a Russian convoy, Bruce receives news in a letter from Micaela Baron: 'One afternoon, Bo had failed to return. His jeep has passed over a mine; wreckage was strewn over a wide area. Bo was blown to smithereens; only his paybook, later discovered in a roadside bush, identified him.' Later, Bo's father, Israel, would describe him to Bruce as 'like a star on an unknown orbit. Someday, someone must trace its course. Perhaps, Naval Person, you?' Back home, Bruce describes him to the grieving Sophie and Ezra as 'a comet, a light, a path to truth. He was right, you know, I learned much from him.' And for a while it is as if all colour has drained from the landscape of Bruce's life.[23]

Variation VI: Bo Baron and the Ineffable Light

Early in 1946 Bruce receives a Yugoslav postcard, post-marked in London, from 'Roger Salzenthal' (Bo's pen-name from their doomed attempt to become rich as playwrights). He calls Bo's mother, Micaela, at once and announces that her son is alive. Israel institutes enquiries that eventually reveal Bo had fought with Tito's partisans under his assumed name and then disappeared, it was thought, to Russia. It appears that Italian partisans had spirited him into Yugoslavia and fabricated his death using another corpse. Bruce's recollection that Bo had written to 'his Great Wise Teacher, Stalin' provokes more enquiries, but 'the Soviets indignantly repudiated any knowledge of Boris Godunuv Baron, alias Roger Salzenthal'. Only after Bo has been returned to England by way of a spy exchange do intelligence sources suggest he may have been taken to Russia for political training then 'crashed into ignominy at the time of Stalin's rupture with Tito, in 1948. As a Titoist, deviationist reptile, he was dumped in one of Stalin's vast zoos, with thousands of others and slowly rotted there, to be cynically plucked out in exchange for a minor spy.'[24]

Aged thirty-two, Bo shuffles with the gait of an old man. Back in London with his parents he is broken and uncommunicative until, hearing his mother answer the phone in Russian, he suddenly recites a famous poem by Yesyenin, 'Letter to my Mother', which ends: 'Tot vyechernyi nyeskazanyi svyet' (That ineffable evening light). Buoyed by this flicker, Micaela hires a chauffeur to drive them around London. Bo rallies at the sight of the wharves and insists on getting out, only to be ridiculed for crying out, 'Workers of the world, unite!' (the only English words he speaks). At Battersea Park he runs ahead to the Big Dipper. 'As Micaela watched, hand to her mouth, Bo rose in his seat and, at the highest point of elevation, spread his arms—Micaela thought wildly of a black bat—and threw himself off. Shrieks, screams, as Bo whirled down one hundred and fifty-two feet, flashing through struts and girders, a plummeting black fowl, then head first into a heap of metal rubble. Bo Baron was dead.'[25]

Given Lindsay Nathan lived on in the United Kingdom (where, having changed his name by deed poll to Lindsay Mason, he married an English woman with whom he had children; they lived in Sussex and he worked at a university), it is clear the final rise and fall of Bo Baron is invented, presumably to validate the heraldic black bird image. However, Sonja Davies does refer to 'many incredible-sounding adventures' Lindsay apparently had in the Army, and to hearing that he was 'with Tito's guerrillas in Yugoslavia'.[26] Exactly where Mason crosses over from heightened reality into total fiction remains, therefore, a matter of conjecture. Apart from creating Bo Baron as a device for grappling with the profound impression Lindsay Nathan had on him, the whole of *Courting Blackbird* may also be seen as Mason's means of critically appraising Soviet-style socialism, a topic he would return to in *To Russia, with Love.*

Performance-wise, *Courting Blackbird* was the last prose work Mason brought to the stage. While presenting *Not Christmas, but Guy Fawkes* in March 1976 at the Christchurch Arts Festival—where the Court Theatre's production of his major play *Awatea* had featured during the 1974 Commonwealth Games—Mason rashly offered to present his full 'Solo Cycle' in sequence, including the premiere of this latest one. But he didn't complete variations III, IV, V and VI until

July 1976. Downstage hosted a Sunday night preview to an invited audience on 9 August. Nine days later—after single performances of *The End of the Golden Weather*, *Men of Soul* (*The Waters of Silence* and *To Russia, with Love*) and *Not Christmas, but Guy Fawkes*—Mason premiered *Courting Blackbird* at The Court Theatre.

He went on to perform it at Gateway, Fortune, Downstage, Maidment, Centrepoint and Four Seasons.[27]

CHAPTER FOUR

SHORT AND SATIRICAL

Pause; The Bonds of Love; The Evening Paper; The Licensed Victualler; The Verdict; A Case in Point; Wit's End; We Don't Want Your Sort Here

'You can't start with a pause!' a theatre critic character exclaims in Tom Stoppard's *The Real Inspector Hound*. But that is what marked the first public production on record of a Bruce Mason play. In May 1944, while he was overseas on active service with the Navy, Mason's short two-hander *Pause* was produced at Otago University's Allen Hall by his bride-to-be, Diana Shaw, who also played the female role. While studying medicine at Otago she was president of the Otago University Dramatic Society.

PAUSE

Pause shared the playbill with excerpts from Shakespeare's *Macbeth* and George Bernard Shaw's one-act 'true to life farce' *Augustus Does His Bit*. The *Pause* script has not survived but ADM's review in the Students' Association newspaper, *Critic*, has done history the service of detailing the plot.

In the first of two scenes, an elated Joe arrives home from the Great War to his bride, Ethel. But in the wake of his experiences, he becomes obsessed with the futility of existence, pacing the room and denouncing mankind's impotence in shaping the world's destiny. Ethel's 'coquettish blandishments' soon revive his good humour, however, and they look forward to starting a family and playing their small part in shaping the new order. They joyously redecorate this home, Joe settles in his armchair and Ethel hands him the evening paper (an image Mason would return to with *The Evening Paper*).

Scene 2 finds them twenty years later as WWII is about to break out. A dowdy, middle-aged Ethel hands Joe the evening paper, sits in her armchair and knits. It is evident they have had no children. A monosyllabic and rude Joe reveals he has decided to enlist again, rendering Ethel incredulous and frightened as he claims he can only attain peace in the turmoil of war: everything will be different once he is back in the Army.[1]

A few weeks later, in *Critic*'s correspondence column, a Catherine Crosse added, 'Diana Shaw's performance was one of the finest I've seen on any amateur stage, and her technique is far more polished than that of many more experienced actresses. When one considers that she also produced the play, one can appreciate the magnitude of her achievement.'[2]

Pause notwithstanding, the true dawning of the 'Masonic age' of New Zealand theatre came in 1953 when two of Mason's short plays were produced by Unity Theatre in Wellington, an amateur group committed to performing plays that were 'real and sincere in their presentation of life'.[3] At its inception in 1940, Unity had strong links to the Communist Party, which were later severed in an effort to avoid substandard 'propaganda' plays in favour of 'good, contemporary, progressive drama [that] drew an educated, politically aware membership and an audience for whom Wellington in the 1940s was a cultural desert.'[4] It was the first New Zealand theatre to produce Bertolt Brecht (*The Caucasian Chalk Circle,* in 1952) but Mason, who felt Unity's earlier commitment to political theatre had been 'suffocatingly narrow',[5] preferred a realism that challenged audiences to come to grips with their own values, attitudes and opinions by offering insights into all sides of an argument.

Both *The Bonds of Love* and *The Evening Paper* reflect desolate views of life, love and sex in early 1950s New Zealand, and may be seen as early examples of Kiwi 'kitchen sink' drama, although they predate the term. 'Kitchen sink' was coined in 1954 by English art critic David Sylvester to describe such works as John Bratby's social realist painting 'Still Life with Chip Frier', depicting the clutter of urban domestic life.[6] It was also applied, usually as a pejorative term, to socially realistic working-class dramas such as John Osborne's *Look Back in Anger* (1956) and Arnold Wesker's *Chicken Soup with Barley* (1958), referring as much to the psychological as the physical worlds of the plays.[7]

The year 1953 also marked the moment Edmund Hillary put

New Zealand on the map by conquering Mount Everest with Sherpa Tenzing Norgay, on the eve of Queen Elizabeth II's coronation in London, and the year Richard and Edith Campion launched The New Zealand Players with *The Young Elizabeth*, an English play by Jennette Dowling and Francis Letton about Queen Elizabeth I. Although we were achieving distinction in some fields, our cultural ties to Britain remained very strong, and in *The Bonds of Love* and *The Evening Paper* Mason uses English characters to comment on the character and nature of Kiwi life. Both plays won prizes in the 1953 British Drama League Playwriting Competition.

The Bonds of Love

The Bonds of Love is a sardonic title taken from a line in the New Zealand national anthem: 'In the bonds of love we meet'. Set in a seedy hotel room, which could be in any New Zealand city, the play depicts English immigrant sisters as sexually degraded by the uncouth attitudes of Kiwi men but, rather than 'send up' the men or the women, Mason gives each individual a strong point of view and leaves us to judge them as we will. Played for truth, with just a slightly heightened realism, a good production should elicit sudden laughs of shocked surprise as audience members confront their own basic attitudes.

Sally, robbed of her English parents and fiancé by the war, is now a housemaid at the City Commercial, where she shares her bed with barman George. The 'usual' for them is a flutter on the horses, a tot of whiskey and routine 'bed'. He refuses to 'make a lady' of her, having been there once: 'Never again.' She judges all men as 'pigs . . . Have your fun and let the devil take the hindmost'—and has banished George from her bed.[8]

Sally's sister Edna, however, is married and turns up having left her husband, Bert, who has blackened her eye after coming home drunk from work, wanting sex and being rejected. Sally's view that 'that's how you keep a man. If he doesn't want that of you, you might as well give up,' is rejected by Edna as 'crude and beastly'.[9]

'I mean a man's not a fish, is he?' is Bert's excuse. He is contrite but fed up with being ignored in favour of the kid. 'I've got some rights, haven't I?' When Sally asks if he loves her, he is not sure: 'What's love anyway? That soppy stuff you see at the flicks when the choir starts singing? I don't want her for that.' But Sally knows romantic love is what Edna wants.[10]

By way of resolution, Edna agrees to look after the baby, cook Bert's meals and keep the house tidy provided he leaves her alone when she wants to be. Warned by Sally that 'he'll go outside for his fun' if she's not careful, Edna shocks her sister by saying, 'Men seem to be like that. If I don't know about it, and he doesn't spend all our money on it, I shan't mind too much'. Bert is so relieved he offers to make his wife a nice cup of cocoa and put her to bed if she comes home with him, which she does. Sally succumbs once more to 'the bonds of love' by allowing George back into her bed and the status quo is largely reinstated with, at best, a faint glimmer of hope for marginal improvement in both relationships.[11]

Mason has painted a very bleak picture, here, of the attitudes some men had held towards love and sex, provoking his audience to examine their own values and behaviour. While it may be easy for middle-class theatre-goers to feel socially superior to the characters depicted, Unity Theatre stalwarts—and Mason himself, who had an admiration for an Old Vic that was 'sustained by the modest offerings of the poor . . . because they liked the theatre and for no other reason'—are unlikely to have seen the play as a middle-class challenge to working-class values.[12] The critique is of male values and behaviour in 'the gender war'. George and Bert coupled with up-market advertising mogul Max in *Zero Inn* (1970) and the men of the landed gentry in his final stage play, *Blood of the Lamb* (1980), suggest Mason saw—or came to see—male dominance and a husband's sense of sexual entitlement in marriage as endemic across all classes.

The perception that New Zealanders are lacking in arts and culture in comparison to the English persists as a point of view in his next play.

The Evening Paper

Where *The Bonds of Love* pits English women who are out to better themselves against the shortcomings of uncouth Kiwi men, *The Evening Paper*, set in middle-class suburbia, subjects Kiwi women to the scathing judgement of a young man born in New Zealand but raised in England. However, it would be simplistic to suggest that men are off the hook in a misogynistic diatribe. While the mother and daughter characterisations may seem grotesquely satirical, Elfrida and Winsome do have real emotional depth. Again, by bringing out the controlling tendencies of men and comparing the failure of Elfrida's husband, Ernest, as a sexual partner with the more sensitive and romantic approach of Winsome's cousin Philip—albeit revealed in the process of rejecting her—Mason mounts a dramatic debate that demands we consider the viewpoints of all four characters. He compels us to empathise with each of them in turn, while considering the social systems and structures that contribute to their circumstances.

It is tempting to compare Mason's Elfrida and Ernest with Samuel Beckett's yet-to-be-written wittering Winnie of *Happy Days* (1961) and husband Willie, who also takes refuge in the newspaper. Elfrida's oppressive living room décor ('*Everything to make the room look over-stuffed and undersized has been done*')[13] may be seen as a prescient variation on Bratby's cluttered kitchen. Elfrida and Winnie are both incarcerated in unfulfilling marriages and endeavour to make the best of their lot by filling their lives with routine. Phrases that were yet to gain currency such as 'suburban neurosis', 'housewife syndrome' and 'sex role conditioning' may be readily applied to *The Evening Paper*. It is also worth noting that Mason's socially pretentious matriarch anticipates British television scriptwriter Roy Clarke's Hyacinth Bucket of *Keeping Up Appearances* fame by thirty-seven years.

Even more of a fright than her mother is Winsome, the large and plain only child of Elfrida and Ernest. Aged twenty-three, she is a misfit at the bank where she works and hopelessly dependent on her domineering mother for guidance. The routine of this family's humdrum life is upset by a visit from Philip, the son of Elfrida's cousin Amy who, although born in New Zealand, has been raised in 'the UK' for the past twenty-eight of his thirty years, because Amy saw England as 'home'.

Philip turns out to be a born-again Kiwi who has worshipped at New Zealand House and arrived 'home' knowing more than his cousins do about the country of his birth. But while he thrills at the Everest-conquering Edmund Hillary's 'We knocked the bastard off!', Elfrida bridles at the coarseness. Philip is fascinated that the idiomatic Kiwi 'hooray' for 'goodbye' has come from the Māori 'haere ra', but Elfrida regards that as 'more for the young' and 'slightly common'. Philip empathises with his maternal grandfather James Gifford's poetic outburst atop the Hochstetter Dome in the Southern Alps in 1874—Mason channels Thomas Bracken with 'I breathed and cried aloud, into that huge Empyrean: Oh God, reclaim your son: behold, at last, a man!'—but all Elfrida can do is squirm in sympathy with Philip's mother over their grandfather, James Gifford's father, being a butcher in Golders Green.[14]

Left alone with the over-frocked Winsome and having suffered her mangling-by-piano of 'The Minute Waltz', Philip launches into a tirade of criticism of her parents, the room, her name and her dress. He challenges her to have some ambition beyond being 'a credit to that gorgon of a mother of yours' and sums it all up as 'The Kapok Castle' (the play explains that kapok is 'the stuff you put in cushions') from which 'your mother puts down the rope for the fairy prince: white silk, a blue sash and a four course meal: that's the bait to lure them into your boudoir . . .'[15]

In considering Philip's rage—against their inability to appreciate New Zealand's natural beauty and the heroism of Edmund Hillary in conquering Everest; against Winsome, her parents, the room, her name and her dress—it must be noted that Mason's angry young man emerged three years before John Osborne's more infamous Jimmy Porter in *Look Back in Anger* (1956). Although Jimmy followed Johnny Strabler (Marlon Brando) in *The Wild One* (1954) and Jim Stark (James Dean) in *Rebel Without a Cause* (1955), Mason's Philip Dalton came first. In 1953, then aged thirty-two, Mason was clearly in the vanguard of scriptwriters challenging the conservative status quo. Philip does apologise for his rudeness, however, and when Winsome insists he tell her what to do, he advises her to go on a diet and get away as soon as possible. Against his better judgement, he obliges her desire to be kissed by him.

When *The Evening Paper* was selected to launch full-length New Zealand drama on television in 1965 (preceded only by Al Flett's shorter *All Earth to Love* in 1963, by which 'viewers were evidently bored by the play's reliance on a "sit around the table and talk" plot'),[16] Mason wrote the scene that had originally taken place offstage and then incorporated it into the revised stage play script. In his sparsely furnished student flat, Philip is packing a rucksack for a trip to the Hochstetter Dome (rising from the Southern Alps' Tasman Glacier) and listening to a Sibelius symphony[17] when Winsome turns up with her suitcase: a runaway, ready to move in with him. Her ignorance of Sibelius, her lack of appreciation of alpine aspirations and her desire to get drunk on rum to help see through her determination to lose her virginity, all work to alienate Philip further. Disproving what the girls at the bank have told her about men 'wanting it all the time', Philip emphatically does not (in marked contrast to George and Bert in *The Bonds of Love*). 'Men are not just appetite, appetite, like dogs or goats,' Philip tells Winsome. 'This thing that can happen between a man and a woman: it's the greatest gift we have. But it's nothing to do with grasping or getting or forcing or insisting. It's got to happen; it's got to steal up on you . . .' She makes him admit he is not attracted to her and then shrieks her fury and is left clenching her fists and drumming her heels as he goes to call a taxi.[18]

Before Mason compares and contrasts Philip and Ernest's attitudes towards sex, he uses the return of Elfrida and Ernest from a night out to play with attitudes towards entertainment. Elfrida has enjoyed being taken out of herself by art: a tragic tale so real it made her cry. But Ernest, who owns a hardware store, prefers broad comedy: 'Split your sides, home to the nest, forget about it, face a new day. That's all the art I want.' They have assumed 'Win' (as ironic a nickname as Elfrida's 'Freed') has gone to bed, until they discover her 'Dear Mummy and Daddy' letter: 'I have gone away for a while. Please don't try to find me . . .' First the girls at the bank and Philip are blamed, then Ernest—living up to his name—criticises 'Freed' for doing too much for Winsome and filling their family life with routine. She counters by asking, 'What have you ever given me, to make it more than routine?' Elfrida reveals she has felt cheated since their wedding night but lacked the words to express her feelings and so resorted to her mother's advice by submitting and taking refuge in routines, realising that 'love' only existed in books, films and songs. Ernest is floored: doesn't she love him? Her reply is a bleak summing up of middle-class suburban life: 'You go out in the morning: you come home at night. I cook the meal: you read the paper. I nag: you talk back. In the weekends you potter, and on Sundays we go for a drive. If that's love, then I love you, Ernest'. Now she is scared of the routine breaking up: 'I'm too old for another'. Somehow, and very realistically, this honesty brings them closer, but his big gesture for reconciliation is to throw the evening paper into the coal scuttle and offer to make her a cuppa.[19]

Lesser playwrights might leave it there, but Mason brings his themes to a head in a way that compels us to determine where we stand on the issues. The return of Winsome, brought home by Philip, prompts a hurt Elfrida to play the 'Oh, do you live here?' card. She then turns on him and his mother (her cousin) for being so critical and trying to change things all the time. 'Oh, we're not critical people,' she says. 'We know nothing of art or culture. There's no history to talk about. But, good heavens, what's that anyway? You don't live on art! You can't feed on history! . . . And this, too. There's more to life than standing on a mountain top and shouting into the wind!' But in one key respect, Philip is actually the opposite of his mother:

> I came here looking for a fresh start, open spaces, new prospects. My mother gave up the chance, to be a half-pie, English phony. So I expected a lot from you, the family that stayed and stuck it out. And I find you dug into the ground like moles! You could have had Paradise here, the Just City! And what have you done? Mucked it. Turned freedom into safety tickets.

Now Ernest, who has hitherto sided with Philip, calls him 'a Pommie pipsqueak!' and Elfrida banishes him: 'Out of my house. At once! And the country too, if you know what's good for you. We don't want your sort here.' With Philip thus dismissed, a contrite and fearful Winsome declares her hatred of all men except Daddy—who still hasn't made that cup of tea. Elfrida gaily tells her they're not all hateful but 'pretty useless' and declares, 'We'll do it. The girls will do it! We'll go to the kitchen and make his lordship his cuppa,' which makes Winsome 'so happy!' Alone and back in his chair, Ernest retrieves the evening paper and raises it like a shield as the Sibelius symphony swells and the lights slowly fade.[20]

This tragicomic ending is positively Chekhovian in that it returns its characters to an unfulfilling status quo while leaving us to ponder the implications for our own lives in a wider social context that cannot be sustained. The comparison is apt, given that in the same year, 1953, Mason wrote a parody entitled *The Three Sisters of Paraparaumu* (see *Wit's End* and *We Don't Want Your Sort Here*) as a revue sketch.

The Evening Paper won a British Drama League prize in 1953 and was broadcast as a radio play a decade later but its impact on the wider New Zealand community would not be felt until 1965, when it became the first full-length play by a local writer to be produced by the New Zealand Broadcasting Corporation (NZBC). In his *New Zealand Drama* contribution to the New Zealand University Press *Studies in New Zealand Literature* series, Mason reveals he was 'quite unprepared for the storm of protest and abuse which engulfed [him] from all over the country'.

> On the night it was shown in the Auckland province, AKTV-2 was jammed by over 1,000 telephone calls, and there were more than 500 letters to the press, which reached me in successive shock waves, as the play moved from channel to channel. I received over 200 myself, of which perhaps 20 praised the play, 100-odd damned it to perdition, and between 50 and 60 were anonymous and some obscene. May I quote some choice remarks.
>
> 'I will willingly contribute to any fund organised to deport you.'
>
> 'I could tear you limb from limb for *The Evening Paper*, (sgd.) New Zealand Mother.'
>
> 'Leave New Zealand alone!'

'You have besmirched the name of this fair land, and insulted all that we hold most dear.'

'May God forgive you for this crime against your country.'

'Anyone can tell you are not New Zealand-born.'

Which, in fact, I am. I quote these, not to show the scars of playwriting, but because they reveal some very interesting attitudes. My play was not, after all, earth-shaking; moreover, it was twelve years old, had been produced on the stage at least six times up and down the country, had won a national playwriting competition in 1953, and had a successful radio production in 1963. But, taking it into half a million households, had given it this ferocious impact.

I had to conclude that what made many people so angry was the experience of simply seeing their environment examined, possibly for the first time in their experience. I wondered had many of these irritated people ever read a New Zealand novel? I came to these conclusions, which I invite you to challenge:

(a) That many New Zealanders still regard art, in the context of dealing with social issues dramatically, as an act of unlicensed prying.

(b) That if a man performs such an exercise, he is, *ipso facto*, disloyal. (To what, though?)

(c) That New Zealand life is beyond criticism and beyond examination.

(d) That New Zealand plays, or art, are simply not, by their very nature, entertaining. Entertainment results from seeing *others* get into comic fixes or tragic dilemmas, but what we ourselves laugh at or suffer from is not dramatic material. Or . . . a new society is a self-justifying work of art in its own right, and to examine it or criticise it, is an act close to treachery.[21]

The Licensed Victualler

As something completely different, Bruce Mason wrote a short operetta for the Wainuiomata Women's Institute. A 'farce in one scene, with music', *The Licensed Victualler* won them the B-grade section of the British Drama League Festival in 1954. It depicts a monthly meeting of the Hikitene Women's Guild in the parish hall of St Wiggleswid's Church. Fictitious Hikitene (a transliteration of Hick Town) is described by the president as God's 'own little acre' protected from an unnamed city, by 'a brace of mountain ranges'. The city is viewed as 'that sink of vice, that modern Gomorrah'—fifty miles away.[22] With licensing trusts barely a decade old in New Zealand, debates over whether communities should be 'wet' or 'dry' was certainly topical in the mid-1950s. The operetta also revisits the male/female polarities Mason explored in *The Bonds of Love*.

Nine women ('or more or less, as the producer sees fit') form two choruses, busily knitting throughout the action. They establish themselves as: 'The source of creative ability/ The fountains of grace and agility/ The seats of legitimate fertility/ And the guardians of family stability/ The guardians, guardians, guardians of/ Morality and stability.' Their avowed aim is to keep Hikitene godly, clean and, above all, dry: safe from the vile demon drink. Mrs Gullett, head of the Temperance Division, reports on a successful sortie to cleanse a Mrs Chamberlain's washhouse of her husband's home-brew paraphernalia. On a show of hands the husbands of all but two—Mrs Gullett and Mrs Brindle—are making home-brew. The president brandishes car tyre valves as tokens of her success in foiling a father's plan to take a convoy of mates to the dreaded city. 'Let them look into our eyes if they want a bright light,' she declares, 'and for sensual abandon, well: they have their gardens, they have their work, and they have us. What more could any man want?'[23]

Mrs Brindle, a new settler from London, is introduced and welcomed to Hikitene, where 'the pure flame of the pioneer still burns . . . For a hundred years now, there have been white people at Hikitene, working away, summer and winter; richer and poorer; to bring the spark of grace to what was once a savage waste.' The competitions for bloom of the month and seamstress of the month—all won by the president—give Mrs Brindle some idea of how they live their lives. Then a letter is delivered seeking the consent of the Women's Guild for 'the erection . . . No!/ Proceed! Proceed!/ Of a public house in Hikitene!', with a promise that, in exchange, the guild will be 'handsomely endowed'. The women's horror at the proposition is robustly expressed.[24]

Before the titular victualler is brought in to be told what they think, Mrs Brindle asks to have her say. Her argument is that a man is 'a hunter: a rover: and the jungle's his natural home'; that women are really the guardians of 'early senility [and] moral sterility'; that 'marriage is a game [and] no man would stand for it that's in his right mind'. The only way to keep him happy is to 'give him something to make him a bit woozy. Get him nice and lively and swimming just a little, and he'll come home like a lamb. Course he'll think he's a lion, and that's the secret. He'll think he's in the jungle again . . .' She convinces them that any husband will get savage and wild if he can't have his tot; that the opening of a pub will see an end to home-brewing; that if he comes home with 'enough under his belt' not only will he think his wife is the Queen of Sheba, 'he'll think anything.' This differs markedly from the way Mason depicts the effects of a father's drinking in Ginger Finucane's family ('The Conch Shell'). Convinced, the women open the door to the Licensed Victualler who bears 'Good cheer [to] free you from strain/ And free you from pain/ In a glass of bottled beer!' They all drink to a rousing chorus: 'All hail the Licensed Victualler/ The family's noble saviour/ The guardian of good behaviour.'[25]

The arguments both sides offer, for and against, in *The Licensed Victualler* are equally extreme and absurd, leaving the audience to weigh up the pros and cons not only of the licensing issue but also of any attempt to legislate for better moral behaviour.

The Verdict

Mason confronts our tendency to rush into moral judgement more seriously with *The Verdict*, written in response to public reaction to the Parker–Hulme murder trial, which had dominated the headlines the previous year (1954).[26] This time the story is hermetically sealed in New Zealand. Although the original Hulme family are English, there are no English characters in *The Verdict*.

The lounge bar of the Tirimoana Hot Springs Hotel, in the off-season, is Mason's choice of place to pit a lone woman, who has travelled a long way, against two couples who turn out to be on their fifth annual golf, bridge and hot-pools holiday together. Barrister Lewis Fisher, '*brisk, professional*', has a young wife, Janet, who '*finds her life easy and pleasant but there is a ruefulness in her expression which is her way of accepting experiences she does not quite desire, but cannot altogether avoid.*' Jack, a '*high-spirited*' extrovert sells liquor for a living, and his wife Mabel '*has a native warmth*'. Barney the barman, who has 'heard it all', is always discrete and operates as a sort of Common Man facilitator as the drama unfolds.

Given it is the talk of the nation, conversation between the couples inevitably turns to the guilty verdict passed on fifteen-year-old Fiona Douglas who 'murdered, according to careful plan, her father, Dr Maurice Douglas, while he was taking his bath.' As they question, discuss and pass judgement, it emerges that 'Mrs Douglas lived eight years, three-in-a-bed,' as Jack puts it, with her husband and a boarder named Moore, 'Never tried to hide it either. Everyone knew, even his patients.' Lewis' know-it-all tone of moral superiority dominates as he observes the deceased was a psychiatrist with 'advanced ideas' who became the 'good, old-fashioned, heavy father' on discovering his daughter was pregnant. Lewis dismisses his wife Janet's comment that it could happen to any of them as 'rubbish. It happened to them because they asked for it. Just deserts.' It is Mabel's inability to comprehend how the mother could 'leave her own daughter, her own flesh there by herself, to hear a life sentence from a judge' that provokes the lone woman to reveal herself as Mrs Douglas.[27]

As they manoeuvre to regain their equilibrium on the shifting ground, Mason employs a clever dramaturgical device by getting Barney to tell her who they are and what they do, so 'she'll know who she's dealing with.' Mrs Douglas then attempts to explain her own situation: she had a delicate and highly strung husband with personal difficulties, and despite her daughter Fiona, her life had 'no core'. When Ronald Moore moved in as a boarder, they fell in love. She had an open relationship with Maurice, who 'seemed to understand', and she and Ronald became lovers; 'Maurice didn't want a divorce, I was still very fond of him, and so we lived together, the three of us, for eight years, until . . . (*A pause*) Was I wrong?' Janet says yes, she was, because she had a child. But as the battle of virtues and values continues, the complacent facades crack to expose their own moral lapses. Mabel can't understand how Mrs Douglas can contemplate sailing off to an aunt in England leaving her pregnant daughter in prison, assuming her baby will be adopted. She goes on to reveal why she believes a mother has a sacred trust to look after her child. Years ago, at the end of her maternal tether, with Jack away yet again for his work, Mabel abandoned their crying child, escaped to a picture theatre, and returned to find little Sarah had smothered herself. Janet confesses that, unable to maintain the role of perfect wife and mother of three with Lewis, she has been unfaithful. When Jack blurts out it was with him—years ago, on their second holiday together and it only lasted for a few weeks—Mabel is reasonably pragmatic, while the outraged and sanctimonious Lewis' main concern is the danger of gossip. 'If you knew what I've got up here,' Barney reassures him, tapping his head, 'you wouldn't ask.'[28]

Pointing out they volunteered their revelations without any coercion from her, Mrs Douglas tells them of her own lone struggle with guilt and asks what she should have done. 'Look: sometimes perfectly healthy people produce a monster or an idiot . . . You can't say, because of this, because of that. There's nothing big enough to hold it! I had a lover: so have others. I neglected my child: so have others. Must that lead to murder? No. Or the prisons would burst their walls. I had to know that. I had to see it.'[29]

When Lewis refuses to dismount from his high horse, Barney has a go at articulating the concept of forgiveness: 'Don't be too hard on the poor beggars who have to make the best of a bad job. You've got your principles: bully for you if you can live up to them. Some of us can't, you see. Or maybe we just live without too many rules and do the best we can. You call it weakness; isn't it a question of where you're strong? Some of us here, some of us there . . .'[30]

But Mason is too realistic to leave it at that. Wider public opinion arrives in the shape of an unnamed reporter whose two-hundred-mile pursuit of his story has been impeded by a puncture. Barney is alerted by a phone call from the front office, but it's Lewis who suggests Mrs Douglas hide behind the bar. Mason ensures his audience will grapple with whose side they're on as the couples and Barney conspire to protect her. They almost get away with it until the reporter spies three handbags. Lewis and Jack form a united front and soon manhandle the intruder out to his car, which causes Mrs Douglas to change her mind about escaping to an aunt in England. She will stay with her child even though she knows it will not be easy. While Mrs Douglas concludes, 'Somewhere, way beyond words, we're all in this thing together' and offers a toast to their next holiday, Lewis remains resistant and ends up sobbing in Janet's arms while Mabel and Jack hold hands.[31]

As a play about judgement, both subjective and objective, *The Verdict* invites each audience member to empathise with each well-justified character's choices while passing judgement on them, just as they do. Mason clearly knows how to engage an audience.

A Case in Point

Judgement also lies at the core of Mason's next play. For the British Drama League's special silver jubilee Festival of New Zealand Plays in August 1957, Unity Theatre premiered Bruce Mason's *A Case in Point*, subtitled (with a nod to Jonathan Swift's *A Modest Proposal*, no doubt) 'An argument on the necessity of hanging children', in which Mason played the hanging judge. This was the same month in which Mason co-directed, with Richard Campion, the New Zealand Players Theatre Workshop's trial run of *The Pohutukawa Tree*.

Sarah Gaitanos, in her biography of Wellington theatre director and teacher Nola Millar, reveals that *A Case in Point* was inspired by a Unity member asking Mason for a donation towards the campaign for the abolition of capital punishment. Instead he offered to write them a play, and the Millar-directed result won the Mavis Ring Cup for the most original production.[32] The death penalty for murder had been abolished by a Labour government in 1941 but a National government had restored it in 1950, allowing eight hangings up to February 1957. The Second Labour Government returned to power in late 1957—after *A Case in Point* had premiered—and the following year Labour made the death penalty inoperative. A conscience vote under the next National government saw capital punishment for murder abolished in 1961, although it remained valid for treason until 1989.[33]

Despite his debunking of New Zealanders who wrote plays set in England, *A Case in Point* is set entirely in the courtroom of the Suffolk County Assizes in 1833: the Britain from which New Zealand's legal system and early colonial settlers would come. The Old World language is not unlike that of Arthur Miller's *The Crucible* (written in 1953; set in 1693).

Employing a cast of ten, plus public gallery extras, Mason dramatises the case of Rex v Prout, wherein eleven-year-old Ned Prout is tried on the capital charge of stealing thirteen pullet eggs. Ned's mother and her two friends reveal the shaky understanding their ilk has of the finer points of the law. Ebenezer Jones, a truculent farmer, has laid the charge and expects the law to take its course. A young lawyer called Laurence Eggers appears for the defence. When Ned pleads guilty, Eggers can only plead for mercy on his behalf, explaining the boy is the third of twelve children. Thanks to a bad winter and a fitful summer, his father is an under-employed field worker who cannot afford even one day off seeking work to attend the trial. The boy stole not for himself but for his starving family.[34]

Ned does not help his case by knowing exactly how much a boy has to steal 'before ye swing' for it: forty shillings' worth, or five shillings from a public place. The eggs he stole were worth one and fourpence ha'penny. He was taught this in prison, while awaiting trial. He was also told he can't be transported, being only eleven years old. But the judge explains he has discretionary powers and, justifying himself at length, he takes a hard line on the grounds that it would cause chaos if he and his fellow judges let young thieves like Ned go. Now that his anger is assuaged, Jones is shocked at the apparent outcome and attempts to withdraw the charge, but the judge will not allow him to 'make the law a harlot'. He dons the black cap and pronounces the death sentence, and Ned is led out amid uproar.[35]

The play ends with an intense debate between Eggers and the judge, alone in the courtroom. Eggers is passionate and emotional; the judge is detached, pragmatic and complimentary of the lawyer's ability to plead the case despite his youthful idealism. He puts a strong case for pronouncing a verdict that protects the future by using the fear of death to subdue 'the evil that lies sleeping in the heart of every man: ay, yours and mine too, ready at the first hint of weakness to awake and engulf us.' Eggers argues that property cannot be more important than people if it causes children to be hanged.

> I declare against your property that not even a starving child may touch without risking his neck, and I say to the future this: better far that our streets be wild and stealing rife, than that our children should be hung for it. I'll take the risk! I'll make the future safe for children, whether or not it's safe for goods and chattels. I'll fight, fighting blind maybe, for the right of a life, once launched, to be lived . . .

Calling him foolish, headstrong and quixotic, the judge warns Eggers he will not succeed; he will have the whole judiciary against him, ruin his career and cover himself with shame without saving a single soul. Eggers is willing to take that risk.[36]

Although the surviving typescript seems overwritten, *A Case in Point* is a powerful play with a very relevant political purpose. As with *The Bonds of Love*, *The Evening Paper* and *The Verdict*, it gains great theatrical strength from Mason's capacity to articulate both sides of the argument with compelling force.

Wit's End and We Don't Want Your Sort Here

Along with one-act plays, locally written revues were a popular form of entertainment in the 1940s, 1950s and 1960s. Mason wrote sketches for a number of Unity Theatre annual revues, performing in some himself. In December 1956 he put together an entire revue called *Wit's End*—'Book, Lyrics, Music and Production by Bruce Mason'[37]—which was independently produced at the Concert Chamber in Wellington and (for one performance only) at the Lower Hutt Little Theatre.

He included 'The Three Sisters of Paraparaumu' (1953) in which over-educated but culturally undernourished Irina, Olga and Masha plead with Private Dmitri: 'Marry me: take me to Wellington!' When the platoon reunion at the Buckle Street barracks beckons Dmitri, they each plead: 'Take me!'—'Take me!'—'Take me!' In his atrocious

Kiwi accent, he replies, 'Well, not today, chicks. Men only. You know: Kiwi-style.' Their demented, hysterical sobbing, waving and screaming at his departure, gives way to a sad, collective sigh, 'When will we get to Wellington?'[38]

Improving on the Bard offers 'The Deposition of Richard II' for juvenile delinquents, 'Macbeth' for commercial television and 'Hamlet' as a pantomime (which preceded Sydney's Nimrod Theatre pantomime *Hamlet on Ice* by Grahame Bond, by fifteen years). A cautionary tale called 'Let's Make a Man of You', played out by Skinnimalinks, Snazzy and Hunk, was included in the first half while the second half opened with 'The Lizzie Boys', billed as 'our answer to the Teddy Boy Menace' and involving Adrian, Lionel, Cuthbert and Bertie.

Herself Surprised takes the theme of a lady entertaining her lover and being interrupted by her husband, and offers it in three variations. 'Lady Brindlemare's Man' by Oscar Wilde (as performed by Wellington Repertory), with Lady Dahlia Brindlemare, Lord Arlington-Portarlington and Lord Brindlemare, is replete with Wildean epigrams. 'Virtue's as Rare as a Snowball in Hell' by 'A Restoration Dramatist' (New Zealand Players), with Lady Lucinda Shakehip, Sir Pimple Overreach and Sir Fullbelly Snakehip, wallows in suggestive loquacity. 'Greasy Hall' by Bruce Mason (Unity Theatre), with Bert the lodger, Maude the Mum and George the Dad, is so monosyllabic it is almost reduced to grunts.[39] Despite the echo of Bert and George from *The Bonds of Love*, Mason's comments in a Television New Zealand *Kaleidoscope* interview twenty-six years later suggest it was not himself he was satirising in 'Greasy Hall', but Frank Sargeson.[40] Noting 'parodies are of their nature, esoteric, because appreciation of them depends on a detailed knowledge of the thing parodied,' Mason wrote sketches that were 'satiric versions, for the most part, of Wellington theatrical productions over the last few years'[41]—hence the stylistic variations in *Herself Surprised*. When they were published in *We Don't Want Your Sort Here*, however, the references to the theatre groups were dropped.

Bill Sheat, who was the business manager for *Wit's End*, recalls Mason's performance as The Herr Professor Eusebius Apfel-Strudel,

PhD, visiting examiner in speech from the University of Mittwoch-am-Breitenspiegel, as a send-up of Maria Dronke, the German–Jewish refugee from Hitler's Germany to whom Wellington thespians flocked for voice lessons. In the sketch, a thickly accented Apfel-Strudel complains that he has heard 'the morst shocking sounts in all my larfe, since arrivink in your sor beautiful Country of Gott' and therefore sets about telling us how to speak English properly, including vowel sounds, how 'the leeps must moof' and 'Diaphragmatic Control'. Demonstrating with a passage from 'Romeo ent Chuliet', an excess of passion over insufficient breath becomes his fatal downfall.[42]

In April 1961, as New Zealand's answer to Victor Borge and Noel Coward perhaps, Mason performed a collection of eleven solo items, some with piano accompaniment (by Leslie Souness), under the title of *Late Night Extra* at the Auckland Concert Chamber. The following year Caxton Press published them along with four parodies, requiring more than one actor, in a booklet entitled *We Don't Want Your Sort Here* (recalling the immortal line uttered by Elfrida Branson to her 'pommy pipsqueak' cousin in *The Evening Paper*): a collection 'drawn from various light entertainments devised over the past nine years'.[43]

A sketch entitled 'A Gastronomic Tour of God's Own Country' is in three parts which work their way up the social ladder. In the title item, Joe, of Joe's Joint in a small New Zealand town, tells his hapless customers there's only chips on the menu and sneers at the demanding, superior types who complain; 'I mean a Kiwi's not like that, now is he?' Over six verses and choruses to the tune of 'Habanera' from *Carmen*, he tells those who ask for wine or salad, who crook their fingers, loiter over their meal, talk too much or come in with any fancy ideas, 'I don't want your sort here'.[44] A suffering Husband's 'Summer Lament' (to an original tune by Mason) tracks the transformation from domestic bliss in the winter to the torment of summer, when 'my wife gets the barbecue itch!' He gets grease everywhere when they 'slum it' and avenges himself on the guests who converge from miles around by seeing that every steak is charred. But this primitive life is sending him 'nutty'; he is ready to see his lawyer.[45] The World President of the Food and Wine Society, Squadron Leader Ronnie Starr—'British, of course'—delivers 'A Matter of Taste' in seven stanzas '*to a vamp accompaniment*'. Alternating his personal self-aggrandisement with critiques of the Cliquot, 'vin spumante' and Beaujolais that he imbibes, he gets more and more pissed and mangled in his locutions.[46]

Mason's 'Good Neighbour Policy' sketch parodies 'Why Can't the English' from *My Fair Lady*. A Kiwi working man, settling with his beer and Sports Edition, reacts to Beethoven's 'Fifth Symphony' blasting from a next door radio by asking why his neighbour—who has a beard, listens to music and draws sketches—can't be the same as him:

> The thing that's fine in the Kiwi line is we're cut off from abroad,
> And if anyone starts muckin' round with the arts, we can chuck 'em overboard![47]

A revised national anthem (to the same tune as 'God Defend New Zealand') is offered in 'The National Song, A Draft for Consideration', imagined with massed choirs in a huge town hall. The Lords of Business entreat the God of Business to keep our markets safe and sweet; The Lords of Government seek to keep 'men of every creed and race' out of New Zealand to protect 'God's Own Country, God's Own Flock/ Can't adulterate the stock'; the Matriarchs worry about their sagging skin, keeping the children free from sin and keeping their menfolk's thoughts pure and fresh and shielded from the lure of flesh in order to purify New Zealand.[48]

The next three items in *We Don't Want Your Sort Here* all use original music composed by Mason. The '*middle-aged and portentous*' man who delivers 'A Cure for Delinquency' is described as '*Chairman of several companies, at the very least, the Director of some large scale enterprise*'. His cure is to, 'Bring back the cat!' (meaning the cat-o-nine-tails), and his targets include those delinquents who fail to appreciate the world they have been given; who have been coddled, spoiled, pampered and pandered to by 'The Welfare State'; who protest the hydrogen bomb: 'We'll crush youth's effrontery from God's Only Country . . .'[49] In counterpoint, 'An Angry Young Man Needs a Cause' (referencing *Look Back in Anger* and *Rebel Without a*

Cause) depicts a '*pale youth, in duffle coat, glasses, and straggly beard*' who, as an apprentice angry young man, has a disastrous lack of something to be angry about. With a pleasant job:

My future's all mapped out from the cradle to the grave
I'll get a decent pension if I promise to behave
But there's more to life than this, there's got to be because!
An angry young man needs a cause![50]

'*A lady of formidable aspect*' from Oamaru in 'La Belle Dame sans Merci' (named after the poem by John Keats and a more recent poem by New Zealand poet ARD Fairburn which attacks the supporters of capital punishment) explains her now infamous attack on a Frenchman in the middle of a rugby game because there's something about a Frenchman that makes her hopping mad, gets her dander up, gets her giddy goat and makes her do her scone. They have the temerity to bring style and elegance to the game, complain about our hotel meals and 'their gabbly talk and manners just drive me crazy.'[51]

At the opening of the 1958 Auckland Festival, Governor General Viscount Cobham opined that all modern artists should communicate and, above all, be intelligible to the ordinary person. This speech provoked Mason to parody another *My Fair Lady* song, 'An Ordinary Man', envisaging its being performed 'at the opening of the New Zealand Fine Art Winter Exhibition, or at the formal opening of the Kelliher Prize landscapes.' The performer declares he is:

Free from any modern taint. An average man am I
And though I hold vice-regal reins, in my veins
There is nothing but decorum and restraint.
A very ordinary man.
But—let—an—Abstract in your house.[52]

Philistinism is also targeted in 'Press Conference' where a Justice Department Chorus introduces the Arbiter Elegantiae Novae Zelandiae (AENZ), a little man who benignly explains himself in eight verses. It was being an 'average chap' that saw him appointed Censor, reading 'every filthy book' in order to conclude, 'This country's not ready for it'. Currently reading *The Decameron*, his:

> Muscles are flexed
> To burrow in antiquity
> Nothing's sacred: (the Bible's next)
> That record of sin and iniquity.

A final chorus hails 'literature's arbiter!'

> Our youth shall not be corrupted.
> The health of the world will be far better
> When authors are stifled and ruptured.[53]

'The Mad Hatter's Gin Party', which mashes up *Alice in Wonderland* by Lewis Carroll and *The Cocktail Party* by TS Eliot, was performed in Unity Theatre revues of 1952 and 1955. Mason regarded it as his 'best parody'. Here, in wondrously absurdist poetic style, the big life-choice Alice, the Mad Hatter, March Hare and Dormouse confront is whether to drink their gin and water without water or without gin.[54]

When the *Evening Post*'s drama critics said experimental theatre was not to their taste, and an editorial categorically damned the blasphemy of *Look Back in Anger* and the cheerless and grubby pessimism of *Waiting for Godot*, Mason wrote versions dedicated 'respectfully to the stern arbiter of taste who wrote the editorial.'[55]

Mason's 'Look Back in Anger' is just one-and-a-half pages long. When Jimmy arrives home from his job at the sweet shop, Alison, at the ironing board, greets him '*in a voice like dripping molasses*'. He shouts at her and she is replaced by Helena, who is clearly attracted to his abusiveness. The scenario repeats with Helena at the ironing board, then Alison returns and her father follows to tell Jimmy, 'Remember always: you are British!' Bells clang; 'Come to Church!' the women plead, but Jimmy confesses then and there that he has sinned and the women cry, 'A soul redeemed!'[56]

Billing his *Waiting for Godot* as 'optimistic, cheerful, traditional, forward-looking comedy', Mason shrinks it to just over a page. Estragon and Vladimir are broadly smiling chaps in '*pin-stripe suits, top hats and old school ties*'. Old boys of Harrow, they sing 'Forty Years On' (also the school song of Wellington College), exchange their top-quality top hats and are relieved that it all makes sense when Pozzo makes Lucky sing the alphabet song. *The Evening Post* is named as part of the trinity that keeps their morals safe.[57]

These short plays, sketches and parodies add further proof that Bruce Mason was a playwright by vocation, compelled to observe and dramatise the world around him for our entertainment and edification in ways that encourage us to look at ourselves and our world afresh. The works surveyed so far already prove his cultural value to New Zealand, but his major full-length works brought his contribution to a whole new level.

CHAPTER FIVE

Blood and Bone Exhumed

The Pohutukawa Tree

Aroha Mataira attempts to reconcile the old and new ways while clinging to the last acre of tribal land. But her daughter's betrayal and her son's angry reaction lead to her loss of faith and life.

The Pohutukawa Tree (1955) is a seminal work of contemporary New Zealand drama, authentic for its time and place, deeply insightful and a true classic in both craft and content. Having made it his business to learn and understand Māori language, culture and history in the 1950s, Bruce Mason was clearly way ahead of the general populace. Early readers who were ignorant of Māori culture may have thought *The Pohutukawa Tree* was overblown, that Aroha's eloquence was too florid, Johnny's desecration of the church was melodramatic and Aroha's willing herself to death was beyond the pale. Yet that was before the collective consciousness of the average Pākehā was raised in the 1970s by the early writings of Witi Ihimaera, the Michael King/Barry Barclay television documentary series *Tangata Whenua*, the setting up of the Waitangi Tribunal to settle Māori land claims, the Māori Land March led by Whina Cooper, and the seventeen-month occupation of Bastion Point. New Zealand's awareness of Māori history, viewpoints, values and oratorical traditions was further consolidated in the 1980s by Geoff Murphy's feature film *Utu*, on which he was advised by Merata Mita (who made the documentary film *Patu*), and by major novels like Ihimaera's *The Matriarch* and Patricia Grace's *Potiki*.

In his 1982 *Kaleidoscope* interview, Mason reveals that his Māori plays arose in part from his love of eloquence.

> The Māori people [have] got this enormous richness of language. Further there is something intrinsically dramatic in the people whose culture we smashed . . . It seems to me now that it's rather a case of 'Father

> forgive us for we know not what we did'. But in fact we did smash that culture. And only now is it pulling itself together. Against the bleats of 'the numbed ones', which is how I look at us Pākehās, there's still this enormous eloquence of the Māori people, which I can only admire and revere. So in my first Māori play, *The Pohutukawa Tree*, I did my best to create a character of this eloquence. And to the extent that it has been taken seriously by Māori people, I'm very flattered, honoured and humbled, because as far as I know . . . no Māori actress who has played the part has felt it was untrue to them or that it was wrong for a Pākehā to write it.[1]

In August 1957, two-and-a-half years after he wrote it, the New Zealand Players Theatre Workshop presented *The Pohutukawa Tree*, jointly directed by Richard Campion and Bruce Mason, four times only, in Wellington. Unsurprisingly, the three leading Māori characters could not be cast from within the permanent company. A feature in the Māori news magazine *Te Ao Hou* (The New World) reveals advertising and auditions secured the roles for hairdresser Hira Tauwhare (Aroha Mataira), who acted and produced in amateur theatre, Adult Education typist Mary Nimmo (Queenie), and Department of Justice employee and medical intermediate student Maia Sullivan (Johnny).

The script describes Aroha as '*a noble looking woman of sixty*'. However, given her children are still teenagers, forty-something would be a more realistic age, with her life experience giving her the face that Mason describes: '*in repose of epic grief, in animation of wonderful warmth*'.[2] The *Te Ao Hou* feature describes Hira Tauwhare as having to 'represent an aged Maori of the old school while she herself is anything but old school. But she has had wide dramatic experience and therefore was able to adapt herself to this new part very quickly.' She is profiled as being very fond of sport and a champion marching team leader whose 'main interests have always been drama and speech'. Actively involved in a number of amateur theatre and musical societies, and concert parties (she sang, danced and performed in comedy sketches during the war), Hira had passed the LTCL examination for speech.

> She told *Te Ao Hou* that she would like to interest the Maori people in speech and drama, for she believes that artistic work, apart from the old traditions, will give them confidence to face the future, for it is the future that is important, and although one can learn from one's own traditional past, other peoples' customs and cultures should be adopted and used to advantage.[3]

It is intriguing to compare and contrast these attitudes with 'old school' Aroha's lone stand for her tīpuna's values alongside her total adoption of Christianity.

After extensive revision, the New Zealand Players Theatre Workshop gave five more performances of *The Pohutukawa Tree* in 1957, three in Wellington during October and two in Auckland during November. Confirming its importance, BBC Television produced it in 1959 for their Sunday Night Theatre series, with Hira Tauwhare reprising the role of Aroha and expatriate New Zealanders and Australians (seen as interchangeable in those days) completing the cast. Mason's own radio adaptation was produced by the New Zealand Broadcasting Service, and aired on ZB Sunday Showcase in 1960, the same year it was published by Price Milburn.[4]

Also in 1960, Mason wrote this in *Te Ao Hou*:

> In the last ten years, the theatre in New Zealand has surged with activity. A recent survey disclosed that only the Soviet Union rivals, per head of population, the volume of theatrical activity in New Zealand, though this has been of necessity, almost wholly of amateur status. We have three professional touring companies, of which the New Zealand Players is the largest and reaches the largest number of people.[5] All these organisations, both amateur and professional have perforce, in their first decades of existence in a newly settled country, given most of their energies to the reproduction of established European and American commercial successes, with, in the more adventurous groups, some attempts at classical drama. But it has for long been clear that theatrical activity in New Zealand could never wholly justify or sustain itself until New Zealanders began writing, designing, dancing on themes thrown up from their own way of life, and as there are two races in New Zealand, inevitably a vital drama

> must involve both of them. A start has been made with a play like *The Pohutukawa Tree*, which showed to many millions on BBC Television something of the relations between Maori and Pakeha . . .
>
> There are, however, some difficulties in arousing the interest and participation of Maoris in theatrical activities in the European tradition, even if these involve the Maori people directly. The peculiar kind of concentration involved in European-style acting stems from the strongly individualistic tradition of Western Europe, alien in many respects to the Maori ideals of community service and performance in a community cause. The sense of being on personal display, the feeling of working alone, sometimes does not appeal to Maoris whose services may be solicited for a play on a Maori theme. The powerful sense of drama that one can sense on ceremonial occasions among the Maori people can often, it seems, take place only in contexts familiar to them from tribal associations. Yet enough good actors have already been produced by the Maori race—Inia Te Wiata is one example, Hira Tauwhare another—to suggest that in the future they will lose this reluctance, and work freely in the kind of dramatic literature now being written for them.[6]

The following year *Te Ao Hou* reported that late in 1960, having seen the BBC Television broadcast, a Mr FG Fisher produced *The Pohutukawa Tree* for the Theatr Fach (Little Theatre) in the small Welsh village of Llangefni, Anglesey.

> Not knowing what a pohutukawa looked like, Mr Fisher sent his designer some 300 miles to Kew Gardens, London, where there was one. The designer returned with a sprig which he said fell to the ground as he was passing! From this sprig, Mr Fisher built a complete tree, flowers and all. For the Maori *waiata* in the wedding scene, Mr Fisher took a 13th century Welsh lament, changed some of the vowels and asked a Welsh composer to set it in a primitive idiom. The result was an interesting combination of Welsh and Maori. It is understood that the play will be taken on a Welsh provincial tour during 1961.[7]

The Pohutukawa Tree did not appear again on a New Zealand stage until Mason himself directed a semi-professional production with the Southern Comedy Players in 1963. Following this he made some 'minor amendments to the text, amounting mostly to reduction of some over-explicit speeches' and reduced his stage directions in response to James Bertram's observation that they 'often try too hard [and] read sometimes like a tourist brochure or a producer's pep talk to a sluggish cast'.[8] It is this second edition that Victoria University Press reproduced in *The Healing Arch: Five Plays on Māori Themes*, published in 1987, four years after Mason's death.

Both editions place the opening scene early on a December evening 'a year or so after the Second World War'; however, an earlier typescript sets it 'a few years ago', which could mean the early 1950s and may be more consistent with Roy McDowell's '*T-shirt and jeans*' (or wind-breaker and jeans in the typescript version).[9] Presumably the move back in time, closer to the war, is in deference to Sylvia Atkinson's husband-to-be George, who has seen active service with the Air Force. Although if Mrs Atkinson is indeed the '*smartly dressed woman of fifty*' specified in the first edition only,[10] Sylvia could well be in her mid-to-late twenties, allowing George to be in his early thirties. The old-fashioned music, played on the portable gramophone and '*badly eroded by steel needles*', is all 1930s, but 'Speak to Me of Love' (presumably an English version of the Italian 'Parlami d'amore Mariu', 1932) in the first publication is replaced in the second with the Bing Crosby's 'Moonlight Becomes You', from the 1942 film *Road to Morocco*.[11]

Te Parenga ('pop. 250'), where the play is set, was created by Mason in 1949 for a short story called 'Summer's End' and is based on Auckland's now suburban Takapuna, where he spent the childhood he would go on to use in 'The Conch Shell' and immortalise in *The End of the Golden Weather*. The titular tree, with its gnarled old trunk, hangs over the porch of the cottage. In Act 1, Scene 1, it is in bloom and the roots are starting to come through.[12] In Act 2, Scene 1, the flowers have gone and it has drooped a little.[13] In the next scene Atkinson says it must be either restrained or cut down,[14] and by Act 3 the tree has come right down over the porch, causing local GP Dr Lomas to call it 'a menace' and Atkinson to curse it when it knocks his hat off: 'Damn that thing! I've told her time and time again to cut it down.'[15] Standing as an emblem of Māoritanga itself, the fear and anger the tree provokes in Pākehā characters is clearly symbolic. The blood that was spilt where it is rooted lies at the heart of the play. For Aroha Mataira, her grandfather Whetumārama's defence of Te Parenga against colonial troops was 'the greatest victory ever won by the Maori against the Pakeha'.[16] It was he who planted the red-flowered tree to commemorate that battle. 'Te Parenga was never taken by force,' Aroha tells the Reverend Athol Sedgwick, newly arrived from England. 'Only by time; Pakeha time. Slice by slice from the whale . . .'[17]

What was once a great tōtara forest has been felled to create what looks like 'rolling English countryside', as Clive's great mate Claude Johnson proudly describes it in his speech at the wedding.[18] Over time the Atkinson family have bought up most of Te Parenga from the Ngāti Raukura, who have re-settled in Tamatea on the East Coast, except for Aroha and her children, who remain on this last acre of tribal land. It emerges that without their daily labour, the Atkinson's orchard of introduced citrus trees cannot survive. 'Dammit, they *were* the orchard,' Clive Atkinson admits.[19] But it is the fate of the land itself that determines the final outcome.

Aroha could have chosen to wallow in hatred and bitterness at the dishonouring of Whetumārama and the land he fought so hard to retain. Instead, at an early age, she embraced Christianity with a fervour Atkinson eventually blames for making her children rebel: 'We've had two thousand years of it. We know how far to take it and where to draw the line. But they don't. No judgement. No common sense. Swallow it hook, line and sinker. Get into a helluva mess and start tearing the place apart.'[20] When Aroha's dual allegiance to Whetumārama, 'the shining star', and Christ, 'the light of the world', is reconciled and in balance she embodies the mana that makes Johnny say, 'Ma. You're too big. The world can't hold you. It's too small out there. You tried to make me as big as you. I tried, Ma. But me, I'm not big.'[21]

The Reverend Athol Sedgwick sees her as 'a battlefield. Christ *and* Whetumarama'. By Act 3 Aroha's deep-rooted convictions, and the scale at which she has attempted to live by them, have been destroyed, not least by her rebellious children. Queenie's love of romance has led to her enjoying sex with barman Roy McDowell, the son of a

Waikato grocer, and becoming pregnant to him. Johnny feels most alive when riding and caring for Sylvia Atkinson's horse Jezebel, and when it is taken away he takes a liking to whisky. Then when Roy refuses to marry Queenie because she is Māori, he desecrates the church in his rage. If Aroha is 'to go on living in the little world', Sedgwick concludes, 'then she'll have to cut herself down to fit it.'[22]

The same questions, challenges and dilemmas threaten the survival of Māoritanga, *The Pohutukawa Tree* and Aroha Mataira; the fates of all three are inextricably entwined. So too are the clashes of genders, generations and cultures that were beginning to seethe beneath the surface of post-war New Zealand. Indeed they remain woven into New Zealand life: culturally specific evocations of universal and timeless thematic conflicts.

It would be futile to seek a character in *The Pohutukawa Tree* who represents entirely the playwright's own viewpoint. Mason is not one to spoon-feed his audience. He creates characters who are worthy adversaries for each other and with whom we can readily empathise or whom we can judge as they evolve through the play's action.

The youthful quest for freedom, identity and meaning in life is explored through three distinctive characters who still need the love and respect of their parents. Johnny's childlike identification with Robin Hood and need for his mother's approval anchor his troubled transition from boy to man: from compliant orchard manager, through hot-headed radical activist, to a level of maturity that may bode well for his future, depending on how we judge his relegation to Tamatea. Queenie's questing innocence, inner pride at her heritage, back-chatting defensiveness, girlish love of pretty clothes and 'bride-as-queen' fantasy, and her underlying rebellion, all conspire to see her deeply disillusioned by Roy's cavalier treatment of her and her heritage. Yet an indomitable quality allows Sedgwick's report that she has become the 'queen' of Tamatea to be entirely credible. Handsome, horny and happy-go-lucky Roy McDowell presents a likeable young man until his fear of being disowned by his parents if he marries a Māori reveals his ignorance and cowardice.

Clive Atkinson's paternalism seems benign enough until his chat with Sergeant Robinson (Act 2, Scene 2) exposes their blinkered racism:

ROBINSON: . . . Law and order: not so easy for them with their background. Not used to it. They see things a bit different. They'll come round to our way of thinking in time.

ATKINSON: No sign of it yet. And they've had a hundred years. No. Scratch them, you'll find savages underneath, ready to break out into violence at the drop of a hat. They've begun to slip. And once they slip, they'll fall fast.[23]

Perhaps Atkinson's discovery that he cannot run the orchard without the Matairas earns them greater respect, but he remains wilfully oblivious to what provoked Johnny's crime, let alone Aroha's profound connection to her tribal land and heritage. Because Isobel Atkinson—who utters the most cringeworthy line in the wedding scene: 'Where are the Maoris! We want our lovely Maoris!'[24]—is the character most changed and humbled by Aroha, it is easy to identify with her as she grows from complacent middle-class mother-of-the-bride and patronising dispenser of charity to self-aware potential campaigner for true social justice. Even so, she thinks it is 'splendid' that the Ngāti Raukura at Tamatea want to receive Aroha 'like a queen' once Sedgwick has facilitated their sale of the remaining land at Te Parenga.[25]

As the voice of Pākehā progress, Claude Johnson is authentically 'blokey' and crass. Sergeant Robinson does his best to be a fair-minded community cop. Dr Lomas, having brought all the children into the world, maintains a strong connection to both the Atkinsons and the Matairas, but even though he has taken the trouble to learn about Māori approaches to health and wellbeing, neither he nor Isobel can comprehend why Aroha's spirits have not been lifted by the way local people rallied to restore the damaged church and raise money to repair the stained-glass window.[26]

The Reverend Athol Sedgwick begins to show his true colours with his idealised view of Tamatea, except his viewpoint does offer a good critique of 'those nagging things that make us so miserable: time, security, money'.[27] Although it hints at the communes some baby boomers will embrace as an alternative lifestyle choice (note: choice), a couple of decades from the time it is set and a decade or so from the time of writing, his desire to park Māori away from mainstream New Zealand life, out of sight and mind, amounts at best to a convenient conscience salver. In fact Sedgwick's pastoral advice to the betrayed and grieving Aroha is tantamount to separatism by reservation (as practised to varying degrees in North America, South Africa and Australia): 'Everything pulls you to Tamatea. Johnny. Queenie. Not even this land will remain in your hands. Accept the Pakeha's conquest by time. Forget greatness: forget history. Find harmony and lasting peace.'[28]

In hindsight we can see Aroha's resolute stand and self-willed death as a portent for the possible fate of Māori and self-determination; of tino rangatiratanga: a concept most Pākehā only began to comprehend in the late 1970s, when the 'Māori renaissance' began. Insofar as Mason used this play to articulate the 'state of the nation', he let the warning speak for itself rather than attempt to preach a solution. But Mason's response to an important article by Dr James Ritchie (Lecturer in Psychology at Victoria University of Wellington), 'The Future Place of Maori Culture in New Zealand Society', offers an insight into his personal views and that of his peers.

> Dr Ritchie summarises four main types of culture in New Zealand society: first as a way of life, totally enclosing, limiting, nourishing and sufficient, for those persons involved in it. In this sense, he points out, Maori culture no longer exists, irreparably severed from its roots by Pakeha conquest and occupation. Second, culture as a set of traditions and customs, cherished and practiced by a group. In this sense Maori culture continues, as we all can see. Third, culture as a creative process, the absorption of certain values, the expression of discontents, tensions and, more rarely, fulfilments in the various art forms available. The spirit of this country, the development of a soul as it were, particular to it, is now slowly expanding, mostly on Pakeha promptings, to involve some consciousness of New Zealand as a bi-racial community. Fourth, culture as a sense of uniqueness, of personal identity, of apartness, in the strict sense of the word, of being 'this' and not 'that'.
>
> From this fourth category, Dr Ritchie draws his major conclusion, that culture in the sense he defines it is 'not an amalgam, but an integrated

> whole'; 'not bits of this and bits of that, but the basis of a person's self-esteem and confidence.' One does not, in other words, acquire culture that can be nourishing and meaningful simply by performing action songs and hakas, not merely by exploring the classic repositories of Maori poetry and lore, but by acquiring something for oneself, by living these activities in a manner which shed light on your whole life, which keeps them living for you.

Mason concludes that 'if this honesty of approach is sufficiently intense and sustained, it can transform and nourish the whole community . . . and show us the shape of our society in the years ahead.'

There can be no doubt that *The Pohutukawa Tree*'s challenge to the principles of Christian and British colonialism, and Pākehā paternalism, is a hugely valuable contribution to culture in every sense of the term. Yet despite its having enjoyed the status of the most produced New Zealand play in history by amateur groups, professional theatres ignored its originality, theatrical power and insights into the lesser-known values of Māoritanga. Is this explained by cultural cringe, wilful ignorance or a prevailing view that theatre's most important role in New Zealand was to emulate the preferences of British and American theatre?

Whatever the reason, it remains a travesty that *The Pohutukawa Tree* was ignored by our professional theatres for decades while they paid regular obeisance to the likes of Anton Chekhov, Henrik Ibsen, Arthur Miller and Tennessee Williams. Mason's play is as worthy a cultural artefact as any of their major works and all the more important to New Zealand for capturing the nature of our society. We can only wonder how much healthier Mason's career as a playwright, and New Zealand theatre in general, may have been had *The Pohutukawa Tree* been more publicly transplanted from the page to the professional stage while Mason was in his creative prime.

Of course, the cast of thirteen would stretch the resources of most professional theatres. The play's design requirements are also a challenge, especially where a large proscenium-arch theatre and back-stage crew are not available. However, when Mason wrote this play, that was the scale the New Zealand Players were operating at, with productions of *The Young Elizabeth* by Jennette Dowling and Francis Letton, Jean Anouilh's *Ring Round the Moon*, George Bernard Shaw's *St Joan* and Arthur Miller's *View from the Bridge*. Over the decades since, most professional theatres have mounted one or two large-cast productions a year, from Shakespeare through the aforementioned modern classics to the latest Tom Stoppard, most of which also require ingenious design solutions, while steadfastly ignoring Mason. The challenge of casting Māori characters is a poor excuse for this continuing lapse, given the Māori Theatre Trust was formed in 1965 and a steady stream of tangata whenua has entered the profession since.

'Since its publication in 1960,' Mason wrote in 1963, '*The Pohutukawa Tree* has been produced in Feilding, Taupo, Murupara, Ardmore (Teachers' College), Dunedin . . . Numerous societies have given private readings of the play, many with Maori actors in the leading parts, some taking the stage for the first time'.[29] It is unlikely that these amateur productions met the performance and production challenges as well as a fully professional production could. Indeed, in the 1982 *Kaleidoscope* interview, Mason reveals, 'There have been times when I have seen *The Pohutukawa Tree* on stage when I have despaired and thought why the hell didn't you write a novel instead? It went so far away from what I had in mind.'[30] Nevertheless these amateur productions, and the play's being studied and sometimes performed in secondary schools, and examined in School Certificate then the National Certificate of Educational Achievement (NCEA), will have contributed to far more copies of *The Pohutukawa Tree* being sold than any other New Zealand play. Its publication also led to its being translated into Russian, although in 1963 Mason wrote that it was 'prevented from production by what the translator is pleased to call the author's "anti-Maori grimace" in the last act'.[31] It seems the USSR required all plays performed there to be socio-politically polemical, rather than observationally accurate.

In the 1982 *Kaleidoscope* interview Mason said, 'I've recently been asked to write a sequel to *The Pohutukawa Tree* for Downstage, who at last wish to do only the second professional production of it that's ever been, the first being for the BBC . . . This I feel I can't do because in 1968 [having written five plays on Māori themes] I more or less vowed that I'd done my best, to the extent that I'm equipped, to turn over the ground of Māori–Pākehā relations, and that any more from me would be presumptuous, from a Pākehā.' He named Patricia Grace, Witi Ihimaera, Rowley Habib and Rawiri Paratene as examples of the strong and vital Māori voices being heard in home-grown literature and theatre.[32]

In 1984, nearly two years after Mason's death and twenty-seven years after the New Zealand Players Theatre Workshop production, Richard Campion finally directed the first fully professional season of *The Pohutukawa Tree* in New Zealand, at Downstage. Elizabeth Murchie, who had played it on radio and with the Southern Comedy Players, reclaimed the role of Awroha. Jim Moriarty, who had played young Hemi in Mason's *Awatea* sixteen years earlier, played Johnny. It won a standing ovation on opening night and did excellent business despite some critical concerns about mixed performance styles and the production being neither of its period nor contemporary.[33] This was also a time when political consciousness was so heightened that perceptions and judgement were distorted by guilt-fed demands for ideological soundness (political correctness), not unlike the Soviet Union position. To some minds, the fact that Mason was Pākehā would automatically have rendered his attempt to represent a Māori point of view as yet another example of cultural imperialism. But as a playwright Mason had cast his critical eye and well-tuned ear over both Pākehā and Māori cultural values and set his play at their point of collision. No character is a stereotype or cipher. Nor can Aroha be said to personify a pan-Māori viewpoint (if there is such a thing) or even be a typical example of her people. She is an isolated extremist, a classic tragic heroine whose fatal flaw, as post-war progress takes hold, is her unshakeable faith in the Christian God of love which she attempts to reconcile with her equally unshakeable reverence for Whetumārama and the land he fought to defend.

In 2009, more than half a century after its initial workshop production, the Auckland Theatre Company staged the first professional production of *The Pohutukawa Tree* in Auckland, and it

Elizabeth Murchie in *The Pohutukawa Tree*, Downstage Theatre, Wellington (October–November 1984). Photograph taken by Guy Robinson. ALEXANDER TURNBULL LIBRARY

set a new company box office record for a classic play.[34] The following year, Toi Whakaari: NZ Drama School produced the play as one of its two graduation shows in its fortieth anniversary year. Perhaps this marks a new lease of life for a truly great play that every New Zealander and visitor to New Zealand deserves to see more than once in their lifetime.

Bruce Mason's first full-length play can now be seen as the taonga it has always been. Its articulation and exploration of timeless, universal themes of human existence, in a culturally specific place and time, qualifies it worldwide as a classic.

CHAPTER SIX

HOW DO WE NEST POST-WAR?

Birds in The Wilderness

In post-WWII New Zealand, a pregnant Juliet Bascombe and her husband Bernie need to settle and nest. But the world arrives and conflicts arise over how best to live.

Between the New Zealand Players Theatre Workshop presentations of *The Pohutukawa Tree* and its being produced for television by the BBC, Bruce Mason wrote his second full-length play 'in three feverish, coffee-stained, smoke-wreathed nights of February 1958' to meet the closing date for the Auckland Festival's tenth anniversary playwriting competition. In his foreword to the unpublished text Mason wrote, 'Diamonds, I know, are formed by the highest pressure, but I make no such adamantine claims for this groggily sustained tour de force; I had misread the expiry date and had to be in like Flynn . . . The third and final bout began after my day's work at 6 pm and ended at 7 the next morning, but the play had been fermenting for months.'[1] Or fourteen years, if its evocation of collective living owes anything to his discarded four-act epic *The Secret People*. This version, however, clearly draws on Mason's wartime experience in the Navy and on his employment in the public service.

Taking its title from a scouting song commandeered by WWII forces in far-flung climes, *Birds in the Wilderness* gathers a veritable aviary of broadly drawn displaced characters in order to confront the whole question of lifestyle and ways of working in post-war New Zealand. In its quest for individual and idiosyncratic freedoms, as opposed to nine-to-five conformity, it has something in common with George S Kaufman and Moss Hart's 1930s Broadway hit *You Can't Take It With You*. But where the antics of the randomly extended Vanderhoff 'family' offered New Yorkers an escape from the Great Depression, it is the depressing spectre of middle-class mediocrity in a new and far-flung nation that Mason asks us to confront with Bernard and Juliet Bascombe.

Birds in the Wilderness won the Auckland Festival competition but the promised production by a leading Auckland amateur group failed to materialise when all those approached refused to take it on. Mason's foreword reveals 'an Auckland spy' claimed this was largely due to 'chagrin that the competition had not been won by an Auckland writer.' An embarrassed Festival committee then suggested Mason direct the play 'with a Wellington team, all expenses of production, construction, transport to Auckland of set and cast, to be borne by the Auckland Festival Society'. Thanks to the good offices of the New Zealand Players director Stafford Byrne, the New Zealand Players Theatre Workshop took it on with part-time professional actors rehearsing, unpaid, in the evenings. An invited audience watched a run-through in Wellington, the production travelled north by train and it opened at the Auckland Town Hall Concert Chamber on 22 May 1958. A matinee was added to the seven scheduled performances 'in response to overwhelming public demand.'[2]

Its critical reception was mixed. The daily papers were kinder than Mason had expected, but he heard from a friend 'that the play had outraged some leading members of the Auckland Jewish community, because it ridiculed refugees (huh?) and, a few days later, Antony Alpers frothed with rage on the radio, beginning one pulverising sentence with "Never, in all my experience of the theatre", and ending another with . . . "this mountainous lapse of taste".' By the third night Tim Eliott, playing the 'Jewish buddy' Jacko Sternberg, was struck with laryngitis and Mason had to take over for three performances. As Eliott recovered Mason, in turn, lost his voice.[3]

Less than a month after the Auckland season, the London Repertory Players staged a single performance of *Birds in the Wilderness* at the Lyric Theatre to an invited audience with a cast that included Prunella Scales (who had trained at the Old Vic Theatre School with Edith and Richard Campion) as Ruby Goalen from Te Kuiti. Reviews ranged from 'totally scathing' (*Daily Telegraph*) through 'cautiously enthusiastic' (*The Times*) to 'ecstatic' (*The Stage*), but a full production did not ensue.[4] One of the invited theatre managers would have been happy to present it if Mason had been prepared to transpose it to Northern Ireland. 'Since this would have made mincemeat, not to say nonsense of my theme,' Mason wrote in his preface to *Blood of the Lamb* (1980), 'I refused.' He therefore offered rights (through Playmarket) 'on the strict understanding that there be no transposition of theme or setting into another country (implying that, say, English audiences lack the imagination to project themselves imaginatively into the South Pacific). This baneful practice must now cease.'[5]

However because Mason felt *The Times* critic, and Dr John Pocock and Professor Sydney Musgrove, whose reviews appeared in *Landfall*, all accurately divined the play's weaknesses, he 'remodelled it, to Dr Pocock's expressed satisfaction, and it was this slightly revised version the Manawatu Repertory Theatre, Palmerston North, staged in December 1962': the play's first amateur production. While Mason acknowledges the play has farcical elements, and deception and misunderstandings are key elements in the sometimes far-fetched plot, he writes that the weaknesses he set out to resolve included 'a thin Act III, which not only did not advance the play, but allowed the farcical elements to dominate.'[6] The single and physically awkward entrance and ladder (to emphasise the 'bottom of the world' location perhaps, or a bird cage) also suggest he was never aiming for pure multi-door farce. Throughout the play, Act 1 especially, the evolving and increasingly bizarre comic situation is masterfully counterpointed by sobering insights into the realities of war, revolution and their aftermaths. Indeed much of the dramatic and comic friction comes from the clash between that horrific past and the quest for a better future that will avoid the same mistakes.

Presumably it was the characterisation of Jacko, and the ambivalent feelings he inspired in all who encountered him, that offended those Jewish sensibilities and possibly Alpers. Had Mason published and performed his prose piece *Courting Blackbird* by then, they may have realised Jacko, who is constantly referred to as a 'wandering Jew', rootless and unlikely to settle anywhere, owed quite a lot to the idiosyncratic Boris (Bo) Godunov Baron, who in turn was drawn from Mason's real-life neighbour and university friend Lindsay Nathan.

In her autobiography, *Bread and Roses*, Sonja Davies describes Lindsay Nathan as 'a slim, dark young man . . . with an impeccable

English accent.' Covering their brief and sexually incompatible marriage, she reveals he was conscripted into the Army and had a habit of arriving home 'on leave with large numbers of like-minded Army mates [insisting] they share our bed and board.' She later heard that he had 'many incredible-sounding adventures in the Army.'[7] Mason describes Bo Baron as '*a short, slim, elegant young man with fine Semitic features*', and wrote: 'The vividness of his conversation, the satisfying geometry of his speech with every word measured and sliced, the English language a formal garden of clipped hedges and tailored lawns, the alert face and intent dark eyes, quite captivated me.'[8] He describes Jacko Sternberg as '*a small, wiry little Jew in his early thirties, gay, spritely, witty*'.[9] While 'gay' did not mean then what it does today, it would be perfectly legitimate to play Jacko that way, given his flamboyance and apparent lack of romantic interest in the opposite sex. He claims 'a dash of Jewish sauce' has helped him to live on his wits. Having hatched 'a plan to catch flying bombs in enormous nets suspended underneath barrage balloons all over London and the larger cities,' Jacko went on to convert old scrap iron, peddle insurance, be a speedway rider, ghost-write for a popular scientist of international renown, write speeches for illiterate great men, get chucked out of a tough nightclub and become a dancing partner in another: 'anything at all, anything, just so I wasn't a slave, crucified to a desk, eight hours a day.' Then he worked his passage to New Zealand as a ship's cook.[10]

At the time of creating his open cage of odd birds, Mason may also have been aware of the New Jersey Jew, Beat Generation poet, politically active homosexual and compulsive traveller Allen Ginsberg, who entered popular consciousness through Jack Kerouac's *On the Road* (1955) and whose *Howl and Other Poems* was performed and published in 1956 (then subjected to a notorious obscenity trial, mainly because of explicit references to sodomy). But if such real-life models as Nathan and Ginsberg do not justify the characterisation of Jacko Sternberg, it may also be argued that he is no more supposed to represent the average post-war Jew than Aroha Mataira, in *The Pohutukawa Tree*, is supposed to typify mid-twentieth-century Māori. Mason created both Aroha and Jacko for clear dramatic purposes that reached well beyond stereotyping or generalisation.

Jacko is compulsively provocative. When he explains how he tracked his Navy mate down through Bernie's mother in 'Whackatain' and Bernie corrects him with the accurate pronunciation of Whakatane, Jacko acts '*mock-shocked*': 'Bernie! Language! In front of ladies! Is that the native tongue? . . . No wonder you had them put down!'[11] This 'gag' from Jacko, who also plays the fool at times by capering about like a monkey, is certainly a shocker but it accurately captures the sort of banter we may assume was common among Mason's wartime naval mates. Here Mason continues his practice of avoiding comfortably sympathetic characters in order to engage us with their all-too-human failings as well as their good points, gaining dramatic mileage from the play's abiding question: how well can we ever say we know each other, even those to whom we are married? In Act 2, for example, when the Jacko-driven wooden goods enterprise, dubbed Woodenit, has failed, Mason gives Bernie this outrageously offensive and defensive outburst, which Juliet does not condone:

BERNIE: (*striding about*) That fool of a Jacko! Craft, he called it. The poetry of the shaping hand. Well, I'm going to show him the poetry of the kicking boot. He's a menace: a wandering Jew, sowing discord. They've got too many bloody ideas. Why don't they do an honest day's work for a change?

JULIET: (*quietly*) Sieg Heil, Mein Führer.

BERNIE: The Kiwi never leaves the ground, he said. Well: so what? Keep on the ground, you're in touch with life. Let him fly away if he wants to. Fast! The Kiwi stays on the ground, feet on the floor.

JULIET: Rubbish Bernie. And racist, at that. You wanted to fly away, don't tell me you didn't.[12]

Birds in the Wilderness is best approached as an allegory for a new colony trying to start afresh in the wake of two world wars only to be pursued and infiltrated by British, European and Canadian influences arriving on a ship called the *Captain Cook*, no less. In an interview with theatre historian Howard McNaughton, Mason said, 'It parodies what we've done in transporting our culture from

Europe. In miniature.'[13] Inevitably the question of New Zealand identity arises: how do we claim the space to let it thrive and achieve distinction; where do we find the point of balance between enriching and overwhelming our culture with external influences? This is explored in microcosm by pitting the notion of nuclear families living in relative isolation against the virtues of communal living. In his 1979 foreword Mason wrote, 'Perhaps it also shot an arrow, of modest arc and trajectory, towards the urban communes of the late sixties and early seventies.'[14]

The allegorical qualities may justify an expectation that characters will typify their generic group. But they are not so much archetypes or stereotypes as sometimes larger-than-life vehicles for reflecting the state of the nation in the post-war environment, where nation-building demands a separation between work and fun, family and community. In every generation some men will empathise with Bernie's resistance to the nine-to-five family 'provider' role. Likewise women will recognise the conflict Juliet feels between nesting in preparation for their first child and cohabiting with a wider range of entertaining people. Importantly there is no earnestness in Mason's exploration of these themes. The verbal sparks that open the play ignite a healthy glow of mutual respect between husband and wife. Through Juliet's mentally agile and very articulate librarian, and Bernie's ex-Navy adventurer, who has returned resistant to settling down and security, Mason proves—to thespians and audiences familiar with the likes of Oscar Wilde and Noel Coward—that Kiwis can be worldly, witty, bright, passionate and eloquent. Consider this example of eloquent verbal sparring which, while not sustained throughout this play, was destined to flourish in *The Light Enlarging / Virtuous Circle*, *Zero Inn* and as a major stylistic element in *Blood of the Lamb*:

JULIET: Bernie Bascombe. We've been married three years. By the devilish art of the female, with black spells in spades, I lure you away from your cosy quartet of poker-playing, dart-throwing, beer-swilling, cud-chewing war bachelors, and you agree to take on with me the full quota of nuptial bliss. The full quota, boy. Right. You do the job, and we come back to a dreary bed-sitter and a ghastly land-lady who shaves—all that, and I could still be divinely happy! And what happens on the day we return? There's a shout of 'Belay, there! Shipmates ahoy! Splice the bricemain . . .'

BERNIE: Mainbrace!

JULIET: And in they come, Charlie, Stiffie and Sockeye, tongues hanging out for beer, darts and poker. As if the war were still raging. As if my marriage vows, spoken with such warmth and passion, were just a gentlemen's agreement, though that's not the word I'd use for your old cobbers, but let it pass—(*He tries to interrupt her; she shouts him down*) A GENTLEMEN'S AGREEMENT! That the old order changeth by not one jot or tittle or itsy bitsy, and that poker, darts, beers, and talk talk talk talk talk will be my lot until Kingdom Come and after.[15]

Although the scenario she describes here does not involve Jacko, this is a set-up for his bringing a collection of ship-mates from the *Captain Cook* into their home. It is tempting to see some of its inspiration in the doomed Sonja and Lindsay Nathan marriage counterpointed by the robust debates we may imagine Mason, Diana and their friends enjoyed.

In their own idiosyncratic ways, other *Birds in the Wilderness* characters also manifest Mason's love of language in its rich variegations, subverting audience expectations as they challenge our value systems. When a momentarily enthused Bernie asks Jacko what he will do in the pseudo-wooden goods factory they are fabricating to impress a buyer, Jacko replies, 'Talk, of course, with all the eloquence for which my race is famous'.[16] Maxwell (Maxie) Waller, the loud-mouthed Canadian ex-British Empire Wrestling Champion (1935–1938), whose egotism hides a fear of obscurity, delivers an extraordinarily colloquial patois, which seems to owe as much to his love of Hollywood movies as to his home country. Here is how he envisions people, recalling his glory days:

MAXIE: . . . Yarin the Town Hall. Crammed to the roof. Ya might get one more in, but if ya did, need a shoehorn! Yessir! Yarall sittin' there, all tensed up, all choked up, an' I come on. (*He strikes a heroic pose*) Here I am: it's me, Big Maxie Waller! An' dames, bewdaful dames, rows of 'em, litters of 'em, all screamin' and blowin' me kisses! Then they see me lick the pants of Whiskers Blake, knock the stuffin' outa the Terrible Turk, give the koop da grayce to Belearic Bert. Yu'd think the Town Hall'd fall in with the noise! Love, that's what it was: love! Two thousand of 'em, all lovin' me at once.[17]

Maxie is a model of manhood, who used to train by running along a beach with a rock in each hand. His larger-than-life caricature, rooted in strong emotional truth, offers a stark contrast to Bernie, Jacko and Ferenc Szabo, a Hungarian refugee lawyer turned toothpick carver. As if in defiance of the yet-to-erupt feminist revolution, Maxie stands unabashed as the heroic fighter and protector who respects and admires a woman who stands up to him, provided he remains in control. Furthermore, Maxie appears devoid of tact and sensitivity. When Ania Szabo explains that she and Ferenc call each other Apus (Pop) and Anyus (Mom), 'to remind ourselves that once we were parents', because their son was killed in the war and their two daughters died in the fighting for Budapest, Maxie responds with '*huge compassion*': 'Say. Say! Ain't life just the end sometimes? All the money ya spent on them gone, smoke, splat, fizz! Gee, I'm sorry.'[18]

As yet another cringe-inducing moment, this exemplifies a key element of the play, which is to track the process from alienation to acceptance; from negative judgement to a positive understanding of the humanity we share beneath our outward differences. Maxie's decree that it will make Ferenc and Ania Szabo feel better if they call them Apus and Bellpush seems crass, but it works. It may also raise some eyebrows when Juliet, now loving her odd-bird companions, describes Jacko's farcical behaviour as having 'a wild poetry' and Maxie's roughing up of Gilbert Stead—the chief buyer from McKelveys chain stores (based on the actual McKenzies chain)—as 'a sudden bout of knightly chivalry'.[19] Mason constantly challenges us to confront and rethink our notions of acceptable attitudes and behaviour as the play unfolds.

Lest we think we have at last worked out whose side we are on, Mason brings in Gilbert Stead to simultaneously counterpoint the protagonists and critique Kiwi values. As an advocate for the

Protestant work ethic, when he discovers their factory is a fraud and Bernie is in charge, he tells them they ought to be ashamed of themselves:

> This is a serious country, and we work hard here. We can laugh with the rest, take a joke with the best, but we don't fool about in our working lives! (*He moves to APUS and BELLPUSH with a snake-like malevolence*) And if you foreign people are to make a go of it here, and return our hospitality, the first thing you've got to learn is to work hard and well, and not waste our time with cheap and senseless vaudeville acts! You're old enough, both of you, to know better![20]

Then just when Bernie is coming down to earth and realising the deeply flawed Woodenit enterprise will neither liberate him nor make them happy, Gilbert becomes a born-again disciple of laughter, fun and learning to wrestle—taught by Bellpush no less, who has

Birds in the Wilderness in rehearsal. (L–R) Grant Tilly, John Gordon, Mollie Parton, Bruce Mason (director), Susan Morrissey (production assistant), Dorothy McKegg (in silhouette), Charles Walker, Dick Johnstone (resident producer), Judi Lenart. Produced at Downstage (March 1968). SALIENT become Maxie's sparring partner as well as the household cook. Even Bellpush is concerned when Gilbert gives up his job and uses his savings to set Maxie up in his own studio of physical culture. 'I've given up wisdom! Given up caution!' he cries *'in a lyrical rapture'*. 'I want to fly as high as a kite and let myself float on the air. I never want to live on the ground again.' What's more, his wife has left him, but he is confident she will be back. 'She doesn't know The New Gilbert! Scared out of her wits! I'm terrifying! Blazing like the sun!'[21]

Meanwhile, Ruby's muteness—an extreme form of hysterical aphonia probably caused by her mother's rejection of Maxie—has offered an ingenious counterpoint to the loquacity of Maxie and the others, until she recovers her voice in the bosom of her new 'family' by bursting into song. But when Maxie wants her to give a farewell speech, she is monosyllabic: 'Been nice here. Thanks.' Maxie is dismayed this is all she has to say after eight years of silence: 'Rube, speech! Eloquence! Noblest gift a man! . . . Ah: what's the use of talkin'?' Her riposte is simple: 'No use. See?'[22] In taking this satirical poke at his own love of eloquence—and that of his other characters—Mason offers the taciturn Kiwi as an alternative and leaves us to take our pick.

Birds in the Wilderness invites us to contemplate its counterpointing levels of happiness and sadness, comedy and pathos, optimism and pessimism, wildness and wilderness, according to our own ages and stages, lifestyles and value systems. Having 'roosted' together through autumn to winter, the choices the local and exotic 'birds' make reflect the options each of us face throughout our lives: conventional nesting by way of securing a future for the next generation (Bernie and Juliet); taking a risk with a new business that will either fly or fail (Gilbert, Maxie, Ruby and Bellpush, with craft artist Apus carving his toothpicks on the side) or flitting about the globe with no fixed abode (Jacko). And so the search for identity—a role, a place, a purpose, a lifestyle—continues, while how we relate to others remains a key factor within the elusive equation. When Bernie and Juliet, who is now heavily pregnant, finally opt for having the house to themselves in preparation for starting a family, their choice may be seen as fundamental to nation-building or as an insular rejection of what the wider world has to offer—again: take your pick.

In contemplating whether New Zealand should 'repel all boarders' in order to nurture a hermetically sealed culture of nuclear families or embrace what northern hemisphere immigrants have to offer to enrich their lives, the parallel with the Māori dilemma of how to accommodate the Pākehā 'invasion' (canvassed in *The Pohutukawa Tree*) is inescapable. The comparison with a fascist nationalist extreme of eliminating those who do not fit the ideal—satirically captured in Jacko's quip, 'No wonder you had them put down!'[23] when he discovers Māori can sound like offensive language in English—is also relevant.

Assuming Mason intended the allegorical implications, the absence of a Māori voice in *Birds in the Wilderness* appears surprising. Having written it so soon after *The Pohutukawa Tree*, he may have felt it would have been tokenistic or insufficient to add a Māori voice into the mix. Of course a producer or director may well cast Ruby as Māori. Her job at the Te Kuiti Railway Station tea rooms, and having had a Catholic upbringing and a harsh mother who is thought to have rejected Maxie because he wasn't Catholic, are perfectly credible for a Māori woman. Her lack of voice coupled with a feisty capacity to take no nonsense from Maxie or anyone else could be seen as allegorical. As with so many aspects of the play, it would be a provocative proposition that added to its engaging qualities.

Wherever we personally perch in watching *Birds in the Wilderness*, the play's robust theatrical perspective on the state of post-war New Zealand explores human experiences and issues that transcend its time and place. As such, it may be considered a minor classic and claim a place of honour alongside Mason's better known plays. In 1968, ten years after its Auckland debut and just over a decade after it is set, Mason directed *Birds in the Wilderness* for Wellington's four-year-old professional theatre Downstage, where it 'ran to packed houses for a month.'[24] Nearly fifty years on from that second professional production, it has not had another.

CHAPTER SEVEN

REMEMBRANCE OF INNOCENCE LOST

The End of the Golden Weather

A solo narrator (unnamed) recalls how the 'golden weather' of his boyhood, and that of the nation, was lost. He tells the story in a scene-setting prologue and then in two acts of three parts each.

Bruce Mason's note to the second published edition of *The End of the Golden Weather* is in script form. He originally wrote it when the NZBC invited him to prepare a television programme to celebrate his 500th solo performance of the play. Although a programme did eventually reach the screen in another form (on Sunday, 14 September 1969, as part of the *Looking at New Zealand* series), his submitted script was not used. Instead, Mason recycled it to introduce the published play to readers. His imagined interviewer asks how it all began:

> Well, in 1959, I'd come to the end of the road. I'd written a few plays, assembled a mountain of criticism, done some producing.[1] I'd had a crack at all the arts and trades of theatre. But it hadn't got me anywhere . . . I just wanted to feel I had a calling for theatre and that this calling would at length be recognised, so that I could give my life and best energies to it. But you can't work in a vacuum. A man won't write symphonies, if there is no orchestra to play them. There was no solid theatrical framework here, no ladder to climb so that, feet on the first rung, you could go upwards to the second. You created no *mana*, no reputation or authority to justify your work. In fact, to most people, it wasn't work at all, just pretentious frivolity.[2]

In his *Listener* account, following the first few hundred performances of *The End of the Golden Weather*, Mason explained that despite being advised to concentrate on one of his many skills, he had gone on as before, 'operating on all fronts, in the hope that I would one day find a basket into which I could drop all these eggs without breaking them'.[3] His strategy would serve him well. Although the New Zealand Players had facilitated a production of *Birds in the Wilderness* and commissioned Mason to write sketches and pieces for their Drama Quartet tours of schools, they had not managed to get *The Pohutukawa Tree* into full production. Edith Campion (née Hannah, of the shoe shop empire) had used her own money to bail them out of financial strife more than once, but the Players would eventually fold in 1960. Given this climate, Mason realised that 'at no stage could I consider that this was opening up a career. It was always and only a spare time job. Hence the desperation.' It was only because he worked in all sectors of theatre that he was able to make the basket in which to gather his eggs:

> I'm a Kiwi, born and bred. We're at our best in a corner: good improvisers, bad experts, as an American critic once said of us. No theatrical framework? Right, then, I would create my own. Touring a play is expensive? Then cut to the minimum, table and chair. Scenery is costly to make and cumbersome to cart around? Do it all with words: appeal directly to the audience's imagination. Casts are expensive? Be your own. Do all forty parts. Play anywhere, in any circumstances, to any audience.[4]

The precedents for solo performance mostly involved high-profile actors presenting anthologised excerpts from the works of world-famous writers such as William Shakespeare, Charles Dickens, Mark Twain or Dylan Thomas. As Mason tells it, the eminent actor and playwright Emlyn Williams, now touring the world on the shoulders of Dickens and Thomas, expressed astonishment that an unknown performer at the backyard of the world should dare to assume he could hold an audience for two hours, not only with words alone but with his own script![5] The only approximate parallel was English actress Joyce Grenfell. Having gained fame in the *St Trinian's* films, in stage revues with the likes of Noel Coward and Max Adrian, and on radio comedy shows, she took to the stage in 1954 with a performance of comic monologues entitled *Grenfell Requests the Pleasure*. But *The End of the Golden Weather* is much more than a series of comic monologues.

The title came from *The Web and the Rock* by American author Thomas Wolfe, whose works Mason had 'devoured' when he was young. In it, Wolfe's narrator speaks of a novel he wants to write, but never does. It would involve a boy's vision of life over a ten-month period, between his twelfth and thirteenth year, and the title would be *The End of the Golden Weather*. Mason had already written and delivered a series of radio talks on his interest in theatre. Because that interest began when he was very young, his talks characterised a host of people who had populated his childhood summers at Auckland's Takapuna beach.

'These [talks] I adapted and wrote another: I had my first half,' he wrote in his *Listener* piece. The rest came from his story 'Summer's End', published in *Landfall* in 1949: 'a study of a man alone, as it were, a variation on the theme that John Mulgan has set down with classic precision for us—the psychosis, as I don't hesitate to call it, which makes physical prowess the summit of all human endeavour. I rewrote it in the first person to make it coherent with the rest of the programme and called it 'The Made Man'.[6]

The voice of the prologue is that of an adult man, setting the scene with Mason's now characteristic critical judgement. This is the same Te Parenga he invented for *The Pohutukawa Tree* but set twelve to fifteen years earlier, between the two world wars. For those who have seen or read *The Pohutukawa Tree*, his references to pohutukawa trees—'single and stunted in the gardens, spreading and noble on the cliffs, and in the empty spaces by the foreshore'[7]—will have a special resonance. The rhythm, flow, colour and texture of the language elevate what could have been historical reportage to the status of prose poem.

As with *Birds in the Wilderness* there are no Māori characters in *The End of the Golden Weather* even though *The Pohutukawa Tree* suggests the Mataira family and some other members of Ngāti Raukura would have been living at Te Parenga during that time. Perhaps Mason wanted a clean break from that epic, or he didn't want to diminish the size of their story by giving them bit-parts in this one, or he'd been unaware of them as a child. Maybe he was reluctant to play Māori characters himself. We can only guess.

In the face of accusations that he had characterised actual

people from Takapuna, Mason would insist his Te Parenga and its inhabitants were entirely fictional. There is no doubt, however, that the era he dramatised was of his childhood. Mason's unnamed boy states he is 'twelve and a bit', so if we assume he is the same age as Mason, *The End of the Golden Weather* is set over the summer of 1933–1934. But it is also fair to assume that the fictionalised Te Parenga demonstration witnessed by the boy in 'The Night of the Riots' was inspired by the infamous Depression riot in Auckland's Queen Street (provoked because a policeman used his baton on a man who'd stood up to appeal for calm) which occurred in March 1932. Perhaps this is why 'The Night of the Riots' is narrated in the past tense while all the other parts are recreated in the present tense.

In a note to 'The Made Man' Mason states that it begins earlier than 'Sunday at Te Parenga' and ends later than 'Christmas at Te Parenga', encapsulating the whole story of the boy's relationship

Is Firpo being conceived in this moment? Mason wins an inter-collegiate sprint for Wellington College at the Basin Reserve (1938).

with the play's most memorable character, Firpo. On the floor of the abandoned bach to which Firpo has been relegated (by the Atkinsons), the boy sees a scrap of newspaper referring to the death of 'Captain Dreyfus, Officer of the French Legion of Honour and victim of the most infamous political persecution in modern history' (prompting Émile Zola's famous open letter to the president: *J'accuse!*). Dreyfus died on 12 July 1935, which would make this the summer of 1935–1936, nearly four years after the riots and when the boy was one year younger than Mason, unless we allow for artistic licence regarding the death of Dreyfus.

Common to both *The Pohutukawa Tree* and *The End of the Golden Weather* are the Atkinsons and Sergeant Robinson. In 'The Made Man' the Atkinsons, who are burdened with the care of Firpo, are 'old and stinking rich.' Mrs Atkinson (Ella) is a 'thin elderly woman . . . hair like an old mop, eyes mild but imploring'. Mr Guy Atkinson

An *End of the Golden Weather* moment: the Mason brothers, Tim (about seven) and Bruce (about twelve).

is 'in a wheelchair . . . a great loose frame of bones, white-haired, white-suited, white-moustached, white tufts sprouting from ears as large as mussel shells'.[8] In *The Pohutukawa Tree*, we have learnt that old Tom Atkinson bought most of Te Parenga from Whetumārama, and after WWI, Tom's son Clive 'worked his land. Planted it. Reaped it.'[9] Assuming Clive was about twenty-two at the end of WWI, he'd have been in his thirties during *The End of the Golden Weather*, when the orchard would have been well established, and in his early fifties during *The Pohutukawa Tree*. So either Clive's father, Tom, has become Guy by dint of artistic licence or Guy is Tom's brother, Clive's uncle. Either way, Guy, Ella and Firpo live on another part of Atkinson land that has access to the beach.

In *The End of the Golden Weather* Sergeant Robinson is described in 'Sunday at Te Parenga' as 'small, fierce-eyed, round and gnarled as a nut' with a 'Victorian sense of propriety' and 'a proper ole dag'. In 'The Night of the Riots' (set a year or more before), he is called 'ole Robbie', and describes himself as 'a nole joker'.[10] Can this be the same Sergeant Robinson who turns up a dozen or more years later in *The Pohutukawa Tree*, described simply as 'the image of small-town authority'?[11] While calling someone 'ole Robbie' does not necessarily denote age in the Kiwi vernacular, he does see himself as senior to the demonstrators in 'The Night of the Riots'. If he were in his late forties in 'The Night of the Riots', he would be about sixty in *The Pohutukawa Tree*.

As with *Birds in the Wilderness*, set about twenty-five years after *The End of the Golden Weather*, Mason uses a Canadian heavyweight wrestling champion of the British Empire as a motif of 'manhood'. If Te Parenga identity Jesse Cabot is the reigning champ in the summer of 1933–1934, he is soon to be beaten by Maxie Waller (champion from 1935–1938). They both train by running along the beach with a rock in each hand, an 'olympian and majestic' image which, in Cabot's case, causes the fantasist Firpo to look 'suddenly strained and old, his eyes bulging with water.'[12]

A recurring Mason theme may be described as 'identity versus nonentity'. It is embodied in Tim Barlow's remaking himself as a new man, named after the South American boxer Luis Firpo (who found fame by challenging Jack Dempsey for the World Heavyweight

Championship in 1923 and knocking him out of the ring before being knocked out in round two).[13] But Mason's central question in this loss-of-innocence, rite-of-passage and coming-of-age play is the one he first posed in *The Bonds of Love* and *The Evening Paper*: what is it to be a man in New Zealand? On the cusp of puberty, the boy is discovering his own value system, largely as he pursues his idealistic quest to help Firpo realise his impossible dream of competing at the Olympic Games. In the process he observes, relates to, and sometimes interacts with, many models of manhood: his popular and entertaining but politically conservative father; his crass and jovially demeaning Uncle Jim; the insensitive but impressively athletic Joe Dyer and Bob Fergusson; the 'physical man incarnate' Jesse Cabot;[14] the respected and necessarily authoritarian Sergeant Robinson; the other-worldly Reverend Thirle; old and nasty Guy Atkinson; and Mr Stephen Irons, the loathed expatriate English teacher, lover of Romantic poetry and scathing critic of this country's 'cult of brawn over brains'.[15]

The boy's innocent delight in the characters on the beach and in his father's entertainment, during 'Sunday at Te Parenga', sets up a dramatic contrast with 'The Night of the Riots', which features no heroic specimens of manhood, and which Mason describes as 'a glimpse of the land of milk and honey, turning without warning, into bread and dripping.'[16] Expecting to witness a bloody fight or an orgy of looting, the boy instead discovers how poverty has drained the pride and humanity from men on both sides of the social and civic divide. The experience leaves him feeling more dismayed and alienated than enlightened.

While the boy is mostly an observer of what happens during 'Sunday at Te Parenga' and of the events that play out in 'The Night of the Riots', he is a very active participant in 'Christmas at Te Parenga' and even more so in 'The Made Man'. The thematically seeded conflicts—right versus wrong, good versus bad, reality versus fantasy, 'haves' versus 'have nots', the individual versus the mob—now take root as formative experiences for the boy, materially contributing to his own loss of innocence and coming of age.

The way the boy stages his Christmas concert, in facsimile of the

traditional theatre with sliding curtains, offers a satirical contrast to the more modern open-stage convention employed in Mason's own solo performance. The trauma of having his artistic endeavours disrespected (similar in some respects to Chekhov's Konstantin in *The Seagull*) speaks to Mason's own maturing as a theatre practitioner. The boy's rite of passage from childhood to adolescence and towards manhood is depicted as a deepened understanding of human behaviour, except this time—in contrast to 'The Night of the Riots'—when his brother admits he played the fool because he was scared, the boy feels compassion and closeness.

'The Made Man' submits the boy to tests of his character as he comes to terms with the Firpo phenomenon and learns to distinguish aspiration, ambition and performance from self-defeating delusion. Having made friends with Firpo and promised

---

'Firpo will have his day and what will he be then, boy? . . . A made man. Made man!' Mason in full flight.

not to laugh at him, and in salutary contrast to the lad who cast his lot in 'with the herd' in 'The Conch Shell', the boy has to resist joining the beach mob as they relish Uncle Jim's lofty mocking of an oblivious Firpo. This, his father's warning to be careful of Firpo, and the pre-Olympics challenge race set up by Joe Dyer and Bob Fergusson—using the boy to convey the message—serve only to increase the boy's determination to become the maker of this 'man half-finished, soon to be made whole'.[17] The English teacher's denunciation of 'this cult of brawn over brains that you all go in for'[18] is classic Mason, pitting 'the mother country' against her uncouth spawn, New Zealand, to provoke personal scrutiny of our own value systems. The doomed attempt to bulk Firpo up with meat, only to find he is vegetarian, sends the boy in search of divine intervention. When he expresses his outrage that the noisy choir practice is stopping his prayers getting through, the boy is banished for his cheek, not least because he has called a Magnificat of the minister's own creation 'so much noise.' Mr Thirle is scathing: 'Choir: did you hear that? You've got a critic here it seems.'[19] (It is tempting to see this as an in-joke, but Mason was not well known as a music critic until his *Listener* column 'Music on the Air' appeared between 1964 and 1969). 'God's deaf, and Firpo's on his own,'[20] the boy concludes, his loss of faith yet another step in his disillusionment.

Mason dramatises the 'half a moll, iddunut?'[21] (half a mile, isn't it?) race to maximum effect, tempting us to share in the dream of victory, before reality and the other six runners overtake Firpo, whose failure is that of a tragic clown: larger than life to a comic degree, yet compelling our compassion. Even more remarkable is the boy's response to being the only one to help the 'gawky albatross' to his feet: 'I feel a sudden sharp warmth. I've never been so happy in my life.'[22] In marked contrast to masochistic pleasure the boy in 'The Conch Shell' felt at becoming Ginger Finucane's slave, this boy is experiencing the joy of offering compassion to his fellow man irrespective of the judgement of others. But lest he commit the sin of pride, perhaps, he is not allowed to bask in joy. Firpo is inconsolable: 'Firpo is finished. That's the end of the made man!' When the boy tries to comfort him by mentioning God, Firpo stiffens. His angry denial of God's very existence—'It's all a cheat, a cheat! How could there be . . . Get out. Get out!'—delivers another blow, terrifying this time, to the boy's innocence.[23]

Hard on the heels of this disillusionment comes moral redemption, when the brother and parents show compassion and respect for what the boy has done and been through. But the dramatic resolution is not sentimental. Amid images of seasonal change, the boy's 'golden weather' finally ends with his discovery that Firpo's bach has been demolished and, according to a gruff Kiwi workman, 'the athalete' has been taken 'off to the nuthouse' where it is believed he will be looked after, get everything he wants and be happy.[24]

Thus the boy's transition from childhood is aligned to the inevitable and natural, if sometimes unwelcome, passing of summer. In this microcosm of Pākehā New Zealand society between the wars, Mason uses the boy's rite of passage to explore themes of justice, compassion and a fair go for all without overtly questioning the status quo. He leaves his audiences, all of whom have seen it a generation or more after the story is set, to empathise and wrestle with the dilemmas anew. Each audience is invited to vicariously share the world view of the boy but, as with Mason's previous plays, there is no rightness or righteousness in the ending. We are left to assess the implications of a realistic outcome. Because *The End of the Golden Weather* has always profiled a bygone era, including for its first audiences, every generation is provoked to compare who we were then to who we are now, and to ask themselves how far we have come.

The first showing of *The End of the Golden Weather*, in August 1959 at the New Zealand Players Theatre Workshop in Newtown, was, according to Mason, 'a disaster':

> I had a mild throat infection, exacerbated by nerves; I collapsed in hoarse shrieks, my lips stuck together, about a third from the end: Stafford Byrne, then Artistic Director of the New Zealand Players, bounded out of the audience and made a chivalrous, gallant speech. I rallied and just scraped home. One of the reviews next day was excoriating, dwelling gleefully

on all the mishaps, calling it pretentious piffle, ending crushingly, 'New Zealand cannot yet, it seems, produce an Emlyn Williams.'[25]

Undaunted, Mason took the play around various small venues in Wellington, giving about a dozen performances by the end of the year, its two halves played on consecutive nights. However, when he took it on a three-month provincial tour of Otago, Canterbury and Wellington the following year, under the auspices of the Community Arts Service of the Regional Councils for Adult Education, he played both halves in one night, with an interval. It is fair to assume Mason then took it further north, given this letter to the editor of Auckland's *New Zealand Herald*, dated 8 June 1960 but unpublished:

> Sir,
>
> May I thank your critic for his encouraging and perceptive review of my performance of The End of the Golden Weather in your issue of 8 June? I am glad to know I am no Dylan Thomas; I can place this useful intelligence beside that of the two southern critics who said that I was no Emlyn Williams, and the one who deplored that I was no Ruth Draper. May I add to the list, for your critic's information? I am no Dickens, no Oscar Wilde and no Mark Twain either.
>
> I am etc.,[26]

Those who saw Mason perform *The End of the Golden Weather* may recall it as an intrinsically Kiwi story narrated in a fruity BBC voice, while the Kiwi character voices came across as foreign accents. Those were the days when having a Kiwi accent was anathema to success as an actor; when many middle-class children had elocution lessons and 'speech and drama' were indivisible. Any radio actor whose voice had been trained by the likes of European émigré Maria Dronke, and who was then required to do a New Zealand accent, had to put it on. Mason himself noted, in 1980, 'the once curious incapacity of New Zealand radio actors to achieve a local accent'.[27] But because the boy who experienced *The End of the Golden Weather* was, in essence, Mason, and this was his own voice now, it is fair to argue that Mason's crisply articulated consonants and roundly modulated vowels were entirely valid.

At some point Mason recorded *The End of the Golden Weather*, probably for radio, although tape recordings were in circulation for private use. The 1970 revised and reset Victoria University Press publication of the play is dedicated 'To BC Deer stalker, friend'. In his note to the second edition, Mason scripts an encounter he had in Christchurch with a self-effacing deer stalker from Hokitika. He took Mason for a beer after a performance and revealed he had heard the recordings at a mate's place, bought the recordings and the published script, and learnt it all by heart, 'Up on the tops, all on my own.' Despite being a self-confessed 'ignorant hooer' with only a fifth-form education, he impressed Mason by saying, 'you showed me that summer is not just a season, but a climate of the mind'.[28] The implication is that the young Barry Crump's realisation that 'I see it; I say it' encouraged him to persist with his own career as a writer. Crump published his first semi-autobiographical comic novel, *A Good Keen Man*, in 1960.

By 1978, when cancer of the jaw curtailed his travelling and performing, Mason had performed *The End of the Golden Weather* some 968 times, most often in small halls throughout the country.[29] In March and April 1981 he re-recorded the play with Radio New Zealand, holding up the sagging side of his face in order to articulate his words with customary clarity. That version contains a number of cuts and modifications that were not included in the simultaneously published *Bruce Mason Solo* collection (Price Milburn with Victoria University Press, 1981).

Also in 1981, Theatre Corporate in Auckland produced a full cast version of *The End of the Golden Weather*, adapted by Raymond Hawthorne and directed by Paul Minifie with a cast of twelve, in which the major roles were consistently played by specified actors. In 1987, five years after Mason died, Murray Lynch created an ensemble version with his company, Tantrum Theatre (Auckland), in which a cast of ten shared the roles around. Lynch, who had stage-managed Mason's solo performance at Centrepoint Theatre in Palmerston North, directed further productions of this version at Downstage in 1990, and with Auckland Theatre Company in 2011 as their contribution to the Rugby World Cup's REAL NZ Festival.

The film adaptation—minus 'The Night of the Riots'—which

Mason had worked on with writer and director Ian Mune, finally made it to the screen in 1991. Mune was nineteen when he stood at the back of the Tauranga Repertory Society Hall and watched Mason perform his solo play, and later came to know Mason while working at Downstage in the 1960s. In his autobiography, Mune writes of Mason's 'struggle to see the distinctive needs of the screen as against the magic of his words', which led to 'long and tortuous discussions' over the adaptation and script edits.[30] While in theatre it is the playwright's words that create a vivid picture in the imaginations of audiences, in cinema it is the role of the camera. In the film, empathy with the central characters, specifically the boy and, through him, Firpo, is the crucial factor for engaging the audience.

It was not until eighteen years after Mason's death that Diana Mason allowed another solo actor to take on Mason's text, when the Museum of New Zealand Te Papa Tongarewa required an iconic play to usher in the new millennium. In June 2000 Peter Vere-Jones produced and performed *The End of the Golden Weather*, directed by Susan Wilson, at Te Papa's Soundings Theatre, recorded an independently produced CD, and then toured it to eight towns from Kaitaia to Christchurch, returning to Wellington for a Circa Studio season at the end of 2001. Although Paul Minifie had performed 'Christmas at Te Parenga' for the opening of the Bruce Mason Centre at Takapuna in 1996, the 2001 Vere-Jones tour brought the first full production of a Bruce Mason play to the theatre named after him.

Stephen Lovatt, who was in the Downstage ensemble production, toured a somewhat edited version of *The End of the Golden Weather*, directed by Mark Clare, around the North Island, beginning in September 2006. In contrast to Mason's clipped tones and Vere-Jones' Maria Dronke-trained voice, Lovatt brought a true New Zealand voice to the role, slipping simply and realistically between

---

The boy (Theresa Healey) contemplates the goal Firpo (Cliff Curtis) has set himself. Downstage Theatre, Wellington, June 1990. Directed by Murray Lynch. Photo by Peter Dinnan. ALEXANDER TURNBULL LIBRARY

'As my mother passes him . . . [my father] sweeps her on his knee': *The End of the Golden Weather*, 'Christmas at Te Parenga'. (L–R) Byron Coll, Sophie Roberts, Nic Sampson, Tim Carlsen, Keisha Castle-Hughes, Elliot Christensen-Yule, Dena Kennedy, Matariki Whatarau. Auckland Theatre Company, directed by Murray Lynch, set and costumes by Brian King (September 2011). MICHAEL SMITH

the wide range of characters with ease.[31] New Zealand's most popular playwright, Roger Hall, was quick to commission Lovatt to perform 'Christmas at Te Parenga' at the Takapuna Beach Reserve on Christmas Day 2006, where it continues to play as an annual event (where entry is free or a donation may be made to OXFAM).

To this day, *The End of the Golden Weather* remains the most widely performed and therefore the best known of Bruce Mason's plays.

CHAPTER EIGHT

THE QUEST FOR LIBERTY: MOTHER VERSUS DAUGHTER

The Light Enlarging / Virtuous Circle

The sexual revolution rocks the safe and complacent middle-class lives of Barbara and John Everiss.

The Light Enlarging was written as a stage play in 1963 and, with a little adjustment, was also submitted as a radio play, but the NZBC rejected it 'on the grounds of immorality'[1]. The New Zealand Indecent Publications Tribunal was also set up in 1963, three years after both Vladimir Nabokov's *Lolita* was banned in New Zealand and the trial of DH Lawrence's *Lady Chatterley's Lover* in London was won by the defence. It must be noted that Mason's play contains no offensive expletives or illegal sexuality. While some off-stage behaviour—extra-marital and pre-marital sex; a staple of drama—may be seen by some as immoral in principle, the play's outcome may also be seen as conventional and conservative. Yet when he resubmitted it to NZBC Radio Drama in 1971, it was again rejected with no further explanation.

In 1980, Mason wrote to a friend:

> My attitude to politics is identical to that of Vladimir Nabokov, my idol and god in literary matters, who observed once: 'My view of politics is classical to the point of triteness. Freedom of speech, freedom of religion, freedom of art. Portraits of the head of state not to exceed a postage stamp in size. No torture and no executions.' Which covers the lot when you think about it.[2]

As *The Light Enlarging*, later to be renamed *Virtuous Circle*, opens, Mason uses Puccini's opera *La Bohème*, set in 1830s Paris, to remind us that sexual permissiveness and hedonism are nothing new. It is a while before we realise that the young dressing-gowned tenor Kevin Hogan (thirty-three), who sings along to a recording of

Rodolfo while declaring his love for Mimi, is the lover of Barbara Everiss (forty-two). The 'Dear John . . .' letter she is writing is to her husband tells him she's running away to England with Kevin. The robust buoyancy of their interactions are somewhat redolent of Noel Coward, although the setting and tone are resolutely small-town New Zealand, and Mason playfully 'deconstructs' his script (four years before Jacques Derrida introduced the term) with witty metatheatrical and literary references:

- 'This is your scene,' Barbara tells Kevin before leaving him to face John.[3]
- 'We're not in Restoration Comedy,' Kevin tells Barbara's daughter, Miranda, when she loudly calls him 'the man who cuckolded my father!'[4]
- 'So it's logic you want,' says Barbara as John struggles to make sense of her actions, 'Kevin: drama; John: logic'.[5]
- Barbara tells her husband of the epiphany she had while making passionate love with Kevin in the back of her 'V-dub': 'What I thought was me wasn't me at all. It was simply a huge piece of fiction, built up every day from thousands upon thousands of thoughts. Fiction! An endless serial with me as the star.'[6]
- John tries to find some degree of understanding via his library book, *The Near and the Far* by LH Myers, set in India, in which 'a good man, a wise ruler' suddenly, at fifty, gives up 'wife, family, palace, riches' to live as a monk 'dressed in rags, begging for food. And he's completely happy. And everyone: wife, kids, courtiers, the lot, think this is perfectly natural,' though John 'never thought of it happening here'.[7]
- When Kevin turns instead to single and pregnant Miranda, Barbara paints the scenario: 'Poor ruined and abandoned girl: I'm like something from an opera. He'll burst into a tenor solo any minute, won't you, Kevin?'[8]
- In negotiating a way forward with the devastated Barbara, John notes, 'I could thrash about in private dramas, too. Couldn't I?'[9]

The play ends as it begins, accompanied by Rodolfo from *La Bohème*.

It emerges that for 'twenty-two years come Pancake Day', Barbara has happily done her duty by her family: John, her lawyer husband; their university student daughter Miranda; and their two sons

Geoffrey and Donald, both of whom now have safe jobs and safe girls to go with them. She has turned to classical music for stimulus and a wider horizon. Three months before the play begins, while attending a small touring opera production of *La Bohème*, she was unexpectedly seduced by Kevin's 'beautifully taken high C'. At her instigation, they began an intense affair. Now, with John in Auckland visiting clients, she has summoned her lover back to their small town (three hundred miles from Auckland). She cannot ease Kevin's residual Catholic conscience by saying John is a bore, a drunkard or abusive in any way; nor is he a bad lover: 'He's a very good one: still is.' John's only failing is that he hates music and won't come to concerts with her. But Barbara is not so much leaving him for that as following her heart. She knows Kevin won't be in love with her forever:

> You'll see a girl on the beach in a bikini, someone in the next seat at the flicks or on a train, and you'll itch. Itch away! Scratch! And then I'll go. It'll be a wrench, no doubt, but I'll weather it.[10]

Irish-born Kevin, whose drunken, violent, womanising father walked out on him and his mother, grew up in Liverpool and joined the Army at fourteen. He was posted all over the world before being demobbed and pausing in Paris for singing lessons, while making his living driving a truck for the Paris morgue. Although he speaks good French and Italian, Kevin is not a top-drawer tenor, so he tours for four months of the year, then 'seagulls' on the wharf while picking up little jobs, 'warbling at smoke concerts and the RSA, putting on the blarney for the old ladies.' He loves Barbara's 'sureness, that directness', but craves substance, a base, 'permanence!', so is having trouble understanding her willingness to give all that away. Kevin also hates England: 'Fogs and misery. Class and spite.' He wants to settle in Sydney because he loves sailing. Barbara tried sailing once and loathed every minute of it, but accepts Kevin's promise to make her love it.[11]

Having engaged audience interest with a range of questions regarding the propriety, advisability and longevity of Barbara and Kevin's escapade, Mason interrupts their getaway with the early return of John with daughter Miranda. High stakes and jeopardy ensure tension and comic release as John discovers why Kevin is wearing his pyjamas and dressing gown. Miranda appears to be highly entertained by it all until, in a volatile exchange alone with Kevin, she reveals her own predicament and her trepidation at how her mother will react. She is four months pregnant and any one of four of the six boys she has been flatting with in Auckland could be the father; the other two were 'busy. With each other.' She takes it for granted 'Mummy' and 'Daddy' will be there to look after her, and, as with her father, it shocks her to realise her mother has other feelings and priorities. In the process of setting out Miranda's options before catching her train, Barbara takes a strong anti-abortion position while Miranda puts up an equally strong defence for it. At four months, however, she has left it too late. Again Mason articulates both sides of the argument to maximise its dramatic value, even though his wife, Dr Diana Mason, now specialising in obstetrics, was destined to join the Society for the Protection of Unborn Children (SPUC) when it formed in 1970 and become its president in 1974. When Miranda declares she is scared, and plays the 'I'm your daughter!' card, Barbara replies, 'I don't own you, Miranda, any more than you own the life inside you.' Of course she was Barbara's responsibility when she couldn't fend for herself but, 'You're a big girl now; you must pick yourself up.'[12]

When John returns '*in a towering rage, wearing shorty pyjamas, and a moth-eaten egg-stained dressing gown*', Mason ensures he has the lowest status of any character at the play's mid-point, and there is a tragicomic tone to his upset. Barbara is significantly different from Mason's other wife-and-mother characters: Elfrida (*The Evening Paper*); Mrs Douglas, Janet and Mabel (*The Verdict*); Aroha and Mrs Atkinson (*The Pohutukawa Tree*) and the yet-to-be-written Sandra (*Zero Inn*). Barbara's years of marriage and motherhood have not made her unhappy, narrow-minded, anxious, stressed, disillusioned or angry. Her passionate affair has rocketed her beyond a complacent, conventional and aimless life of safety, security and reliability into an expanding enlightenment (hence *The Light Enlarging*). Where her choices affect other people, she sees that as a positive: 'You know the phrase: a vicious circle, one bad thing leading to another? Well, there are virtuous circles too. One good thing leading to another.'[13] Hence *Virtuous Circle*.

When Barbara accuses John of wanting her to be safe, of wanting to defuse her 'unexploded bomb', he replies, 'Of course I want you to be safe! How could we live, with everyone like an unexploded bomb? Safety: security: our lives are built on them. They must be.' Mason uses Barbara's response to elevate the argument beyond the domestic realm:

> You're right: we're eaten up with it, eroded and gutted by it. We're a family: all right, protect it with roof and four walls, fences, gates. Outside, the street, the town, the nation. Guard them. Police, armies, navies, air forces, hydrogen bombs. Isn't that security? And it all leads straight to war and death. Can't you see that? And this country! Look at it! More security and less fun than anywhere I can think of. Nothing to warm it up but the odd ghastly crime, and the Maoris, bless them, who couldn't care less about security. Well, that's what I'm resigning from; not just you, hearth and home. Safety. Security. I'm walking out on that, John.[14]

But this classic Masonesque critique of New Zealand and its Allies is not where the argument ends. In a brilliant twist, Kevin and Miranda announce they are leaving together. Kevin has realised the relationship with Barbara won't work, what with him wanting to settle down and her wanting liberation into a wider world. His plan is to look after Miranda at his two-room shack 'up the coast', at least until the baby is born. There is a touch of *The Taming of the Shrew*'s Petruchio to her Katherina in Kevin's treatment of Miranda: 'I shall slap you in a moment'; 'Shut your face'.[15] The audience is left to ponder whether the sparks will produce passion or disaster.

A devastated Barbara is left with John declaring her 'blinding light' has touched him too: 'Darling: you can't keep light to yourself! It falls on others! It's not your private passport to Higher Things . . . I too can explode like the stars and fill the heavens with music.' He claims to be another beneficiary of her 'legacy of clarity'. She has hammered away all the flaky old plaster, 'And what's left? The naked bronze, girlie, awful and terrible. What's safe, what's secure about that?' He is looking at her now for the first time in years: 'Every line, every fissure, all toil-worn for me, dear Mother Machree! Kiss me, you bag.' Her response is tentative at first, then passionate, but she will keep her bag packed for a while. John's final flourish sees him order Barbara, military style, to turn on the radiogram, unleash Rodolfo from *La Bohème*, then go into the kitchen: 'Coffee and liver sausage sandwiches for your lord. I'll sit here like the god I am, listening.' She weeps a little before recovering, touching his head and going with a parting, 'Yes, sir. Right away, sir.' As the music swells the lights fade leaving John in darkness, '*with a pencil of light falling on the suitcase.*'[16]

This ending is problematic, as with Shakespeare's *The Taming of the Shrew*, which was yet to attract opprobrium from feminists. By the time *The Light Enlarging* premiered in 1978, however, *The Taming of the Shrew* was either off the list for production or presenting challenges for socially aware directors, actors and their audiences. Ibsen's *A Doll's House* (1878) is also worth referencing, given its exposé of a more unwitting kind of repressive male chauvinism (the acclaimed film of Christopher Hampton's adaptation, starring Claire Bloom and Anthony Hopkins, came out in 1973). Like Shakespeare and Ibsen, Mason is not telling us what to think or whose side to take: he's provoking us to take a position. The situation and the spouses' responses to it are entirely credible, if not ideal, and each actor/director partnership has to interrogate the characters' actions in order to determine how to play them. Is John's attempt to appreciate music going to be enough? If he is sincere, why the 'alpha male' routine? Is he trying to emulate Kevin or send him up, or has he gone mad?

Does he really think this is what Barbara wants or is he just playing at being unpredictable? Is Barbara tragically trapped in her role? Was her 'blinding flash' and quest for change a hormone-induced fantasy? Has she come to her senses, or is she facing an inexorable truth in tandem with her husband's sense of humour? Each member of the audience will have their own ideas as to whether this is a sad or happy ending, and that makes for stimulating theatre.

The Light Enlarging / Virtuous Circle is Mason's 'finger-on-the-pulse' response to what would become known as the 'sexual revolution' and the 'midlife crisis' (a term not coined until 1965 by Canadian psychoanalyst Elliott Jaques). British poet Philip Larkin identified the year Mason wrote it as the start of the 'swinging sixties', as in his 1967 poem *Annus Mirabilis*: 'Sexual intercourse began/ In nineteen sixty-three/ (which was rather late for me)/ Between the end of the *Chatterley* ban/ And the Beatles' first LP.'

It is also relevant to note that this play, *Swan Song* (1967) and *Zero Inn* (early 1970) addressed these issues before Germaine Greer's *The Female Eunuch* (1970) and Gail Sheehy's *Passages: Predictable Crises in Adult Life* (1976) were published. Barbara in *The Light Enlarging / Virtuous Circle* and Sandra in *Zero Inn* both seek liberation after decades of marriage and motherhood. Although, in the end, both remain with their husbands, this should not be seen as Mason's preferred position but as his provocative take on probable outcomes in New Zealand at the time (echoed in Roger Hall's 1977 hit play, *Middle Age Spread*). While *Zero Inn*'s Max and Sandra face a different and uncertain future together, John and Barbara are either starting afresh or regressing to something medieval; either way, Barbara's suitcase remains packed. In *The Evening Paper* (1953/1965), Mason addresses the long-term effects of a wife's sexual disappointment. A different solution to an unfulfilling marriage is examined in *The Verdict* (1955), albeit with a shocking outcome and an open verdict concerning the cause. In *Swan Song*, Jenny Lucas does break free of her controlling husband, so Mason cannot be accused of always letting the husband win.

It was not until 1978 that *Virtuous Circle* had its world premiere. It was produced by The Company Theatre in Tauranga, a semi-professional enterprise which did not employ a company as such. *Virtuous Circle* followed *The Evening Paper* (incorporating the scene developed for the television production) in a double-bill entitled *Suitcases*. The same four actors performed in both plays and Mason was their director.[17]

In 1978 New Zealand boasted no fewer than nine professional theatres: Mercury and Theatre Corporate in Auckland, Gateway (which closed that year) in Tauranga, Four Seasons in Whanganui, Centrepoint in Palmerston North, Downstage and Circa in Wellington, The Court in Christchurch and Fortune in Dunedin. Bruce Mason had been a playwright for twenty-five years and had followed the short plays surveyed in chapter four with *The Pohutukawa*

Tree, *Birds in the Wilderness*, *The End of the Golden Weather*, *Awatea*, *The Hand on the Rail*, *Swan Song* and *Hongi*, His five plays on Māori themes had been published in *The Healing Arch* collection (1974). Despite this unsurpassed portfolio which, along with his much-performed solo works, earned Mason the status of New Zealand's leading playwright, he was obliged to premiere *The Light Enlarging* (as *Virtuous Circle*) and direct it himself with a semi-professional theatre group fifteen years after it was written.

CHAPTER NINE

CONFRONTING POLITICAL AND ARTISTIC SUPPRESSION

To Russia, with Love

Three character studies set in Moscow embody the state of Soviet Russia (based on Mason's visit in 1958 and responding to events in 1968).

Of the solos originated by Bruce Mason, only *The End of the Golden Weather* (apart from 'The Night of the Riots') and *To Russia, with Love* are dramatised in the present tense so that their characters can more successfully 'come alive' on stage.

Mason was a vice-president of the Downstage Theatre Society from 1964 to 1976 and, more than once, when its struggles to find and retain its professional footing brought Downstage to the brink of collapse, his solo shows helped turn the tide. Diana Mason used to say Bruce had a photographic memory, which was why he was able to create and perform his solo shows in extraordinarily short order, but she would 'tick him off for reading off the inside of his eyelids.'[1] With each new show, he found it a challenge to become fully present to his audiences, and yet no one in New Zealand has proved his equal in getting a solo play on its feet so fast.

In March 1965 Mason performed his well-seasoned *The End of the Golden Weather* at the tiny Downstage Theatre Café (still in its original Walkabout Coffee Lounge space; capacity sixty). Immediately after, Downstage staged Ben Jonson's *Bartholomew Fair* at Victoria University's much larger Memorial Theatre in the hope of making more money (given only the six core professionals in a cast of twenty-seven were paid), but it bombed. The following month Mason attended a crisis meeting where it was revealed that, despite full houses for the five small-cast shows so far staged at the theatre cafe that year, debts were mounting and 'unless we could present a completely new show, for one actor only—we could not afford to pay any more—Downstage would founder within a week'.[2] Rising to the challenge, Mason conceived, wrote and learnt *To Russia, with Love* within one week and premiered it on 3 May 1965. His translation of Vercors' famous work on the French Resistance, *The Waters of Silence*—reworked from the point of view of Werner, the Nazi officer who tells how the hostile and very upper-crust French father and daughter were forced to billet him—followed at Downstage in July. Mason performed it in English and French on alternate nights.

When he took *To Russia, with Love* to the Auckland Festival that same year, he added a piece called 'The Last Supper'. Set in America, it dealt with nuclear contamination and was based on an article in *Look* magazine. Calling the double bill *The Counsels of the Wood*, he performed it at Downstage, which had now expanded into the next-door space, in 1966. But when he revised *To Russia, with Love* in 1972 (three years after the Soviet invasion of Czechoslovakia), he discarded 'The Last Supper' and instead preceded it with *The Waters of Silence*. He called the new coupling *Men of Soul*.[3]

Mason's introduction to Marxism and Soviet communism under Stalin is revealed in *Courting Blackbird*, which he had laid aside in 1952 after completing 'just two variations and the coda.' Six years later, when the world-famous Russian violinist David Oistrakh performed in New Zealand for the first time, his Wellington concert was boycotted by most of the invited diplomats in protest against the executions of four counter-revolutionaries in Soviet-occupied Hungary. In his weekly 'Theatre and the Arts' column for *The Dominion*, Mason argued that although 'the noises coming out of TASS [the Soviet news agency] were sickening cant, it seemed inappropriate and unjust to take this revulsion out on a musician', especially when 'no one in this vile century has clean hands'.[4] Some weeks later, in October 1958, he was invited to be part of a three-person cultural delegation (with artist E Mervyn Taylor and Julius Hogben, chair of the Auckland Festival Society) to the USSR and Czechoslovakia. Almost ten years later Mason wrote 'An open letter to His Excellency Boris Yakovelich Dorofeev, Envoy Extraordinary and Minister Plenipotentiary for the Union of Soviet Socialist Republics in New Zealand', which was published by Wellington's morning newspaper *The Dominion* on 5 September 1968, and occupied a full page. It was translated into Czech and sent to Pragopress in Prague, and into Russian and sent to TASS in Moscow. 'No report was ever received of its fate in these places,' Mason noted, 'but one can guess'.[5]

Mason had met Dorofeev during 'an hilarious evening . . . at the house of Fred Turnovsky, who left Prague in 1939 to escape disgusting tyranny.' His letter praises the 'fabulous hospitality' the delegation had experienced in Russia, and notes how 'at home' he felt with the people of the USSR. He also reports on the furious wrangles he had had with their interpreter about the Hungarian revolution, his shock at realising WWII had left Russia with six million war widows, and the grief the delegation shared with their Ukrainian interpreter at the German's slaughtering of Jews, which included her parents.

> We wept for her loss, for man's inhumanity. And Rada, recovering, said that she wept for the Germans too, even for her parents' killers. Because 'they did not know what they were doing.' This is perhaps the most luminous moment of charity I have ever experienced.[6]

It is possible this experience influenced his decision to play *The Waters of Silence* from the point of view of the Nazi officer.

But the main objective of Mason's letter was to protest the Soviet invasion of Czechoslovakia on 21 August 1968, to halt the liberal 'Prague Spring' reforms being introduced by Alexander Dubček, an invasion which had been greeted with 'grief and anger . . . all over the world'. Referencing the worldwide student-led cultural revolution precipitated by the war in Vietnam, Mason argued that Dubček:

> . . . has proclaimed his loyalty to the ideal of communism in a federation acknowledging Moscow as its head, but equally, he insists on a national identity within it, and he has thus become a symbol for the young, who insist on theirs. Above all, they insist on free discussion and exchange of information to which they have a right, and it is this, finally, which so terrifies your leaders. In the name of Pushkin, Tolstoy, Dostoyevsky and Turgenev (I can't very well say 'God' to you), why? Why are you so afraid of words?[7]

Mason writes of his reaction to the 1958 Nobel Prize for Literature being awarded to Boris Pasternak and its aftermath:

> I could have wept for joy that once again the great stream of Russian literature would irrigate the soul and imagination of the world. My grief was bitter when I heard that Pasternak had refused the prize and was the target of every time-serving, toadying, lick-spittle hack who came to sneer at a talent incomparably greater than theirs . . . The spectacle of a great nation, possessed of a marvellous culture, driven to ignoble spite over the work of a great poet, is simply heart-breaking. It betrays the very spirit of the October Revolution and violates the principles of the Soviet Constitution.

He ends with an English translation of words he found in Prague, in 1958, on a statue of Jan Hus (priest, philosopher, reformer, burned at the stake for 'heresy' against Catholic Church doctrine): 'Love the truth. Let others have their truth, and the truth will prevail'.[8]

In this passionate and eloquent letter we see how Mason values the West's social revolution of the 1960s, including the right to free discussion and exchange of information. He also places a high value on the maintenance of a national identity, as affiliations with larger entities become more pervasive, and the right of writers to 'irrigate the soul and imagination of the world' without fear of suppression or punishment. We sense how his own work is driven by these values, not least in his ability to write opposing characters who each have their 'truth' so that we may freely determine ours.

The 1972 version of *To Russia, with Love* replaces references to the United States of America's Secretary of Defence Robert McNamara with the Secretary of State Henry Kissinger, and the Soviet vilification of ballet dancer Rudolf Nureyev (who defected to the West in 1961) with that of novelist Aleksandr Solzhenitsyn (a 'non-person' from 1965; expelled in 1974). In a departure from earlier requests that his plays be set as written, Mason gives permission, in 1973, for those names to be 'changed and brought up to date without acknowledgement'.[9] The piece could not, however, be set later than Gorbachev's *glasnost* (openness) and *perestroika* (restructuring) initiatives in the mid-1980s, which Mason would not live to see.

To Russia, with Love is set in Moscow and comprises three separate scenes for a solo performer who plays a different character in each. Mason shares his concerns about Soviet Russia by exploring its truth from three very different perspectives: the genial but crass American businessman, the naïve young American lawyer on his 'OE' to broaden his mind, and the literature-loving Russian dissident who is loyal to the socialist principles that Soviet communism has betrayed.

I

Eugene B Timms, a boisterous businessman from Castroville Texas, USA, is staying in a third floor apartment of the ornate old Metropol Hotel in Moscow. Mason's device is that prior to being picked up by his interpreter, Irina Dolganova, to go to *Swan Lake* at the Bolshoi Theatre, Eugene tape-records his impressions of Russia for his wife, Grace, and for the folks back in Castroville, not least her Book of the Month Club friends.[10]

While sending up Americans with this archetypal tycoon, Mason uses Eugene to satirise the Kremlin's reputation for bugging hotel rooms. He searches for microphones, plays up to what might be one under the bed, goads the Kremlin with key words like atomic energy, Kissinger and uranium isotopes, and cracks quips about being James Bond. Mason also uses Eugene's tape to introduce Irving Davis Jnr, a young law graduate from San Francisco who is taking six months off to 'see how the other half lives' before settling down. Irving raises cash by reading back-copies of *Time* or *Newsweek* magazines in the hotel lobby and selling them to Russians who ask to buy them. Eugene confesses he found Solzhenitsyn's *The First Circle* (which Grace put in his luggage) 'dry as a bone', so he has given it to Irving. When Irina Dolganova (he calls her 'Irene') arrives he gets her to record 'good evening' on tape in Russian, then howls and wheezes at the result.[11]

The monologue works well until the voiceless Irina arrives. At this point Eugene's one-sided conversation becomes even more contrived than the standard onstage telephone call convention, where what the unseen caller is saying has to be echoed or implied in the audible responses. The second and third scenes suffer similarly.

II

Rather than voice all his main characters, as he did with *The End of the Golden Weather*, Mason sticks with the convention of one-sided 'present action' conversation.

In the hotel lobby, Irving Davis Jnr reads Solzhenitsyn's *The First Circle*, fends off attempts to purchase his clothes and greets Mr Timms and Miss Dolganova in passing. He then gets into conversation with a rather evasive Dmitri Alexeyvich Doroshenko who, after telling him he shouldn't be selling that book here, invites him to his room. Saying he wants time to think it over and have his dinner, Irving gets Dmitri to write down his address. Once Dmitri has gone, he calls the American Embassy for advice, is shouted at for not knowing the phone line is 'open' and accepts the instruction to get a taxi to the Embassy.[12]

III

Now it is Dmitri's side of the conversation that Mason articulates, and in this scene the concerns he expressed in his letter to Dorofeev come to the fore.

Dmitri lets Irving into his room, locks the door, offers vodka, jokes as to the fears and suspicions that may have made him so late, then becomes grave at being told Irving has been to the American Embassy, who brought him by car. After they've shown each other photos of their fiancées and drunk more vodka, Dmitri reveals his curtained-off shelves of Western magazines and books. On being given *The First Circle* by Irving, Dmitri launches into an eloquent appreciation of Solzhenitsyn, 'our great underground hero', who achieved fame when Krushchev allowed the publication of *One Day in the Life of Ivan Denisovich* only to have *Cancer Ward* and *The First Circle* rejected; he was treated like Pasternak, who was hounded to death. 'But Solzhenitsyn is still young, unquenchable: all the toadies and lickspittles and arse-lickers in the world will not crush him!'[13]

Mason's political voice remains strong as Dmitri speaks of the limits put on him as an art teacher, having to teach symmetry every day to 'unload' Lenin on Soviet children, watching them change from freely imagining five-year-olds into unimaginative disciples of the 'Heroes of the Soviet Union'. The vodka-fuelled Dmitri likens all 'sober citizens giving no trouble' to Stravinsky's straw puppet, Petrouchka. Recalling how, when he studied English at Moscow University, he 'devoured history, novels, plays', Dmitri calls for a toast: 'Peace and friendship. And the courage for us to be not Russians, not Americans, but men!' He describes going to Red Square on the night the Soviet tanks moved into Prague and compares it with Ivan the Terrible blinding the architect of St Basil's Cathedral so he could never build another church. Dmitri equates himself to a Russian novel that cannot be written down and must only be spoken to a sympathetic listener. Although he is left-handed, and paints that way in private, he is obliged to make his pupils paint right-handed. 'But the left is also the side of the heart,' Dmitri points out. 'The left wing in politics was always the more humane but when, as in Russia, the left becomes the right, the heart becomes the right, the left is crippled. But both must work together!'[14]

The dramatic tension begins to build as Dmitri recognises Irving, who is falling asleep thanks to the vodka, as 'a man of soul' and reveals the secret recess that holds copies of their underground *Chronicle of Current Events,* which they smuggle out through Amnesty International. He calls it 'the voice of the Loyal Opposition, telling truths that would make your American blood freeze', like the way dissenters are held in psychiatric prisons and 'processed, by terrible drugs'. He talks a reluctant Irving into taking a copy, explaining he is their only hope. Dmitri cannot leave Russia, 'the country of the Great October Revolution . . . of Pushkin, Turgenev and Solzhenitsyn . . . I am Russian! I breathe with its breath, I beat with its heart!' He asks Irving to forget all he has said but 'tell my story of the heart, and how it beats here, if faintly, on the left side.' Toots from the waiting Embassy car summon Irving, and Dmitri sees him out. Soon after that car is heard leaving another arrives with '*a scream of brakes*'. As footsteps pound on the stairs, Dmitri frantically tears secret papers and drops them into his stove. The loud knocking stops with the door splintering and being kicked in '*as the lights fade to black.*'[15]

This, then, is the solo work Mason wrote, learnt and performed within one week in 1965, then revised in 1972: flawed as a piece of live theatre but powerful in the message it carries and arguably his most politically polemic work. In his 1982 *Kaleidoscope* interview with Helen Paske, Mason notes that *To Russia, with Love* is the only one of his solo works that did not have him as the first-person narrator, which makes it the most amenable to being performed by others. More importantly, he reveals:

> *To Russia, with Love* [is] perhaps the one I feel most about, because it was the fulfilment of a commission made to me in Moscow in 1958 by a young man called Igor. I was the member of a cultural delegation and he tried to pass to me the manuscript of an underground novel. Well I was a guest of the state and I felt if this were found on me I'd be in a terrible situation and it might implicate him too. So he said, 'Well if you can't do that, will you tell my story?' I said, 'Well you'd better talk fast' because we had only an hour together. So I got just enough out of that hour together to make a 'moa bone' [from which he created the whole skeleton] and I had to—from my limited knowledge of Russia, which I later did my bit to extend by studying Russian and so on—I had to create the character which I call Dmitri Alexeyvitch Doroshenko. And that, to me, of my four solo pieces, that was the best thing I was able to do.[16]

In the same interview, asked about his interest in Māori themes, Mason said he was interested in eloquence, 'Hence my attraction to Dmitri Alexeyvitch in *To Russia, with Love*, because if the Russians are not eloquent, nobody is.'[17]

It was financial pressures that required *To Russia, with Love* to premiere as a solo piece. Because its flaws are entirely related to that limitation, consideration might well be given to adapting it for a cast of four.

CHAPTER TEN

SHINING LIGHT WHERE TRUTH LIES

Awatea

The high expectations placed on 'Dr Matt' by his father, Werihe Paku, and the Omoana community come to a head as the truth is revealed.

It is thanks to Inia Te Wiata, the London-based world-class bass-baritone (and master carver), that Bruce Mason wrote *Awatea* and the three other Māori-themed plays that would eventually be published, along with *The Pohutukawa Tree*, under the collective title *The Healing Arch*. Because the New Zealand Opera Company had secured a special dispensation to produce Gershwin's *Porgy and Bess* in 1965 with an all-Māori cast, led by Te Wiata, William Austin (head of radio drama for the NZBC) commissioned Mason to write a radio play that would feature the renowned singer as an actor and utilise the whole cast of *Porgy*.

Three ideas formed that would make the most of the 'priceless asset' Mason had to work with: 'a bass voice of huge range and richness'.[1] Although Inia Te Wiata turned fifty in the year he played Porgy (the romantic lead), the three roles Mason conceived for him were older men. He wanted that 'great instrument' to characterise the old Māori ways and imperatives that were fast disappearing: a theme strongly established in *The Pohutukawa Tree,* which, eight years after its workshop airing, was now in the production doldrums.

The idea Mason settled on initially combined two real-life stories he had come across. First, a young Māori man he had known well at university brought mana to his district by being the first to gain University Entrance. In a flush of idealistic optimism he enrolled for a medical degree, but found it too complex and dropped out. Too ashamed to show his face at home again, he changed his name and got a job as a freezing worker. Second, a young Māori woman working in the city had met and fallen in love with a doctor. They were married in the far north where her father was a prominent rangatira. Only after the magnificent ceremony and honeymoon did she discover her husband was a bigamous house painter whose wife was in hospital with their third child. What intrigued Mason most was that everyone accepted he was a doctor without seeking proof.[2] From these sources Mason envisaged:

> [A] long deception by a gifted and articulate young Maori who, like his real-life counterpart, achieved University Entrance and chose medicine as a career in the same spirit of high-mindedness. Again as in life, he cannot complete more than a couple of terms, and is unable to face the father [to be played by Te Wiata] who had sold his land to make the course possible. So he acts out the role of doctor by returning once a year with the money he has saved from the freezing works. And his return slowly becomes the occasion for an annual hui, the only event which has the power to assemble the now dispersed members of the tribe, who unite once a year to welcome back the hero.

By making the father blind—'with useful Homeric parallels for those who like such things'—Mason was able to use the postmistress as the 'messenger' who brought the son's letters and read them aloud. 'Old Werihe Paku . . . would live in the ancient oral and tactile world of the Maori.'[3]

Mason drafted a treatment, entitled *The Hui*, describing the seventh annual gathering and thirteenth visit of the heroic son, 'Dr Matt', to his home at Omoana (the place of the ocean). This time, however, he has lost his job at the freezing works and has had to commit crimes to maintain the pretence. The postmistress and police, who are the only ones in the know, connive to let the hui proceed for fear of the truth killing the old man. When the postmistress receives news of Matt's court case and sentence, she keeps it from the old man. '[The] play, as originally conceived, ended with him still blind to the truth,' Mason writes, 'in a spirit of—I hoped—poignant dramatic irony.'[4]

The way Mason tells it, Te Wiata's first reaction to the treatment was unfavourable, so the playwright spent 'two rather desperate weeks' writing up the two other ideas he had: 'an old Maori father, devoted to the old ways and imperatives, searching for his wild son, who had lost them in the city' (*The Hand on the Rail*) and 'a bardic Maori bursting joyously through the narrow straits of Pakeha feelings and emotions, finding his true image and stature only in death' (*Swan Song*). But Te Wiata did not like these either, and 'mature consideration made him accept [the play now named] *Awatea*, which he thereafter warmly championed'—but not before he and his actress wife Beryl let Mason know, from London, that they were disappointed he had not better explored 'the implicit dramatic material at the end'. Mason agreed and reworked the epilogue, so that 'the old man learns the truth about his son and, instead of being broken by it, accommodates it in what later became the most controversial scene of the play.'[5]

Given the kudos that was accorded English playwright Harold Pinter for immersing himself in the argot of his 'kitchen-sink drama' when writing such plays as *The Room*, *The Birthday Party* and *The Dumb Waiter* (all 1957), it is important to note that Mason researched the setting, language and characteristics of *Awatea* by spending a holiday break on the East Coast.

> I stood for two weeks solid in various Gisborne pubs, filling notebooks with the *argot* of young Maoris of the district; thus I will defend against all comers and objectors, the colloquial passages of the play . . . I moved up the East Coast and found my site, which I describe accurately in the play, and, for some weeks on end, I thought Omoana into existence; I could walk imaginatively over every foot of this ground and recite its total history. I saw the tribe as a sub-branch of Ngati Porou (though I was not foolish enough ever to mention this name), becoming isolated in the twenties, with poor land leading to a slow migration away from it. Its permanent residents now would hardly number three or four families . . . I came to know Omoana so well that I could describe the contents of every room in every house, and Werihe's cliff-top eyrie I knew to the last flaking weather-board.[6]

The title, *Awatea*, means daylight and refers to Matt, whom his blind father calls 'my light, te awatea, the bright sword that flashes though my dark.'[7] Later, Detective Inspector Brett likens Matt to

Lucifer, the angel closest to God, who got hurled out of heaven into hell.[8]

Awatea the radio play was recorded in April 1965, its large cast headed by Te Wiata as Werihe Paku, Pat Evison as Emma Gilhooly and Don Selwyn as Matt Paku. It was broadcast the following month on ZB Sunday Showcase, then repeated in August.[9] The epilogue found Te Wiata 'in magnificent form' on radio, Mason noted. The following year he offered the Maori Theatre Trust a two-year option on his stage version, on the understanding that Inia Te Wiata would reprise the lead role, and showed it to Dick Johnstone, whose early work at Downstage Theatre had impressed him. Johnstone declared himself determined to direct it. They proposed a touring production, to rehearse and open in Gisborne early in 1967, but the Arts Council refused the grant application of £9,000 and the project was abandoned. The radio version was repeated on Waitangi Day that year and Johnstone proposed the stage play for the 1968 Pan-Pacific Arts Festival in Christchurch, but a cash-strapped City Council was unable to fund it.[10]

When Johnstone was asked to return to Downstage, following the premature departure of its imported artistic director, he made directing *Awatea* a condition of the job. The production became part of a series of engagements engineered by Arts Council chairman Bill Sheat to make the most of Te Wiata's return visit in 1968. He would perform a concert of great operatic arias and well-known songs for the NZBC, play Osmin in Mozart's *Il Seraglio* for the New Zealand Opera Company and play Werihe in *Awatea* for Downstage Theatre.[11] Te Wiata would also play the title role in Mason's new radio play, *Hongi*. Johnstone cast George Henare as Matt and English character actress Davina Whitehouse as Emma Gilhooly, and planned to stage it at the larger Paramount Theatre with a set designed by landscape artist Peter McIntyre. They were well into rehearsals with the mostly Māori cast (the play has eighteen named roles plus almost as many 'extra' women and children), pending the arrival of Te Wiata for the final two to three weeks, when Johnstone saw a bus drive past carrying an advertisement for the show at Wellington's Town Hall. This was the first he knew of the change of venue. The way he tells it, he rang Bill Sheat (also president of the Downstage Theatre Society),

who said, 'I knew you'd find out eventually.' (As Sheat recalls it, the Town Hall was always the intended venue.) The Wellington City Council's Parks and Reserves Department provided five truckloads of flax, cabbage trees and other foliage for the set. It was all stored in the small courtyard behind Downstage so that it could be rained on before the 'bump in'. But no one told the garbage collectors, who cleared away the lot, and it all had to be retrieved from the tip.[12]

In September 1968 the large capacity of the Town Hall allowed for a short season of four evening performances and one matinee, but the venue proved problematic. While it 'dealt splendidly with anything of a ceremonial nature', it reduced the more intimate scenes to 'wafer thinness' and presented major problems for the epilogue. Mason conceded 'the great cry of Werihe Paku, the anguish and frenzy which followed it [had been] thought through in sound alone' and did not translate well to the stage.

The cast of *Awatea*, the radio play, at Broadcasting House. (L–R) William Austin (producer), Bruce Mason, Don Selwyn, Sam Stevens, Ngaire Karaka, Hannah Tatana, Diana Winterburn, Newha Taiaki and Inia Te Wiata (1965). Radio New Zealand Photographic Collection, Ngā Taonga Sound & Vision

> In rehearsal, with a group of actors and a few visitors sitting within feet of Inia Te Wiata, these passages were awesome and blood-congealing. Moreover, we saw it without scenery and filled in the gaps with our imaginations, much as radio demands. Stepped out, spelled out, as it had to be in the Town Hall, watching Inia totter up and down what we all knew were the organ-loft steps of the Town Hall, it took on a stagey quality that, from the circle at least, did not enmesh the emotions in the same way.[13]

Despite being Mason's biggest box office success to date (9,000 admissions over five performances), the critics—apart from *The Dominion*'s Russell Bond, who 'praised it highly and followed a warm review with a thoughtful editorial two days later'—were rigorous:

Inia Te Wiata as Werihe in *Awatea*, the stage play. Downstage at the Wellington Town Hall, directed by Dick Johnstone, designed by Peter McIntyre (September 1968).
TERENCE TAYLOR

The critic in the *Evening Post*, however, Owen Jensen, while conceding the evening a victory against the odds, dismissed the Epilogue in terms that I found hard to read, and provoked a fierce correspondence . . . Mr George Webby . . . was offered a full page in *Salient* . . . to examine the play and its production. He did so in several thousand words of lacerating invective, disembowelling not only the play, but the author. That Mr Webby happens to be one of my closest friends made his polemic no easier to read. I learned, among much else, that I had sold out to the New Zealand establishment, whatever that might be, and was counselled at the end to retire to an attic 'for a terrifying reappraisal'.

I find it remarkable that in a country where the arts, far from flourishing, have barely taken root, an artistic failure can evoke a furious satisfaction. Were one a scientist, conducting an independent experiment which failed, it would not lead to professional extinction; one would try again on another tack; unless this were so, no Department of Scientific and Industrial research could possibly survive or even justify itself. The right to fail is conceded everywhere to scientists but not yet to artists. We assume of course that the scientist is objective, working on inert matter which does not take on the context or colour of his personality, but that a writer spinning his material spider-like from his innards, must be identified with it; that if it fails, then it is as much a failure of nerve or character as of talent.

Most writers, I believe, would declare that their best moments seem to happen of themselves, as illuminations which descend unsought and unbidden—much of *Awatea* for example, had seemed to write itself—but this news has not reached many critics that I know of. By signing one's name to a piece, one becomes an accessory to the crime of authorship (or so I bitterly concluded).

Mr Webby's eloquent fury was complemented some weeks later by the review of Jack Shallcrass, also a close friend, which appeared in *Act*, the magazine I edit for Downstage. This was a much more sober, temperate performance, but he too found the play unsatisfactory.[14]

Mason was initially baffled: 'The play was, after all, a huge popular success under the most adverse conditions; I recall, and am grateful for "couldn't see, couldn't hear; loved every minute of it." It had been received in the warmest way after its three broadcasts, both from the press and from numerous private letters. What on earth had happened?' And so he began his reappraisal:

> [Not] in Mr Webby's attic, but quietly at home, less terrifying than laborious. I realised suddenly—perhaps this was what Mr Webby and my other critics were saying, in essence—that Matt's future must come from within himself; any imposed solution, however well intentioned, however pure the motive, from a Pakeha, must insult him. And further, unless this solution were somewhere locked within the play as it stood, then the whole structure was worthless and I might as well throw it on the scrap heap. I sifted the play with an almost desperate zeal. And then suddenly I saw it—it was a moment of bliss—and it had been there, hidden, all the time. I no longer had an epilogue but a fully developed and worked out Act III.[15]

If the overall structure and location of the story was to be maintained, Matt could not be present for Act 3. The resolution that grew from within himself would have to be implied through a scene between Werihe Paku and Emma Gilhooly. For being provoked to write a new draft of *Awatea*, Mason expressed sincere gratitude to George Webby, Owen Jensen and Jack Shallcrass:

> Each gave me, according to his temperament and persuasion, a shock, numbing at first, but later, in the moment of thaw, invaluable. Thus, in setting one's name to a text, one does not so much proclaim authority as declare a convention: this is much less 'all my own work' than evidence of a series of collaborations, of cross-fertilising from people one has known, from producers, actors, audiences and critics. *Awatea* represents a synthesis of all these collaborations.[16]

It was this new draft which The Court Theatre produced, directed by Mervyn Thompson as part of the Commonwealth Games Festival in January 1974. Don Selwyn played Werihe Paku and Pat Evison reclaimed Emma Gilhooly: the role Mason had written for her and which she had originated on radio. Although Davina Whitehouse's bicycle-riding Gilhooly had been a crowd favourite in the Downstage premiere, Jack Shallcrass had spoken for many in saying, quite rightly, that her eccentric English characteristics were all wrong for a postmistress who had lived her entire life in Omoana. The Court's more intimate space served the story much better than Wellington's cavernous Town Hall, but Thompson decided to set it in the 'now' of the 1970s, which Mason believed subverted its credibility. In his 1978 Note to the Second Edition he wrote: 'I suggest that the mythical substructure of the play, the multiple deceptions on which its action rests and by which it is propelled, would simply not be plausible after, say 1962. This would mean that Matt's long masquerade began in 1949, when Omoana would be truly isolated, and Matt free to be anonymous in the city and a hero at home.' The stage directions for Act 1 in the posthumously published text (1987) therefore includes: '*It is New Year's Eve in the early nineteen sixties, just before television ended Omoana's isolation forever.*'[17]

The play depicts the tiny settlement's seventh annual hui (meaning 'gathering' in this context) and hāngī. All but Sergeant Jameson, Detective Inspector Brett, a shocked Gilhooly and the audience continue to believe the highly anticipated and long-overdue Matt Paku is a successful young doctor. He returns, as ever, to his father's place in his latest flash car with a keg, pays for the party and cures the ills of his whānau with his healing hands. The formal ceremonial elements maintained by old Werihe are contrasted with the ritual of picking a Queen of the Hui by ballot. Her prize is to spend the night with Matt in a cave down at the beach. Being no later than 1962, it cannot be argued that the post-pill, flower-powered, free-love ethics of the sexual revolution have already influenced this remote East Coast settlement, or even the larger towns and cities most of the hapū have moved to. The notion that each New Year's Eve, Matt gets to choose his woman for the night, leaving the others to indulge in 'free love' between themselves, either reflects Mason's field research (although his notes make no mention of this), extrapolates from Margaret Mead's *Coming of Age in Samoa* (1928; comparing stressed adolescent American girls with their well-balanced, carefree and supposedly sexually active Samoan counterparts), or is conceived as a contemporary echo of the Bacchanalia of ancient Greece. It is important to note, in this context, that the moral imperatives of Christianity that loom so large for Aroha Mataira in *The Pohutukawa Tree* are never mentioned in *Awatea*. The suggestion that there may be 'two or three little tamas round here can call [Matt] Dad if they want to'[18] is comparable to the Reverend Sedgwick's report of Tamatea (also on the East Coast) that 'the paternity of the children isn't always foolproof'.[19]

Other details of Pākehā–Māori relationships are surprising. Although Werihe delegates the bossy Gilhooly to tell everyone Matt's letter has arrived and the hui is on,[20] it is still a shock when, much later, after a long wait and with midnight approaching, Gilhooly and Jameson take it on themselves to order everyone about on what is designated the hapū marae for the occasion, in preparation for Werihe's emerging to 'say a few words.'[21] But when Werihe appears he chooses to speak in English 'for the sake of the young', who make quietly derogatory comments about how 'fagged out' he looks. It could therefore be argued some protocols do not apply here, in the early 1960s (some decades before the 'Māori renaissance'), especially given this site is only designated as a marae once a year. When Gilhooly interrupts Matt's introducing of 'Dr Brett' to his father, Werihe does publicly tell her off: 'Hush, woman. Keep back and know your place.'[22] Later, when she brings Werihe and Brett 'whisky and water for thirsty talkers' and includes a glass for herself, the old man dismisses her in '*thundering*' tones and grumbles, 'Meddler. Never knows her place.'[23] The younger men resist Jameson's authority when he tries to wind up the party after Werihe retires to sleep. 'You're not the boss!' one of them says,'Only a guest here!'

The value of cultural cross-fertilisation is affirmed, however, when Werihe explains to Brett that Matt's letters, well written in English and read out by Gilhooly, have improved his 'Pakeha' to no end, while she has gained a good command of their language because he dictates his replies in Māori. 'So. Two streams mingle,' says Werihe. 'I keep Matt's Maori green; he makes my Pakeha grow.'[24] In common with *The Pohutukawa Tree*, however, Pākehā are critiqued from a Māori perspective when Matt rails to Brett against the expectation that rural Māori will readily take to Pākehā education:

> You don't get it, do you? None of you Pakehas get it. Have you got any idea how complex your world is to us? You've got science in your blood; numbers are your second language. Can you imagine what it was like to meet Stage One Physics head on? A country lad like me? You take it in like air, like a breath. But us, what do we have to start us off? Myth, memories, mana.[25]

And later in the same conversation, the critique of the new generation of Māori comes from Matt, one of their own, as his cousins party on down at the beach:

> Up here, an old man sleeps and dreams. His mana's secure. Down there, the young sing, dance, make love: don't give a cuss for mana, money or time. And that's the race! The old deceived, the young indifferent. And all blind.

Asked where he stands, Matt's reply is both literal and metaphorical: 'Me? . . . Straddle. On the cliff-top, between the two.'[26]

As with *The Pohutukawa Tree*'s Johnny Mataira, Mason has made a direct causal link between cultural dislocation and young Māori men in trouble with the law.

Comedy of ruthless abuse helps *Awatea* avoid the 'wonderfully cheerful' idealised picture painted of the Ngāti Raukawa in Tamatea by the Reverend Sedgwick in *The Pohutukawa Tree*.[27] In the opening scene, hard task-mistress Pera calls her hāngī-pit-digging husband Kani, a Māori version of the henpecked commedia archetype, a 'lazy sod', a 'lazy damn heap' and a 'lump of rubbish'.[28] Then Pera, with Ana, derides Irapeta's seductive designs on the yet-to-arrive Matt: 'Here's a thought: how's he going to find his way around under all that fat?'[29] In Act 2 the young men mock the dressed-up Gilhooly: 'Hey! Here comes the Queen Mum!' and she rises to the bait: 'Fizz off! Fizz off the lottyas!'[30] But in Act 3 the abrasive banter between Gilhooly and Jameson could be seen as a strange form of flirting.[31]

The relationship between Werihe and Gilhooly is also a 'love-hate' one. Despite the anger and irritation she has provoked in him, at midnight when she calls for a kiss from 'Mr P', he responds with a gentle hongi—and Matt's kiss reduces her to tears: 'Always makes me cry, New Year does . . .'[32] In the new Act 3, when she brings the old man a letter from Matt, supposedly in Sydney, and reads it out, there is a delighted playfulness between them—until Werihe senses something is wrong: 'Where is his work? Where are the people?' Gilhooly's attempt to block his sudden determination to go to Sydney makes him even more suspicious: 'That was not his voice. You think I don't know, after all these years of listening?' He demands the truth and is immobile as she reveals Matt is in prison, he was never a doctor and the deceit was all for him: 'Keep your pecker up, your mana!' Werihe '*gives a low rumbling growl, broadening into a great cry of rage and torment.*' He rejects Gilhooly, the lies in the letters which he unbundles and flings into the air, the patronising protectionism of the Pākehā in collusion with his son, and declares that Matt may 'not put his face to my hand again! Never!'[33]

It is one of the older letters, read aloud by Gilhooly in the midst of her collecting them up, that sparks the resolution. The vivid account of the latest incident involving the Hiroti family, now understood to be as fictitious as his doctor's surgery, makes her realise: 'He's a writer! Matt's a writer!' But when Werihe asks if Matt could live by it, Gilhooly concedes, 'Well, not at first, maybe, no'. But the point is, 'he's a voice: he sings! And it's all him, only him, nothing but him! No one said do it, it's good for you, write and prove something: it just come! It's not lies, Mr P, not lies at all; it's true, because we believe in it! It's—(*awed pause*)—art! He's a torch, in the dark! Shining away on places never seen the light before!'[34]

This is how Mason achieved the challenge he had set himself in response to his critics: 'that Matt's future must come from within himself'. It had indeed 'been there, hidden, all the time'; his new Act 3 just had to bring it to the fore. Mason's decision to make writing Matt's true vocation, of which he wrote in May 1969, may be seen as prescient in that it preceded the launch of Witi Ihimaera's writing career, given the *Listener* published his first short story, 'The Liar', in 1970, and his book *Pounamu, Pounamu*, the first collection of short stories by a Māori writer to be published, appeared in 1972. It was for the 1978 second published edition of *Awatea*, however, that Mason appended four sample letters from Matt to his father, dated from 1959 to 1962. Rich in fictional character studies and social observation from a Māori perspective, they quietly prove Mason could still hold his own alongside the emerging Māori writers.

Dramatically, the reconciliation between Werihe and Gilhooly works as something of a love story. Having agreed not to destroy Matt's letters, Werihe gets Gilhooly to rub his back, implies an apology for being hurtful to her, then asks why she has never married. 'You'd know why if you could see,' she replies '*with a playful bitterness*' and goes on to reveal her father was a roving Irish sailor who passed this way fifty-two years ago: 'Left a bundle on the beach, a little piece of flotsam. Me. My mother died when I was six. After that, orphanage.' The Pakus have become the only family she has ever felt part of and Matt is like a son to her. Werihe concedes it feels that way to him as well. Their mutual support and interdependence is consolidated as they work together to compose a new letter to Matt.[35]

It is with a masterful combination of heartfelt comedy and drama, then, that Mason compels our empathy for all the key players as he arrives at the play's key conclusion: it is patronising for anyone to withhold the truth on the grounds that it may hurt someone. Matt's initial deception of his father puts the play's conclusion in an inter-generational context; the involvement of Gilhooly and the policemen adds inter-cultural implications. As for the more complex question of responsibility for the value systems that made Matt feel he needed to perpetrate the hoax in the first place, that is there to be pondered and debated after the play is done.

Mason's vision of *The Pohutukawa Tree* and *Awatea* being played in repertoire on the same set was never realised in his lifetime. Indeed, given The Court Theatre's decision to make it 'contemporary' in 1974, he never did see *Awatea* professionally produced as he had finally written it. Of course the large cast, born of Mason's brief to involve the entire cast of *Porgy and Bess*, has always been well above what professional theatres could sustain in auditoria that seat 250–450, although performing arts students and/or members of Māori cultural groups could be seconded to fill the bit parts and 'chorus' roles on a semi-professional basis. Alternatively, given the relative intimacy of much of the story, judicious cuts and revisions to reduce

the on-stage cast may be justified if that makes the difference between quality production or continued invisibility. With the blessing of the Mason estate, this solution allowed Auckland Theatre Company to mount a Colin McColl-directed production in 2012, with a cast of ten speaking roles plus five 'whānau' extras. Of special note was the casting of George Henare as Werihe Paku, forty-four years after he played Matt to Inia Te Wiata's Werihe. That this production, which was as successful as Auckland Theatre Company's *The Pohutukawa Tree* (2009) and *The End of the Golden Weather* (2011), rescued *Awatea* from obscurity after thirty-eight years is cause for both celebration and bewilderment.

'He rupahu! Lies!' Werihe (George Henare) roars at his son's deceit in *Awatea*. Auckland Theatre Company, directed by Colin McColl, set by Tony Rabbit, costumes by Nic Smillie (July–August 2012). MICHAEL SMITH

CHAPTER ELEVEN

GENERATIONS AT RISK OF LOSING THEIR GRIP

The Hand on the Rail

'Ko wai koe? Ko wai tō tūpuna? Kei hea tō kāinga?'
Who are you? Who are your forebears? Where is your home?
These questions haunt both Hingawaru Karani and his estranged son, Rangi, who took off from Matakaiti to Auckland ten years ago and is now wanted by police following a fatal brawl.

The Hand on the Rail and *Swan Song*, for which Bruce Mason hastily drafted outlines in early 1965 when Inia Te Wiata did not warm straight away to *Awatea*, were eventually produced by the NZBC Radio Drama although the great bass baritone did not play the roles written for him. Don Selwyn, who was in the New Zealand Opera Company's *Porgy and Bess* with Te Wiata, and played Matt to his Werihe Paku in the radio production of *Awatea*, played Hingawaru Karani in *The Hand on the Rail* (recorded February; broadcast April 1967).[1]

In 1974, buoyed perhaps by the successful Court Theatre production of *Awatea* directed by Mervyn Thompson with Don Selwyn as Werihe Paku, Mason reworked *The Hand on the Rail* as a stage play. He made it contemporary for 1974, extended it by more than a third, employed a twenty-six-scene narrative structure akin to radio and television drama, and 'demand[ed] a series of projected slides.'[2] The language also became more realistic, including expletives that could not have been broadcast but had now claimed their place in modern stage plays.

Despite requiring fewer actors than *The Pohutukawa Tree* or *Awatea* (it could be done with an ensemble cast of seven, maybe nine), it was not picked up for professional production by either Christchurch's Court Theatre, Auckland's Mercury or Wellington's Downstage. In 1974, Sunny Amey's final year as artistic director, six of Downstage's ten main bill productions were new New Zealand plays. The average cast size for that year was 8.2. For their tenth birthday production in November 1974, they staged Bertolt Brecht's *The Good Person of Setzuan* with a cast of seventeen. The following year, with Mervyn Thompson as the new artistic director of Downstage, Thompson's *O! Temperance!* with a cast of twenty-four played the main bill, then went on tour. Overall, a professional cast of nine was not uncommon in the 1970s, but despite the embracing of ensemble casts and other theatrical innovations in that revolutionary decade, no one picked up *The Hand on the Rail.*

Mason was aware that 'the large casts of *Awatea*, *Hongi* and *The Hand on the Rail* make them inaccessible to most amateur groups and almost impossible for professional.'[3] Nevertheless, he felt frustrated that his five plays on Māori themes (the other two being *The Pohutukawa Tree* and *Swan Song*) were either gathering dust on bookshelves (only *The Pohutukawa Tree* had been published) or could only be read in manuscript form. In 1978 he wrote:

> I know that a play does not really exist until it is performed, yet equally and paradoxically, it cannot join its country's literature until it is published. This seems to me, in its small way, emblematic of the larger climate of recession and diminution, the current shrinkage to atrophy of the audacity of vision in which our country was founded.[4]

'Audacity of vision' is a perfect phrase for Mason's continued commitment to telling New Zealand stories on stage against all odds. The conservative middle-class subscribers to companies like the Mercury and The Court preferred the tried and tested, finely honed, 'best-of-the-best' plays from overseas, which could be rehearsed in three or four weeks. They were also easier to market than a brand new work. Even when a local play did win professional production, it was automatically judged alongside the crème de la crème from overseas by audiences resistant to raw, culturally organic, home-grown works.

The Hand on the Rail finally made its stage debut in 1981. Auckland's largely amateur New Independent Theatre had intended to do *Awatea* but were concerned about fitting the large cast into their modest premises. Director Ray Waru asked Mason if he had anything else in his 'bottom drawer', which he did. They engaged Don Selwyn to recreate the role of Hingawaru Karani and it premiered on 27

June 1981. In the preface prepared for its subsequent publication, Mason wrote, 'Ray Waru's stunningly scrupulous production became the most unexpected success of my career, named by several critics as Auckland's "best play of the year".' Mason had made 'some tentative suggestions for a sequence of projected colour slides to enlarge and comment on the action. I was not prepared for the astonishing authenticity of these in Ray Waru's production, which added, as I hoped they would, a new dimension to the play.'[5]

As with Mervyn Thompson's production of *Awatea*, Waru chose to make the present action of the play contemporary with its production, causing Mason to add this to his preface:

> With respect, I ask that, in future productions, the play take place in 1974. I also urge that Elvis Presley be restored on the sound track as King and chief expander of Rangi Karani's imaginative world. No-one else (as I all-too-vividly recall from my own children in the sixties) enlarged young minds with the eloquence and resonance of that great artist.[6]

The abiding questions which open the play (in voice-over) are: 'Ko wai koe? Ko wai to tupuna? Kei hea to kainga?' Who are you? Who are your forebears? Where is your home? In the present of 1974, farmers in a 'Matakait' pub opine on the news, reported in the *Herald*, that the Karani boy (Rangi), son of 'ole Hingawaru', has killed someone in a brawl in Auckland. As the play proceeds, flashback scenes bring significant moments from the past into present action. It is 1960 when Rangi, aged fifteen, first tunes into 'the one and only Elvis P!' on the Hit Parade—'Jailhouse Rock' being a prescient choice—and 1964 when the nineteen-year-old Rangi takes his hand off the titular rail, turns his back on the family farm and becomes subsumed by the city. A flashback to the late 1930s recalls when Hingawaru and Miriam first met.

The title arises from Hingawaru's attempt to explain the importance of whakapapa:

> There is this great rail for our fists to grip, room for every hand that wants to clasp it. And you can stand firm beside the rail, as a people.

> Behind us, the atuas, slowly loosening their grip; ahead, the young, learning the proper clasp. That is the race, the iwi. That is why I grieve at the whakaringaringa loosening . . .[7]

The Hand on the Rail is the third play in which Mason uses the device of a young Māori man in conflict with the law as a way of dramatising his recurring theme of cultural dislocation. In *The Pohutukawa Tree*, set in the late 1940s, Johnny Mataira becomes an alcohol-fuelled vandal, raging against the Christianity that has betrayed his sister, his mother, himself and his people. In *Awatea*, set in the early 1960s, Matt Paku resorts to uncharacteristic violence and theft to cover up his failure to live up to the expectations of his father, his hapū and himself. In *The Hand on the Rail*, Rangi Karani's cultural identity crisis, alienation from his family and stress from city living have left him disillusioned, angry and violent.

Both Johnny and Matt have only one living parent. There is nothing to suggest that the trouble they get into is directly attributable to the loss of Johnny's father or Matt's mother, although both are burdened by the remaining parent's expectations. Rangi's parents are both alive, however, and his behaviour is directly related to the conflict between their value systems. His dad is feeling the loss of his Māoritanga, having 'gone Pakeha' for Rangi's mum, Miriam, who believes it is Rangi's lot and station to marry a local girl and continue working the unforgiving land her father bought from Hingawaru's iwi. Rangi rejects that future and feels pulled apart by his mother's attempts to prepare him for a test about Chaucer, the father of English poetry, while his father frets over his own inability to remember waiata, karakia and his whakapapa. The only thing that speaks to Rangi is Elvis Presley's 'Jailhouse Rock' on the Hit Parade. But when he attempts to find a new life in Auckland, Rangi is seen and treated as Māori or, more specifically, as a 'Hori'—which engenders resentment, disillusionment and an angry backlash against Pākehā so-called civilisation. Like 'Jake the Muss' in Alan Duff's *Once Were Warriors* (1990), Rangi is stuck in the gap between two cultures, unable to embrace either, and so resorts to violence.

All three plays have older Pākehā men showing significant compassion and going out of their way to understand how it is for the young men in trouble. In *The Pohutukawa Tree* this role is shared by the Reverend Sedgwick, fresh from England, and Sergeant Robinson, a long-term fixture in Te Parenga. The urbane, pipe-smoking Detective Inspector Brett steps up in both *Awatea* and *The Hand on the Rail*. It would, however, be a mistake to suggest these men represent Mason's own position. Whether we agree with their attempts to reconcile the cultural conflict or see it as typical Pākehā paternalism, Mason is articulating one of many authentic voices in a debate that remains current today.

In *The Hand on the Rail*, Hingawaru and Rangi are subjected to instances of overt, covert and casual racism, which impact as dramatic provocations. We are invited to empathise simultaneously with them and their tormentors, and thus to examine our own deep-set views and unspoken thoughts. The drama is also strengthened because neither Hingawaru nor Rangi are merely victims of other people's ignorance; both are to some extent complicit in creating the circumstances they are driven to confront.

In a flashback scene, hot to foxtrot with Miriam at their first meeting at a late thirties 'hop', Hingawaru goes along with her decree that 'you people have to go Pakeha now', which means a lifetime of hard graft from dawn till dusk. He marries her with those conditions implicit. Only when their second daughter, like the first, marries a Pākehā, does he voice his regret that his mokopuna will become even more removed from Māoritanga. Indeed he himself is already losing his grip on what he has learned as a boy from a grandfather who spoke no English, was 'full of waiata and karakia' and taught him his whakapapa 'right back to Hoturoa and the Tainui.' Rangi chooses to side with his mother:

> It's about time you realised, Dad, that Maoritanga is dead and dying. It says nothing, answers nothing. Just a list of names and customs; telling us to do what there's no point in doing any more.

He angrily challenges his father's attempt to explain it with the 'hand on the rail' metaphor, demanding to know when he last participated in anything Māori. Hingawaru's explanation is poignant:

> I threw in my hand, Rangi. For your mother's sake. I went Pakeha. She taught me I have to live in this world, not in the other. So, I made my choice. But I can still hear the music of the past, and I would wish that your ears could hear it, also. You are my blood, my seed. And blood binds, Rangi.[8]

Distilling the cultural conflict within the family unit intensifies the drama as Rangi seeks escape from 'the blood that binds' only to have his own blood, and that of others, spilt in Auckland. When he is treated by others as Māori, he retaliates by raging against Pākehā values, in the pub,[9] at work,[10] in a rugby club changing rooms,[11] and in his relationships with girlfriends,[12] with finally tragic consequences. The violent anger that erupts because of his refusal to acknowledge and value his Māori heritage, to keep his 'hand on the rail', may be seen as his fatal flaw.

It is intriguing to compare the rugby scene (16) with Greg McGee's *Foreskin's Lament* (first seen early in 1980 at the New Zealand Playwrights Conference, before it premiered in October that year at Auckland's Theatre Corporate). The cyclostyled typescript of Mason's 1974 stage adaptation of *The Hand on the Rail*, held at Playmarket, confirms Mason was well ahead of McGee in characterising the brutality of rugby football, even between players in the same team. Both have young men wrestling with the 'individual versus the team' dilemma when the hypocrisy of so-called 'team spirit' is revealed. In McGee's play the challenge Foreskin issues—'Whaddarya?'—is provoked by twice witnessing his team-mate, the ironically named Clean, kick their own captain, Ken, in the head. In *The Hand on the Rail* a player, George, accuses 'that bastard Hori' of grabbing him 'by the knackers' and twisting them to stop him scoring a try, only to have Rangi reveal it was in retaliation for what George did to him: 'I had that ball; it was only a foot away. And that bugger knuckled me! Right under the bloody ear!' George's excuse is, 'No bloody Hori's going to get the better of me.'[13]

It becomes apparent that Rangi's deep-set and unresolved anger has led to his beating up more than one girlfriend. The latest girlfriend, June Bartlett, ditched her boyfriend Jimmy for Rangi, to whom she has now become pregnant. The fatal fight at the party is precipitated by Jimmy's confronting Rangi, discovering he has no intention of supporting June and abusing him: 'You filthy Hori creep. You rotten, slimy, greasy bum!' Rangi attacks him, grabs a bottle and the fatal blow is struck. This causes Hingawaru to describe Rangi as 'a waka adrift' in a city devoid of brotherhood: 'No ground! No support! No whakaringaringa! . . . No hand on the rail. Not even mine! Not even mine!'[14]

In contrast to his son, Hingawaru maintains great dignity when June, who has had the baby boy at the National Women's Hospital, says such things as: 'Twenty years from now, or less if I know you people, he'll be muckin' some poor girl's life about. That's men, mister. That's what they do,' and, regarding her intention to adopt him out: 'Hard to get rid of little Horis.' To be fair, her antipathy is directed more towards men than Māori. Her comment that 'when I had to take it quiet an' he couldn't get his bit, he just cleared out, six weeks ago,' recalls the attitude Bert has towards sex in *The Bonds of Love*.[15]

Less easy to rationalise as a dramatic provocation is Brett's behaviour on finding and reading a letter left on a table in the Huia bach Rangi has escaped to. In *Awatea*, Mason's initial inclination was to have Brett and Gilhooly connive successfully to keep the truth about Matt—that he was not a doctor and the letters he wrote about all his patients were pure fiction—from his father. Thanks to feedback from Inia and Beryl Te Wiata, and from theatre critics, Mason has Werihe wring the truth from Gilhooley, who is duly castigated for thinking she had a right to withhold it. Yet in adapting *The Hand on the Rail* for the stage (following the Christchurch season of his revised *Awatea*), he still allows Brett to take a similar position of patronising paternalism with the suicide letter Rangi has written just before—as we are about to find out—he drowns himself. 'It's pathetic,' Brett tells his Sergeant. 'He started to write to his father. "My dear father, I saw you today, but"—and that's all he says. The rest is obscenity. And then, at the bottom of the page, "arohanui". Much love. Finally, he couldn't explain anything.' Brett then burns the letter, in what can only be described as an arrogant act of protectionism with little dramatic value because there is no dramatic follow through or payoff.[16] No matter how kind Brett thinks he is being, it remains a smug, sanctimonious and unconscionable act for him to deprive Hingawaru of the knowledge that his son has at least attempted to explain himself to his father; to deprive him of the opportunity to interpret the so-called obscenities for himself and to read 'arohanui' at the end as Rangi's chosen sign-off, despite his professed rejection of all things Māori.

Maybe Brett's respect for Hingawaru does deepen after the old man arranges for himself and Miriam to adopt June's baby, fathered by Rangi. Perhaps Mason is alerting us to Brett's colonial insensitivity by having him wish Hingawaru 'the best of British' so that when he follows with, 'I don't know how to say it, quite; it's been a privilege. I admire you more than I can properly say,'[17] we have to wrestle with how that equates with Brett's belief that he had the right to withhold and destroy a private and personal letter. There is, however, no indication that he regrets his action and will be conscience-stricken by it.

It is poignant that Hingawaru only recalls the lament he could not remember in Scene 8 as he cradles the lifeless body of Rangi. His soft crooning of 'Tangi mo Pango' at the end of the scene reinforces the value of the language and traditions he fears will soon die out.[18] When Miriam meets Hingawaru at Taumaranui station she is, of course, shocked to discover they have a grandchild and have adopted him. In this case his withholding the information until she was in no position to say 'no' rings true and the struggle ahead is made clear by her telling him off for talking to the baby in Māori: 'You know where that leads: no place, fast!'[19] In the final scene, as they both fuss about getting a bottle for the baby, Miriam draws attention to how old they will be as the boy grows up and wants to know why Hingawaru is willing to go through it all again. But for him, 'Each time, it's new. A new life, startin'. An' blood. It's blood, bindin' us.' She remains stubborn, but realises this is how it is for him and she cannot change him. She feels compassion at his excitement that the baby has gripped his finger—'Whakaringaringa! He's got his hand on the rail, Miriam! Whakaringaringa! Pai whakarere!'—but then stares bleakly into the future, '*accusingly it could seem, at the audience*', the stage direction reads.

The lights narrow and hold them frozen as a triptych, in melancholy parody of a Holy Family tableau: the grim woman, the tender old man, the child. Slow darkness, from which a Maori chant swells and dies.[20]

The allegorical implications of the final image are clear: Hingawaru is Maoridom, needing to reconnect with their all-but-lost cultural values; Miriam is Pākehā New Zealand, confronted with that reality; the baby is the future, dependant on how his elders resolve this issue. In resolving the drama, Mason leaves us with a status quo that clearly and accurately represents the lack of resolution in the cultural conflict at the time. The attitudes held by Miriam, Rangi and those he comes into conflict with, not to mention the well-meaning Brett, permeated most strata of New Zealand society in the 1950s, persisted through the 1960s and were probably shared by many who heard *The Hand on the Rail* broadcast (1968, 1969, 1971). In the Pākehā world especially, and also among many 'assimilated' Māori, there would have been few ears willing to clearly hear the concerns being raised by Mason's Hingawaru.

The breakthrough towards the beginnings of understanding would come in 1974—the same year Mason re-conceived his play for the stage—when, gathered around New Zealand's single television channel, the country had its collective consciousness raised through the six-part documentary series *Tangata Whenua*. Bruce Mason was as prescient about looming social changes in New Zealand as Anton Chekhov was about political unrest in Russia. Chekhov enjoyed great popularity, however, before the revolution rendered him suspect and out of fashion (until British theatre rediscovered him), whereas Mason's plays on Māori themes were not fully appreciated at the time they were written. Once the Māori renaissance revealed the plays' true values, his being Pākehā worked against their becoming championed as the insightful social dramas they have always been.

Mason's specific articulation of eroding cultural values is as timeless and universal as any Chekhov classic. Even if New Zealand has moved on, socially and politically, *The Hand on the Rail* stands as an essential insight into a period in our history that must never be forgotten, lest it be repeated. More than forty years on it cannot be said the cultural conflict is resolved. For example, the populist 'one law' policy of politician Don Brash (first aired in his 2004 'Orewa Speech' as leader of the National Party, in opposition, and regurgitated in his 2011 election campaign as leader of the ACT Party), disregards all notions of 'lore' and amounts to a call for Māori assimilation into the dominant Pākehā culture.[21] There is little doubt this view is still shared by many New Zealanders. The play's opening questions—'Who are you? Who are your forebears? Where is your home?'—will never lose their importance, least of all to those of minority cultures, be they indigenous or immigrant.

The Hand on the Rail is another Mason play we should all be familiar with through seeing it in professional production. At the time of writing no such production has occurred.

CHAPTER TWELVE

AN OPERATIC RAGE AGAINST THE DYING OF THE LIGHT

Swan Song

Two stories converge at a snow-bound winter resort, where a dying man and a fleeing soprano help to liberate each other. Italian opera is the motif for repressed human passions.

Of the three plays Bruce Mason first conceived in 1965 potentially to feature Inia Te Wiata, *Swan Song* is the most playfully confronting and theatrical, not to say operatic in scale. Mason describes it as 'a tissue of recollection, fast-forwarding, back-tracking, splicing in scenes from the past, as a television biography, say, uses old film clips to shed light on the present. Its chronology is imaginative and poetic rather than blankly sequential.' He adds: 'The music of *Tosca*, and particularly that of 'Vissi d'arte' from Act 2, should thread through the action at appropriate points.'[1] It is also the only one of the four plays Mason wrote for Te Wiata that involves his character with opera, although as James Smithson rages in his own special way against the dying of the light, he only gets to sing a snatch of *Tosca* very softly on his deathbed.[2]

The radio version of *Swan Song* was recorded in November 1967 and broadcast the following year, with Don Selwyn in the role of Smithson.[3] As with *The Hand on the Rail*, Mason's 1974 stage adaptation of *Swan Song* was not published in his lifetime, nor has it been professionally produced in the four decades since. The play has twelve named characters, some of whom can be doubled or tripled, and while 'decorous' dancers are suggested—to evoke the 'varsity hop' where Smithson and Isobel first meet, in 1934—they could easily be imagined by the audience. A cast of nine (six female, three male) could do it. Given their daughter, Kura, is described as 'thirtyish' we can assume the play is set in the mid-to-late 1960s and must remain so, given the relevance of WWII within the story.

The many scenes, which are not numbered, are grouped into three parts. The main setting is within and around a fictitious South Island winter resort called Tiromoana (invented a decade earlier by Mason for his short play *The Verdict*), set amid 'unsurpassed grandeur' and owned by 'the Department' (the Tourist Hotel Corporation, happily known as the THC). Flexible staging accommodates a post office calling box and bus stop, the inside of a travelling bus, the resort's lobby, reception office, bedrooms and lounge, limbo, a dance hall, a cemetery, and the stage and dressing room of an opera house in Rome. As a progression from the flashback device used in *The Hand on the Rail*, the heavily medicated Smithson—very near death and in a delirium—interacts in live action with the spirit of his dead wife, recollects their first meeting, and then reveals his secret love of an Italian opera singer during the war that separated him from Isobel for three years.

Written just before the birth of the women's liberation movement (generally regarded as 1968), *Swan Song* reveals Mason's awareness not only of the isolated Māori position (a variation on Hingawaru's cultural dislocation) but also of how life can be for women. In our first encounter with Jenny Lucas, on the bus with her mother, Mrs Fancourt, we discover she is trying to escape from her controlling husband, but he is on her trail. 'If you're Geoff you take everything by force,' Jenny tells her mother. 'Everything.'[4] This implies she was subjected to marital rape long before the term became current, let alone acknowledged in legislation.

Mason's ongoing critique of some Kiwi men is offset by some challenging depictions of women in the play. It will emerge that Smithson's late Pākehā wife, Isobel, attempted to control him and his life, and he remains very bitter about it. Before we learn the details, he tells his ever-censorious daughter Kura—as they, too, travel on the bus—that her mother was 'the dullest, nastiest-minded, joy-quenching piece of deep-frozen coconut ice I've ever tried to take a bite out of.'[5] As with Hingawaru and Miriam in *The Hand on the Rail*, perhaps this is better seen as an allegorical critique, with Isobel (the same Christian name, incidentally, as *The Pohutukawa Tree*'s Mrs Atkinson) representing the moral repressions of Pākehā New Zealand. And Mason would go on to depict a similarly acidic relationship within the all-Pākehā marriage of dying travelling salesman Charlie Jameson and his dour Baptist wife, Dora, in his 1982 teleplay *Do Not Go Gentle*.

Facing death from advanced leukaemia, James Smithson—who now signs his name 'Hemi Mitihana, address: the universe at large', to the consternation of Alice on the front desk—takes great pleasure in challenging his dutiful but judgemental daughter Kura's sense of propriety. She sees him as 'destroyed by pleasure' after turning his back on a promising career. 'Promising? I was the hope of my race,' he retorts, echoing the position of Matt in *Awatea*, although Smithson's academic achievements are real: 'MA with First Class Honours, not the first, but almost.' Smithson's quoting James Joyce's 'The Dead' and a snippet of Shakespeare's *Richard II*, 'I wasted time, and now time wastes me,' proves his intellect is still intact.[6]

When a medication-fuelled delirium produces an unwelcome visitation from his late wife, Isobel—'What's your heavenly name? Sister Constipata?'—it emerges, through re-enactment, that she engineered their first meeting via an excuse-me waltz at a 'varsity hop' (an echo of how Hingawaru and Miriam met in *Hand on the Rail*), having worshipped him from afar: 'Best student of his year. Captain of the football team. Built like a God.' Isobel explains that she comes from three generations of formidable women—her mother being the first woman doctor in Taranaki, while all the men failed in some way—then interrogates Smithson to discover he has no knowledge of his Māori lineage and sees himself as 'a piece of flotsam, thrown up on the beach of Maori-Pakeha relations. Adopted at an early age. Brought up Pakeha.' When she declares this is 'perfect', envisages him as prime minister, then suggests they get married as soon as he has finished his degree—'then you join External Affairs, we get posted abroad . . .'—he escapes back into the dance. But the music segues into Mendelssohn's 'Wedding March' and back in the hotel bedroom Smithson can barely believe he fell for 'that crap about prime minister.' Isobel's explanation speaks volumes about pre-WWII Pākehā attitudes to Māori and the way even highly intelligent women were relegated to living vicariously through their men:

> You *were* irresistible. Maori yet not Maori; no tribal nonsense, no hints of back to the mat. Origin shrouded in romantic mystery, intelligent, dreamily good-looking, plus little me to help you, to pray for God's

> assistance and tap, at full bore, those mysterious sources of energy that run through the women in my family. But you faltered; you slackened. All my prayers, all my hectoring: you balked, you slackened, you slid out sideways, you scuttled like a crab, you sank like a stone. Like my father. My grandfather. My great-grandfather. Same brush, all of them. Same tar. Men! Men!

Smithson reminds Isobel it was the war that 'knocked it all for six'. Despite her plan to get him declared unfit—by adding soap to his food, in order to give him a false temperature and stop him joining the Māori Battalion—he went to war. What he has never told her about, until now, is his life-changing encounter with an Italian opera singer, Graziella Marcelli. Can he show her? 'James: it's your delirium,' she replies, 'I've no existence outside your thoughts. Think it, and it'll happen.' This metaphysical whimsy and metatheatrical device may owe something to Noel Coward's *Blithe Spirit*, which premiered in 1941, although in that play the late wife wilfully acts to disrupt her husband's second marriage, while in *Swan Song* Smithson has manifested Isobel not only to confess to his affair but also to reveal his true feelings about her and the life she tried to impose on him. When he suggests she might not like it, she scoffs: 'After all I've suffered? Try me.'[7]

Thus we observe how Smithson, as a soldier on leave in Rome, is exposed—in stark contrast to 'pinched, flinty' New Zealand—to passion through Italian opera: Graziella as Tosca singing 'Vissi d'arte, vissi d'amore' ('I lived on art, I lived on love') to an indifferent Scarpia: 'Sei troppo bella, Tosca, e troppo amante' ('You're too beautiful, Tosca, and too loving'). Images of occupied Italy's liberation are suggested to bridge Smithson's progress to Graziella's dressing room, where Tosca is clearly identified as the symbol of liberation: the living human spirit, counterpointed by her painter lover, Cavaradossi, who was tortured by Scarpia and executed despite her efforts to gain their safe passage to freedom. Impressed by Smithson's understanding of Italian, Graziella accepts his invitation to the Forces Club, and so began—Smithson tells his late wife, back in the suite—the six weeks in which he 'learned for the first time the meaning of words like radiance, richness, fire and song. Above all, song! The ecstasy of the blood and heart.' But Mason's critique of Pākehā New Zealand is also embodied in Graziella's rejection of his plea to come and live with him there: 'You say no music in New Zealand? I would shrivel, wither.' If she has awoken his spirit from its 'long Kiwi sleep' then it's up to him to show his wife what 'the life of the blood and heart' means; to put a bomb 'under the blancmange.'[8]

Mason characterises post-WWII New Zealand in Smithson's descriptions of Isobel and Kura, the last in a long line of matriarchs: 'with your pinched, flinty faces, sharpened by grasping, by wills fixed to your mean little souls with an iron clamp, by the effort you both made—and how brilliantly successful!—to smother all ripeness, and blight any blooming.' Consummate dramatist that he is, Mason ensures Isobel is Smithson's equal in debate. This is especially interesting given this Isobel is manifested in Smithson's imagination; he is using her to interrogate his choices and examine his own conscience. Thus when she challenges his 'mad' decision to walk away from External Affairs and expected postings to Paris, Moscow and London, to join a road gang, and he tries to justify himself—'I found my people there. Oh, not only Maoris. Pakehas, too.'—she robustly derides the idea of his finding the 'song of the heart' in a pneumatic drill. Despite Isobel's insisting she's proud of their schoolteacher daughter, who is destined to become a headmistress, he writes Kura off as a 'bloodless, lifeless little virgin, implacably doing her duty by me' and is pleased to think 'the long line of pioneering queen bees' will die out with her. While not privy to her parents' exchanges, Kura is subjected to residual invective about her mother and questioning about what will become of her when she is parentless, single and unloved. The audience is challenged to judge the validity of Smithson's, Isobel's and Kura's actions and attitudes, at both personal and allegorical levels.[9]

The play's unifying theme is passion versus repression and Part 3 brings its two main plotlines together: Smithson versus Isobel and Kura; Jenny versus Lucas. An impromptu concert for, and by, the snowbound hotel guests, begins with a 'family travels' slideshow from the Reverend Timothy Benson of the Lamb of God Church in California, and Mrs Fancourt has launched into her piano recital when Jenny's psychiatrist husband, Dr Geoffrey Lucas, arrives at reception to reclaim his wife. On realising Jenny is about to sing opera, he asserts it is 'unfitting' for her to do so in public: an astonishingly extreme form of repression by which Mason notes how controlling personalities may be attracted to psychiatry. The opening bars of 'Vissi d'arte' bring Smithson downstairs. Smithson is deeply touched by Jenny's rendition of the aria and, in response to Kura and Geoff's overbearing attempts to curtail their mutual appreciation and empathy, he asks Jenny to take him back to his room, which she is happy to do, despite her mother's dismay and Kura's fury. The dying Smithson casts himself as a wheelchair-bound Cavaradossi as, elsewhere, Kura and Geoff commiserate over coffee and bond in their shared displeasure. Geoff reveals how Jenny went along with his attempts to reform her through 'deep analysis', then rejected it and him; 'back home to mother and music. This singing, of course, this arbitrary turning of everything into art, into concord of sweet sound, solves nothing: a useless waste of energy.' Kura agrees, citing her father's 'disastrous refusal to grow, to develop, to assume responsibility!' Meanwhile up in the suite, knowing he is near death, Smithson offers Jenny his final observation:

> There's only one language for men and women: song. Flesh and roses. Once it was our native tongue. And conquest has turned it into nuts and bolts. Yes, that's what Europe has done to us. Extinguished song. If we can sing, then all else takes its due and rightful place. I learned this too late. But you mustn't.[10]

It is difficult to reconcile this accusation with Smithson's emotional and spiritual liberation in a European opera house (which he then sought to sustain in a road gang) unless one equates the misappropriation of 'civilising' values in New Zealand with Geoff's abuse of psychoanalysis to serve his own desire to control. As an allegorical thesis, the argument needs work, and it is a shame this play never had the benefit of a development workshop let alone a rehearsal process for a live theatre production. A dramaturg may suggest changing 'Europe' to 'British civilisation' so that the line reads: 'Yes, that's what British civilisation has done to us. Extinguished song.' But that would still leave us to ponder the proposition that being a diplomat is a 'nuts and bolts' occupation while working in a road gang is not, unless it is known that Smithson and his mates sang while on the job, whereas public servants never would.

In bringing *Swan Song* to dramatic resolution, Mason continues to challenge our values and sense of propriety. Smithson makes Jenny lock Kura and Geoff out of his suite, and he dies in her arms. While a funeral service is evoked, with the Reverend Benson officiating and Jenny singing, Geoff and Kura drink in the bar. When it turns out Kura is planning to leave with Geoff, Jenny's offer of a handshake—'No hard feelings, I hope'—is spurned by Kura as Geoff insists they must leave ahead of the bus. With all the guests gone and Tiromoana 'silent as the tomb', Alice and Mrs Jevons conduct a brief post-mortem, commenting on the beauty of the funeral and 'Miss Smithson in the bar, the whole time. She and Dr Geoff Lucas were both as stewed as owls when we came in.' Jevons quotes a saying of her mother's—'There's nowt so queer as folk'—to give the play its end.[11] Along with everything else, a modern audience may feel moved to contemplate more clearly than 1960s or 1970s counterparts the implications of a drunken Geoff driving off through the gorge.

While it is tempting to assume both Smithson and Jenny carry Mason's 'message' about the flawed value systems that prevail in post-colonial and post-WWII New Zealand, they themselves are flawed enough to require us to separate the principles under scrutiny from the people who dramatise the argument. We may well question the integrity of the characters as the drama unfolds. Is Jenny's running back to her mother a 'cop-out' or the best way to recover her self-esteem and love of singing? Is Smithson the victim of a manipulative woman or the author of his own misfortunes? Is Kura heartless or is she deeply hurt by her father's abuse of her mother, even after she has died? What does the future hold for Kura and Geoff, and for Jenny? Since the last word is given to observers of these 'queer' (in the original sense) folk, it is fair to assume Mason is once more provoking us to wrestle with these issues ourselves and come to our own conclusions.

CHAPTER THIRTEEN

A CHIEF, A KING, SOME GODS AND MUSKETS

Hongi

Inspired by his meeting with the King of England, whose gifts enable him to purchase muskets, Hongi Hika returns home to wage more inter-tribal war in defiance of the New Testament teachings of the Reverend John Cutler.

Hongi was written as a radio play for Inia Te Wiata, who played the title role on his return to Wellington for the Downstage Theatre production of *Awatea* (staged in September 1968). Billed as 'a radio portrait of Hongi Hika (c.1777–1828)', the play was recorded in August and broadcast in November 1968.[1] Mason's stage adaptation of *Hongi*, ironically subtitled 'The Noble Savage', was first published in 1974, then posthumously in *The Healing Arch* (1987), but was not produced professionally in his lifetime. In fact, in 2015, there is still no record of its ever having secured a live theatre production. As with *The Hand on the Rail* and *Swan Song*, *Hongi*'s genesis as a radio play doubtless liberated the story from the prevailing modes and perceived constraints of live theatre production. However, the conventions of Elizabethan and Jacobean drama, Brechtian epic theatre, and ensemble theatre in general have always been available to bring *Hongi* alive on stage. There are no designated acts or scenes; the action moves from England—a coach road, Eton College (exterior), Windsor Castle (exterior and interior)—to The Bay of Islands: Cutler's colonial home (interior and exterior); stylised battlefields (night and day); a wayside stopping place, hāngī site, and Hongi's last resting place.

Once again, Mason was way ahead of his time in perceiving, articulating, dramatising, critiquing and satirising the clashing and congruent beliefs and value systems that underpinned the meeting of Māori and British cultures in the early 19th century. In the published edition's 'Note to *Hongi*', he points out the 'historical liberties and deliberate inaccuracies to prevent others doing so.' They include his omission of the other rangatira, 'Prince' Waikato, who accompanied Hongi and Kendall to England, and his endowing Hongi with great fluency in English and 'sophisticated thought and Biblical eloquence' on the basis of his having learned the alphabet in Port Jackson (now Sydney, Australia) in six days. Mason goes on to clarify his central theme:

> What this brief work is principally concerned with is the concept of 'the noble savage' which seduced, and in part corrupted, the philosophical energy of two generations, from about 1770–1830. By then it was completely exploded. Thus George IV, I argue, would listen with attention in 1820 to a man whose freedom from the corrupt conditioning of civilisation was widely assumed. (cf. Jean-Jacques Rousseau, 1712–1778, 'L'homme est né bon; la société le déprave.') The call everywhere was towards a primitive and, hence, uncorrupted simplicity and virtue. Pure in heart, the responses of the noble savage would also be pure. And, in the reverse direction, many Ministers of the Gospel assumed that their 'tidings of great joy' would enter, unimpeded, into simple, untutored minds.
>
> The truth was very different. The missionaries soon discovered that some Maori minds were of great agility and suppleness, able to adapt the Gospel to their own purposes by a swift and cunning logic. Thus Hongi Hika returned from England neither chastened nor subdued by his experiences, but confirmed and even strengthened in bellicosity.[2]

Mason also claims it is historically accurate that the missionaries 'were forced to subsidise the traffic in arms to ensure some tribal protection. Thus they fomented and kept active, against their faith and against their will, the bloody inter-tribal wars.'[3] The very fact that such information was rarely included in mainstream New Zealand history curricula then, and most New Zealanders remain unaware of it now, only increases the importance of Mason's play and emphasises the travesty and tragedy of its remaining unproduced. Generations of New Zealanders have become more familiar with Bertolt Brecht and Margarete Steffin's *Mother Courage and Her Children*, for example, than Bruce Mason's *Hongi*, which is arguably just as 'epic', political and provocative, and even more relevant at every level. Such marginalisation must be addressed and redressed in the twenty-first century if New Zealand theatre is to recover, reclaim and honour the true depth of its existing repertoire.

As with *The Pohutukawa Tree*, Mason interrogates the role of Christianity in changing Māori behaviour, but whereas Aroha Mataira experiences inner turmoil at the loss of tribal land while dutifully embracing the New Testament's 'Prince of Peace', Hongi finds the Bible's Old Testament is more to his liking. Set some 135 years earlier than *The Pohutukawa Tree*, and twenty years before the Treaty of Waitangi, *Hongi* focuses on the power of monarchs and muskets. It pulls no punches in characterising tribal warfare as it was and as it became when Hongi purchased muskets with gifts from the King of England, then acquired more through what we recognise as a protection racket. Hongi's power as a warrior chief equates to that of a monarch, gang leader or mafia boss: a syndrome common throughout human history.

In the play's first scene, Mason draws us into empathy with Hongi as the celebrity rangatira comes to grips with the heart of the British Empire. The scholars of Cambridge University have listened to him with respect but not awe, which is, as north country parson Thomas Kendall explains, preserved for the King who 'rules by the Grace of God and for the Prince of Peace' and who has others to fight his battles for him. The boys of Eton are racist and abusive in their ignorance, and although Hongi's scripture-laden wrath is backed up by Kendall, the parson wishes Hongi had drawn from the 'softer' Gospels rather than the Old Testament prophets. Hongi replies firmly, 'There is no word in the Gospels that yet speaks to me.' Thus the key values of vengeance versus the principles of peace are set.[4]

At Windsor Castle, Hongi scandalises Kendall and the courtiers by failing to kneel before the just-ascended and yet-to-be-crowned King George IV. Mason dramatises the famous and historically well-documented exchange by having Hongi thrust out his hand and boom, 'How do you do, Mr King George?' After a horrified silence, an expansive George IV reciprocates, 'How do you do, Mr King Hongi!' to the relief of all. The king's witty banter is self-effacing as he expresses admiration for Hongi's mastery of 'our rough island tongue'. Mason's love of eloquence is reflected in Hongi's observations of England so far: 'Your crop is people. They flow like the sea; like the sea, they bite the land. They move on it so thick, there is no place for trees . . .' The limits on people's movements, the spectacle of hanging, the Tower, coalmines, cotton mills and the zoo also come in for comment. Although George IV asks his guest questions, he objectifies Hongi by commenting about him to Kendall, as in: 'Tell me: how are you presenting King Hongi? Is this Monsieur Rousseau's Noble Savage? Unspoiled child of nature, until we ravish his innocence? Something of that kind?' Kendall is cautious in his response: 'Unspoiled: perhaps. Innocence? It's a wide word, sire.' When Hongi suddenly questions George IV about his ability to rule by the will of the Prince of Peace, by the Ten Commandments, he gets the message that it is not so easy: 'The commandments hang above our lives, like stars in the sky. Our merciful Lord is our guide and example. But in the clamour of day to day, He seems often far away.' Hongi's murmured, 'I am answered', prompts the King to dismiss his courtiers and Kendall, so he and Hongi can converse alone.[5]

The scene of high-stakes 'gallows humour' satire that follows should be as familiar to every New Zealand student of dramatic literature and history as any from the classical canon. The rangatira and king converse as equals; in fact Hongi sits on George IV's throne at his behest. Hongi's nine wives are compared with George's two: the woman he loves and married but had to disown, and the 'German sow' he was obliged to marry to keep his crown. Asked what he would do with a troublesome wife, Hongi calmly replies with a rhetorical flourish that also serves as a set-up for his later commentary on the Christian ritual of communion: 'I would hang her from the nearest totara, and cook her in my umu [then] eat her, wipe her grease from my fingers and forget her.' But apart from this being against his customs, George IV feels his wife would not 'taste well'. Hongi tells him to invoke his mana: 'A king must rule. Or he is no king.' When he advises George to pray to the Prince of Peace and is told, 'I am not a praying man,' Hongi is suddenly jubilant: '*E tika!* Now I can crush Kendall like a grub. Prayer is for women. For kings . . . Action, action, action!' Inspired by this gift of resolution, George IV quizzes Hongi about his desires, realises he will have to use force to increase the dominion of his rule from the north to all the land, and gives him an inscribed musket and a ruby ring to sell for more. 'I must not seem to be your arsenal,' he explains. 'My church would not care for it.' Then, in response to Hongi's fear that his enemies will also acquire muskets, George IV commissions 'a full suit of plate' and thanks him for the gift of resolution. As soon as Hongi has left, George IV tells the Lord Chamberlain, 'We proceed against the Queen!'[6]

Mason admits he has taken a liberty here: 'In no work that I have consulted is it suggested that His Ventripotent and Britannic Majesty was encouraged to prepare the completely fraudulent and scurrilous public trial of the morals of Queen Caroline on the advice of a native chief. But the dates allow it and, in my version, it is at least plausible.'[7] (History tells us George IV's attempts to divorce Caroline were unsuccessful, but she fell ill on the day of his coronation, claimed she had been poisoned, and died three weeks later).

Mason cleverly reinforces the adult desire for strong leadership by representing the chaotic alternative in childish behaviour, back in the Bay of Islands. Sarah, daughter of the Reverend and Mrs Cutler, has upset 'the tribe' by defending her father against insults from Hongi's daughter Makarora. 'She said when he comes back, he will kill you and eat you,' Sarah tells her father. 'I said, when he comes back you will cut off his head and cook it in an iron pot . . .' Utu sees the Cutler's home ransacked. 'Would Hongi were here!' Cutler exclaims. 'Only he can command them. Let us hope that the ways of the Prince of Peace have commended themselves to him.'[7] But we, in the privileged position of all-seeing audience, already know they have not, and why not.

In having Hongi state his position on his arrival from Port Jackson, Mason expects us to know that Tū is the God of War and Rongo is the God of Peace: 'He pukai to Tū, he pukai to Rongo,' he tells Cutler. 'Let us render unto Tū the things that are Tū's and to Rongo, the things that are Rongo's.' When Cutler realises Hongi has returned with 600 muskets and exclaims, 'Merciful God!' Hongi replies, 'Your God may be merciful, but ours is not.' Cutler is even more appalled at Kendall's open admission that he willingly helped Hongi to exchange his royal gifts for the weapons in Port Jackson, ensuring he got a fair deal. Kendall's argument that 'these guns are your only protection' echoes the way governments to this day rationalise their arms dealing.[9]

Mason simultaneously satirises the British class system and points to similar hierarchies in Maoridom when Hongi, having invited himself and his entourage to breakfast (Mrs Cutler has to cater for twenty), requires his party to sit on the floor: 'In the presence of their King, they will squat. From here we will throw them scraps from your table.' Hongi treats Cutler as his subordinate as he derides the missionary's false doctrine of peace by pointing out his king's security and power is gained through fear and violence; that, as he witnessed in Kendall's home town, British law allows children to be forced into labour and savagely beaten by brutish devils. 'Would I, savage as you have often called me, ever make such savagery? What are you doing here, missionary? You have work to do at home.' He gives Cutler the right of reply but despite his having taken communion many times with Cutler, Hongi is contemptuous of the idea that the Christian sacrament of 'eating the body and drinking the blood' makes him 'part of His Sacred Body'. Having provoked Emma Cutler to denounce the Māori tradition of 'kai tangata'—'A revolting sin! A disgusting, heathen abomination!'—Hongi calls them fools for thinking Māori eat human flesh to gain the strength and mana of their enemies. They eat it to degrade it: 'If my enemy becomes my food, if I take him down into my gut and bowels, he is insulted to eternity. Only war can avenge him. If my God becomes my food, I insult him, also. Think on that, missionary.'[10] This is powerfully provocative theatre.

The challenge to Cutler's Christian faith builds to Hongi's rhetorical suggestion that he could test it by splitting the head of Sarah, 'she of the blabber-tongue', with his mere, so Cutler can make her whole again. Comparing the power of his tohunga (priest), Tawhaki, to 'kill a man by thought' with Cutler's inability to perform miracles, Hongi claims his gods are therefore greater than Cutler's and offers to protect him 'from utu, and the promise of utu, from sunrise to sunset, every day, every year.' Emma is right to fear a trap is being set; Hongi's price is lead, powder and more muskets. 'You can order them, where we cannot,' he reasons. 'And, consider: when you order them for us, they have God's blessing! Then we give you food. It is a good bargain. Tū will be pleased. Christ will be pleased. I will be pleased.' Cutler's attempt to argue the greater value of axes, hoes, grain, and learning crop and animal husbandry does not work because the Māori already have that equipment and knowledge. Hongi is blunt: a refusal to supply arms and ammunition will result in 'Utu. Pillage. Insult. And from you, what? The other cheek. A thin cheek. A starving cheek. A bad bargain, e hoa.' Despite his wife's outrage, and in response to his daughter's hunger, Cutler gives in: 'Well, we must eat. Emma: we must eat! We have to live!'[11] This scene also stands as a fine piece of stringent satire that should be iconic to students of dramatic literature.

To dramatise the ensuing warfare, Mason scripts the sounds and visual images of haka, musket fire, screams, fires and warriors, and a warning conch being answered with a gong banged by a terrified European woman, culminating in Hongi Hika, in the full armour gifted by George IV, waving a taiaha. A letter Cutler has received describes how Hongi has slaughtered thousands, including his closest friend, Hinaki, and pulls no punches: 'Hinaki's death was terrible. Hongi swallowed his eyes while he was yet alive and drank his blood from a chalice.' As Emma rails at the foolishness of the 'noble savage' myth, Cutler feels anguish at his complicity in preaching God's Word to make these wars possible. Stylised war imagery and battle sequences bridge a series of exchanges between people in the street, which report on and mythologise Hongi's progress over five years. With a body count of ten thousand so far, one man asks another, 'Is it extermination they want? Do they want to kill themselves off for us? Do they want to leave the land open for us to walk in on?' Such critiques of Hongi's actions discount any possibility that Mason's play can be seen as the product of liberal Pākehā guilt. Further commentary juxtaposes the physical reality of Hongi—'nothing much to look at, for all his fierce ways. I saw him once, taking a breather between wars. Way up north, it was. Meek as a mouse, well-spoken, quiet-spoken. Just sitting there, wrapped in a blanket, brooding'—with his legendary ability to avoid death. Even when a bullet passes through his chest, he stays standing, calls his warriors to deal to the foe and partakes in a victory hāngī, eating with relish. The stage instruction,

'*He tosses a thigh bone in the air*', may well be a reference to the famous opening sequence in Kubrick's 1968 film *2001: A Space Odyssey*, depicting the start of our evolution as tool-using, weapon-bearing beings. 'He who preyed on life, laughs at death,' Mason's vox pop commentators conclude. 'He was the toughest old totara in the stand. We won't see his like again.'[12]

By continuing to articulate all perspectives in the final sequences, Mason provokes his audience to wrestle with the moral dilemmas while simultaneously recognising the parallels this story has with epic legends. As they watch the dying Hongi arrive by waka, Cutler quotes the Old Testament: '"And Saul has slain his thousands and David his ten thousands." Ay. He is carved from the heroes and prophets.' His wife sees Hongi as 'hemlock! Poison! Venom!' but Cutler refuses her urge to condemn him: 'From what assumptions? No precept of mine can command him, no code of ours enrol him. He is the stuff of myth and legend. Watch him, now: gliding along a river to his death, like Arthur to Avalon, in dark majesty.' Even when Emma commends him to Hell, Cutler counters that Hongi will 'be received as Lucifer. Fallen angel. Inordinate and outrageous.'[13]

The final battle is one of wits between Cutler and Hongi, who claims the cycle of peace and war is 'the way of the world, eh hoa. Of my world, of your world, of all worlds.' On learning a five-year-old boy 'waits without' to be cooked and fed to Hongi in morsels, a horrified Cutler retrieves and unties the boy, despite the attempts of warriors to stop him. When Hongi explains he is 'The grandson of a chief. I slew him in battle and dined on his body. Eat this morsel, I dishonour his ghost, to Kingdom come and Kingdom go,' Cutler asks him to give the child to him. 'No,' says Hongi. 'You will stuff him with the Gospel. Better that I eat him, pass him through my bowels. I would do less harm to eat him thus.' When Cutler pleads to be allowed to bring the child up as his own, as 'a pledge of love, twixt me and you', Hongi relents, despite believing this will break the boy as he himself has been broken, by 'the new babble' (a pun on Bible, no doubt). The last words Mason writes for Hongi becomes a critique not only of 'the Word' but of the power of the written word in general, presumably in statutes as well as all areas of education:

> The mind is split in twain. Forward or back? This way or that? The iwi once was a rock, but your words make it pebbles. When we knew no letters, we knew no sin. The iwi was once great force, but you slice it to the size of a man. Words, words, words, and paper.

As '*a shower of paper*' slowly buries a sleeping warrior, Hongi declares the new words will bury them and their old ways. He asks Cutler not to teach the boy to read, otherwise 'give him to me. Better that I eat him.' Cutler refuses and Hongi decides he has no appetite now. 'Tonight I dine with Hine-nui-te-Po. Her kai is good; she knows my taste.' Chuckling at Cutler's admiration that he can 'jest on the brink of eternity', Hongi is '*seized by a paroxysm of coughing*' and he dies amid keening from the women. In darkness: '*A faint radiance shows Cutler leading the boy off into darkness; another faint glow shows a Maori warrior with the putatara. Its hoarse, straining bark ends the play.*'[14]

Arguably the most challenging, provocative and political of all Mason's plays, *Hongi* confronts aspects of our past that must always be acknowledged and debated. If this had happened in response to a production staged in Mason's lifetime, who knows where he would have gone with such themes, his decision to leave further plays on Māori themes to Māori writers notwithstanding. But Mason's focus in the five *Healing Arch* plays has been on Māori–Pākehā relationships. In the *Kaleidoscope* programme recorded in 1982, when interviewer Helen Paske noted Mason had said all along that he was not speaking for Māori, he agreed: 'I take themes which in themselves are intrinsically dramatic, I think. The clash between the oral culture of Māori, before the language was spelt out into characters, and the highly literate—that is to say, literate in the sense of being visually orientated—European [culture]. The clash between those is fundamental and it makes drama. There's no getting away from it.'[15] He would, however, include Māori in at least two of his subsequent plays: in *Zero Inn*, Kuni is described as looking '*at least half-caste Maori*' and she identifies her people as Māori, and a back-story in *Blood of the Lamb* describes an East Coast Māori community in detail.

CHAPTER FOURTEEN

WHEN DROP-OUTS DROP IN

Zero Inn / The Chance of a Lifetime

Consumer culture meets counter-culture
one fateful Christmas Day.

Bruce Mason was editor of *Act* magazine for Downstage Theatre (1967–1970)[1] and senior copywriter for Wood and Mitchell Advertising Limited (1969–1971)[2] when Christchurch's Elmwood Players, in celebration of their twenty-first birthday in May 1970, secured a Queen Elizabeth II Arts Council grant to commission a new play from him. (This was the year before Christchurch's first professional theatre, The Court, would open with *The Prime of Miss Jean Brodie.*)

As usual Mason had his finger on the pulse of social change well ahead of most middle class New Zealanders. Given the way *Zero Inn* resolves, it is worth noting that although the Riverside Community in Motueka was established in 1941 and James K Baxter set up his 'Jerusalem' on the Whanganui River in 1969, most New Zealand communes evolved in the later 1970s. While this new play certainly captures the zeitgeist of its time, the issues canvassed—concerning gender roles, respect for ancient cultures, environmental degradation and alternative values and lifestyles—have become more mainstream in the decades since. Picking up on the question, 'How do we live our lives?' that concerned earlier generations in *The Evening Paper* and *Birds in the Wilderness*, the play's central clash is between the materialistic, progress-loving values of Maxwell Tully (fifty), who heads up a successful advertising company, and the counter-culture values of three unexpected visitors. Hector, Ben and Cunégonde (Kuni), who is in the last stages of pregnancy, are 'drop-out' musicians in their early twenties. It also taps the well of resentment Sandra (forty-eight) has built up over nearly three decades as Max's 'loving wife', mother of two (she had her tubes tied after the stillbirth of her third child in quick succession) and now the grandmother of five. Her role in the service of others has clearly taken precedence over other options.

Marooned in the titular edifice on a remote shore of Te Moana o Whaitiri (Thunder Lake) on Christmas Eve, with no prospect of her children and grandchildren arriving as intended (because one of them has scarlet fever), Sandra and her mother, Leila (sixty-nine), are left with wrapped gifts in the wrong place and a turkey far too large for three. Zero Inn is a brand new open-plan lakeside house that '*looks as if the contents of a junk shop had been emptied into it*',[3] including superseded radios, a '*a battered Hi-Fi*' and a TV: the jetsam of an advertising executive's constant acquisitiveness amid ever-changing fashion and planned obsolescence (an inspiring challenge for a set designer). In the darkness beyond the panoramic window someone roars about in a motor boat. It becomes apparent it's Max, expressing rage that his largess has been rejected by the children. Sandra's scathing commentary includes 'blasted heath' quotes from *King Lear*. She is also very clear she has no intention of being stranded at Zero Inn, so-named because Max was in the Air Force and 'you zero in when you come in and land.'[4]

This Christmas story offers a stark contrast to *The End of the Golden Weather*'s 'Christmas at Te Parenga', wittily referenced in an exchange between Sandra, who snorts at its idyll of giving and abundance, and Leila, who says Mason made her cry when they saw it last year. 'Oh rubbish,' counters Sandra. 'It's not like that. That's not Christmas!'[5] Sandra's relationship with Max has become a habitual battle zone. Her private girls' school education followed by a brief flirtation with first-year English at university is a major point of contention, given Max never got beyond the fifth form. When she puts him down for not recognising Cunégonde as a character in Voltaire's *Candide*, his attack is venomous: 'You bitch. You snob. Literature. Scraps, and jottings, and clippings. Little bits of junk to do the crossword with, or play scrabble with, or score off me with. Literature! Useless Junk!'[6] Their volatile conflict is dramatised throughout with a perceptiveness that contradicts Mason's assertion, a decade later, that only when reading Marilyn French's *The Women's Room* in 1980 had he discovered that 'women had needs and options I had never considered.'[7] Although Germaine Greer's *The Female Eunuch* did not hit the bookshops until after *Zero Inn* opened, plays like Ibsen's *A Doll's House* (1879) would have alerted him to such issues. And as an astute observer of society, Mason clearly knew the status quo did not serve New Zealand women well when he wrote *The Evening Paper*, *The Verdict*, *Birds in the Wilderness*, *The Light Enlarging / Virtuous Circle* and *Swan Song*. But *Zero Inn*'s well-educated Sandra is much more bolshie than Elfrida, Mrs Douglas, Juliet, Barbara or Jenny. At the cusp of the sixties and seventies, then, Mason was clearly more cognisant than ever of female frustrations.

In the third act, it emerges that Max first told Sandra of his dream of a Zero Inn haven in September 1945, when she was the war hero's blushing ex-nurse bride. Since then she has selflessly supported him in his stellar advertising career, from 'Base Camp A . . . to the promised land at Z for Zero Inn!' Now she sees Max as a 'deadly stinking bore' and their marriage as 'a safari. He's been up ahead on the elephant; I'm the oppressed native, ten paces behind, carrying the packs. He's never turned round, even to look at me!' Even his recent decision to make her his trustee and put her in charge of the money has made her see herself as a 'Madam in his gilt-edged whorehouse'.[8]

The relatively naturalistic marital antagonism between Sandra and Max plays out amid the gradual discovery of the stories of their 'night visitors': Hector, Ben and Kuni, who is '*mountainous in the last stage of pregnancy . . . barefoot and looks at least half-caste Maori.*' There is a touch of 'magic realism' in their post-midnight arrival amid thunder and lightning, heralded by bells on a horse-drawn cart: a conflation of Santa Claus, the Magi and the Virgin Mary. The sudden flooding of light into the room to reveal them in rough hippie clothes, long-haired, beaded and (the men) bearded suggests a biblical tableau, more redolent at first glance of the shepherds than the three kings. When Max bursts in from his boat to demand, 'What the hell is going on!' Sandra retorts, 'They saw our star in the east,' and the visitors are enigmatic: 'We followed the signs. Fire over water.'[9] Later it becomes apparent this refers to the *I Ching*. Whether they are wise and bear gifts of true value remains an open question as the trappings of materialism are pitted against their alternative lifestyle.

It emerges, from persistent questioning by their initially reluctant hosts, that neither of Kuni's companions is the father of her impending child, but they all sleep together 'for warmth', and she has no intention of giving birth in a hospital, where they would 'bring out the baby all crook.' They sing as a group called The Hellovit in randomly found public places and often get offered food and shelter when some official moves them on. Hector studied History, Sociology and Political Science at university, and his father is a lawyer. All three have dropped their family names since their families dropped them. Hector explains they are wanted by the police because sometimes, when there is 'a crisis—violence in the crowd' and 'the young get rough and riled', they 'cool it, with joints . . . They want our supplier. They don't mind us so much.' They 'play the *Ching*' to discover their path: 'We were told to look for a place of thunder, of fire over water, in the south east. That's why we're here.'[10]

By Act 2, after the visitors have slept through most of Christmas Day, Sandra has dressed Kuni in one of her three unwanted negligees (gifts from Max) and the young men are wearing ill-fitting items of Max's clothing: costumes that look clown-like on them and parody the society they have rejected. The gifts Sandra and Leila redirect to their guests also comment on seventies consumerism. A make-up and perfume set 'for the pink and gold gloss girl' makes Kuni giggle, 'They come to the wrong face!', Hector likewise has no use for one of Max's many electric razors. Although he doesn't smoke, Ben does oblige by parading '*in a parody of the model's preening strut*' in the '*brocaded satin smoking jacket and embroidered Garibaldi-type cap*' Sandra had intended for Max, who declares he would have felt a 'right Charlie' in it. Sandra is '*slightly nettled*' that no one thanks her for the effort she and her mother have made to garner these gifts at the last minute. Max fails to impress the young ones with the technological precision of the electric razor and the fact that the make-up kit's packaging won an award in Japan. But the visitors do not verbalise their criticism. In fact they have fallen off their vegetarian wagon by eating the slow-roasted turkey, causing Kuni to declare, 'I love meat,' and Ben to reveal he once worked two seasons in a freezing works, which put him off meat for life.[11] As a lapsed Anglican who still claims to pray, Max's pride at selling 20,000 brass Buddhas last year, made in Birmingham, Alabama, with a campaign that was adopted all over the United States, exemplifies how product-oriented his world has become. Of course Sandra sides with the visitors in characterising it all as 'nothing but junk'.[12] The constant marital sniping between Sandra and Max compared to the laid-back trio also accentuates the generation gap.

Sex threads throughout the play to surface in various forms. In Act 1 it is established that Max and Sandra have not slept together for eight months. When Sandra asks if the arrangement between Kuni, Ben and Hector is 'some kind of "ménage à trios"', which Ben interprets, 'I think what she means: are we living in sin', Kuni simply '*laughs, gently*': 'Sin? Oh . . . sin.'[13] It is some time before the story of her pregnancy is revealed. Having learned that neither Hector nor Ben is the father of Kuni's child, both Max and Sandra are less than receptive to the trio's habit of sleeping together, 'for warmth.' But when Sandra notes they only have single beds, it is Leila who points out Sandra has a double that is 'only half occupied' whereupon Max, who has been sleeping in his boat, offers to sleep with Kuni. This idea is instantly vetoed by Sandra. It is also Leila who suggests to Max, out of earshot of Sandra, that he might just find his wife 'receptive' tonight, even to sharing a single bed with him, which 'wouldn't be for the first time, surely.'[14]

In Act 2 it becomes apparent that Max has asserted his 'rights' with Sandra in the early hours of Christmas morning. When he calls her a teaser for living in the luxury he provides—'lapping it all up with a mocking laugh. Gimme gimme gimme with one hand and with the other, a smack in the chops'—then dares to gloat, in front of the others, about getting his way last night, she rages at him: 'Rapist! The snatch and grab man! . . . Looter! Pirate!'[15] The supposed legitimacy of marital relations looks decidedly sordid in this context, by comparison with the 'illicit' arrangements between Kuni and her two friends.

Rape is also the term Sandra uses to describe Max's work with Tully Associates. 'An aggressive, thrusting agency. It's on their letter-head: true, it is! Sounds like rape. It *is* rape. The rape of the unsuspecting. Giving those who don't know what they want, what they didn't know they needed.'[16] Later that night, Sandra is alone with Hector. After smoking a joint and explaining to him the genesis of Zero Inn and her determination that Max 'should have nothing to tax me with, no shame, no blame. Kids reared, food cooked, socks darned, and marriage bed virtuous,' Sandra declares she wants 'a great big beautiful screaming affair' with Hector. He declines to be a pawn in her game against Max. 'Listen I've mortgaged my whole life to keep Max in the air and build Zero Inn,' she argues. 'And it's all been a fraud. A nothing! Future, future, always future! I want here and now! Experience! Meat!' But Hector won't be her 'naked lunch . . . for chewing, and spitting out at Max.'[17]

The stories of why and how Kuni, Hector and Ben dropped out offer compelling comparisons with the Max and Sandra story. The fifth girl in her family, Kuni got her name (Cunégonde) when her mum asked the lady in the next hospital bed to read aloud the first name she came to in the book she was reading, which happened to be *Candide*. After her mum died of tuberculosis ten years ago and her dad shot through to the city with another lady, Kuni was brought up by her nana while she in turn brought up all the little ones who had come after her. She worked in a milk bar where the manager was a 'persistent sod' who pinched her and felt her up 'even at the counter when I was serving' and one day 'followed me into the john, just stood there, and . . . He was a real pig. A proper filthy swine.' Hector walked into the shop and she gave him a milkshake, even though he had no money, simply because she liked his face. When he wasn't able to pay the manager rang the police, so Kuni paid for it herself and walked out with Hector. She was three months pregnant at the time, to the abusive manager no doubt. Hector had a guitar so they would busk in parks; he would play, Kuni would sing, and they would attract people who listened and sang along. That's how they met Ben with his harmonica.[18]

In the face of Max calling them 'A troupe of shiftless vagrants! Wandering gypsies!' Hector outrages Max even more—as a taxpayer whose sixty-seven cents in the dollar paid for Hector's free education—by revealing he 'flunked finals. Deliberately.' He found third-year history meaningless so wrote a quatrain about the French Revolution as his whole paper and scored two per cent for his trouble. 'I sat that paper in the afternoon,' he explains: 'In the morning I read that the Prime Minister of Canada was paying his farmers to destroy their wheat to keep prices up; that two students were shot dead by

National Guardsmen in Mississippi, that a busload of Israeli children had been machine-gunned by Arab guerrillas, and that a Colonel in the Police in South Vietnam had evicted a war cripple from a derelict shanty and burnt his crutches—that poor bastard hopped down the street on his stumps, screaming for succour; and then you ask me to sit that paper.'[19]

Ben dropped out of the building trade after serving a three-year apprenticeship, 'humping concrete in barrows up ramps in freezing weather.' It was the 'two identical buildings, facing each other, twenty floors high' that turned him off. Having worked on the first one, while building the second, he would watch the office workers gather 'like colonies of white ants, like packs of cards to be sorted and shuffled and dealt out, room by room.' He got to know the occupants opposite only to find, when they moved up a level, that 'every floor was the same, the same bloody same: colonies of paper prisoners, spending bright days shuffling and sorting, sorting and shuffling. It made me want to scream and weep.' He is unimpressed by Max's news that concrete is pumped now: the office workers are still 'being put in the slot at 8 and coming out at 5.' One day he just walked off the job to join 'a girl standing by the bus stop; she wore a red coat and her hair was black and shiny as liquorice . . . [We] went off for three days in the bush, to a hut I know in the Tararuas. We made love like gentle grizzly bears, washed off in mountain streams, fell asleep in each other's arms by a roaring brush fire. It was gorgeous! And I came back, blood bouncing, eyeballs flashing, rarin' to go, ready for a million barrowfuls; I tell you I loved the whole goddam world, even the foreman! But that surly bastard just gave me my cards and told me to get the hell out of it.' Ben now rejects the city as a 'snarled up heap of litter and garbage', full of cars and pollution, and the suburbs as 'warrens' where people 'flop down in front of the telly to daze their poor little brains to the point they can chew on paper again the next day.' The wonders of plumbing and electricity, extolled by Max, are no compensation; nor is dentistry's high-speed drill. Ben sees decay in general as part of life and thinks thirty is a long way off; meanwhile 'let's all have a bloody great party!'[20]

When Max asks, 'What's going to happen to Kuni's child?' and Sandra says, 'Obvious. It'll be adopted or boarded out,' Kuni is instantly alert: 'Like hell it will!' She answers Sandra's concerns for the child's welfare and hygiene by pointing out her people got on perfectly well before the Pākehā came. Education comes back into focus when she echoes Rangi in *The Hand on the Rail*: 'I learned two things at school: the climate of Ecuador, hot and wet, and Thomas-a-Beckett, the father of English poetry.' Hector sees the new child's education as being based on 'The natural world. The forces of the universe.'[21]

Through these three, then, Mason deftly articulates 'anti-establishment' views that still have currency in the new millennium. He also counters them through Max and Sandra, with well-reasoned arguments. The only flaw is the concept of marijuana joints being given out to pacify aggressive people. 'We don't smoke ourselves, now,' Hector explains in Act 1, 'But sometimes, there's a—crisis—violence in the crowd. The police may start it; the young get rough and riled. So we cool it with joints. Settle it down.' Aside from the lack of credibility in doing such a thing when the police are around, such an offer to an anti-hippy agitator would more likely make him even angrier, as exemplified by Max when they produce the pot pouch in Act 2. Even if the person who 'cut up rough' did accept a joint, doing so alone would be against the convention of sharing it as a communal experience. For Hector and Ben to agree that Leila needs a joint and then to abstain themselves seems unlikely, given Hector calls it 'harmless' and Ben calls it 'mouth to mouth resuscitation' and then tells Leila to 'pass it on' to Sandra. 'Don't you and Hector?' Sandra asks when she hands it back to Ben. 'Not now,' says Hector. Kuni's explanation for never having smoked dope is more credible: 'I've got all the colours I can deal with, right here in front of my nose. Why stew it all around? Things are mashed up enough now!'[22] Perhaps Hector means they have attained a higher state of enlightenment; this air of superiority does ring true for some of his ilk. Maybe Mason has taken this tack to accentuate their wisdom as latter day Magi. It is also possible a development workshop would have seen this section revised.

That said, the juxtaposition of Max's cigar-smoking with Leila and Sandra's pot-smoking allows some good satirical points to be made, and his escalating aggression as Leila accepts Hector's invitation to play the *I Ching* to 'ring the changes' while she and Sandra become quietly stoned, makes for some richly entertaining dramatic dynamics. A comic twist comes from Sandra suggesting that Hector throw for Max, who dubs it 'Necromancy. Witchcraft!' until the hexagram reveals 'the superior man'. There is a touch of pathos in Max's immediate conversion to the *I Ching* and in his '*sudden scalding tears*' when Sandra refuses to play along with his gloating and Hector says, gently, 'Max: nothing's been proved.' The juxtaposition of his door-slamming departure with the trio singing an original carol, interspersed with Leila's and then Sandra's languid and lyrical stoned raves, brings Act 2 to a well-wrought close.[23]

In Act 3, Mason ensures the unfolding action is equally unpredictable and that 'taking sides' will not be easy for the audience. Leila tends to side with Max (who has taken off in the car) regarding the marijuana. While she vows never to smoke pot again, declaring it has 'a vile taste!', she fondly recalls being stoned and is clearly drawn to the *I Ching*'s suggestion that she 'sit in the meadow and wait for the gate to open.' Sandra, on the other hand, claims she was unaffected by the pot. With Leila, Ben and Kuni gone to bed, Sandra pitches for an affair with Hector and is rejected. His *I Ching*-inspired claim that 'care of the cow brings good fortune' depresses her even more. That her 'supreme good fortune' is apparently to be achieved by her taking 'the middle way [as] the strong and docile cow' is a far cry from the 'trumpets' she was hoping for. Any suggestion that Sandra might reconcile with Max seems doomed when he returns to announce he has been into town to call the police commissioner and a squad is on the way to arrest their guests. Her horror is somewhat assuaged by his having also arranged for Kuni to be admitted to St Helen's Hospital and be attended by an obstetrician. But her withering sarcasm flares once more when Max goes along with Hector's face-saving acceptance of this turn of events: 'I knew it! There was an uncertainty in the hexagram!' She does, however, obey Max's command to go upstairs and wake Ben and Kuni.[24]

At this point Mason brings the clash of values between Max and Hector to a head. While it may seem clear, at first, that Max is the villain and Hector is the more righteous, it does not play out as simply as that. Initially Hector is surprisingly resigned to their impending fate as Max lectures him on 'discipline!' and insists on providing 'protection and care' for Kuni. As for the 'back to the land stuff', Max insists it is 'so much hogwash', given the farmer whose land they dug over for supper and shelter 'has a tractor plough that can carve up that patch, better and deeper than you did, in ten minutes flat' and a machine on order 'that can plough, sow and reap a whole crop untouched by human hand.' The farmer let them dig for healthy exercise, that is all. What a shock, then, when Max asks Hector to come and work for him. The 'hammering' he got last night, plus the *I Ching*'s revelation that he is 'superior man', has made him rethink himself as an architect of the future, and he wants Hector for his decency, humanity and vision: 'You can tell us what a city should be and how it should be shaped—decently, humanly shaped. Then we can come in and build it!'[25]

Hector isn't interested. He writes off Max's generation as those who turned this world into 'Poluto'. It is clearly a speech he has delivered before: 'You've had it, all of you: H-A-D, had it! H for Hiroshima, A for Auschwitz, D for Dresden.' It turns out Max got his DFC (Distinguished Flying Cross) over Dresden, which Hector sees as 'a fire-storm. Of no military necessity or significance.' He wants to start again from zero, working the land. Max rejects a return to the darkness before electricity; he accepts they have made mistakes but sees the solution in better progress through technological advances. Hector turns out the light and draws attention to the silence of Thunder Lake, which once 'hummed with presence' until Max and his kind 'blew up a whole world of resonant myth! That's what your light has done for Kuni and her people!' He rejects Max's call for 'a new myth . . . Progress! Abundance! Leisure! Creation!' as an old myth that has played out 'to the last gasp.'[26]

Because Mason has ensured both Max and Hector are articulate advocates of their diametrically opposed revolutionary zeal, and are therefore worthy adversaries, his audience is compelled to confront their own values, assessments of the past and visions for the future. Meanwhile the real and present world arrives from upstairs in the form of Ben who, to Hector's horror, knees Max in the crotch for what he has done as the police car approaches. In true 'Masonesque' style, the resolution handsomely pays off what has been so astutely set up. Leila, who thinks what Max has done is 'monstrous', responds to Kuni's anguish over what is in store for her by deciding to go with them. She will use her savings to 'take a little place in town', and promises to be there as Kuni's nanny until she (Leila) dies. As they go to meet their police escort, a mutually respectful Max and Hector vow to each other they won't give up, and a belligerent Ben promises 'total war' before Max is much older. Alone together, Max points out to Sandra that she could have gone too and wonders if this means she wants to stick it out with him: 'Or am I crossing a bridge that hasn't been built yet?' She is enigmatic, non-confrontational and astonished to discover Max has rejected his life of peddling junk, offered Hector a job and now wants to give Zero Inn over to him and his friends to 'start their little commune: see how they do with it.' Realising they have listened to each other 'for the first time in months, years maybe', they face their uncertain future as a 'tough old bull' and a 'strong and docile cow'; the 'Zero' and 'Zeroine' of what is to come.[27]

Although this looks like a happy ending, it is not one to leave us complacent. *Zero Inn* provocatively dramatises the core conflict that the cultural revolution was bringing to mainstream New Zealand society in the 1970s. The immediacy of the unfolding action is so compelling that only in retrospect does it become apparent how cleverly Mason has articulated the debate, not just in contemporary terms but also by reaching back to the birth of Christianity, the colonisation of New Zealand and a war that destroyed priceless cities and spawned nuclear warfare. This elevates the play from being merely topical and distils an essence that will always be present where humans try to coexist.

Even so, *Zero Inn* is not perfect. Like any play it would benefit from a comprehensive development process that sees its over-writing trimmed back, its internal logic tuned up, the emotional drivers and consequent behaviours of its characters 'road tested' for credibility and audience accessibility, its staging requirements and dramatic conventions streamlined, and its structure strengthened, so that its audience would feel free to willingly suspend disbelief and engage with its abiding truths. A single amateur production rehearsed part-time over a few weeks could not have achieved all that.

To compare Mason with Chekhov again, New Zealand theatre

has never had the luxury of the eighteen-month rehearsal periods for new plays that the Moscow Art Theatre enjoyed. Chekhov was aghast, apparently, when his last play, *The Cherry Orchard*, which Mason translated for radio in 1960,[28] was only allowed six months rehearsal. Mason's most respected work, *The Pohutukawa Tree*, did evolve through what were called workshop productions, only to be ignored by professional theatres for decades. In the late 1970s, when our professional theatres became more established in their operations, they were not primarily focused on the development of new works. The first New Zealand Playwrights Workshop took place in 1980, too late for Mason, who had to defer to 'emerging talent' when it came to such opportunities. By 1980 Mason had already had one operation for cancer of the jaw, not that he let that stop him. But as with his earlier plays, had *Zero Inn* proved its full potential soon after he had written it, who knows what else may have followed.

In 1971 Mason wrote what may be described as a deconstructed version of *Zero Inn*, a play in one Act that he called *Chance It!* or *Chancey Business* or *A Game of Chance*, before settling on *The Chance of a Lifetime*, largely because of the role the *I Ching* has in the play. He explicitly turns theatrical convention on its head by opening with a deus ex machina (used in Greek tragedy to resolve the drama and later decried by Horace). A Chinese 'god of the machines' called Ch'ien Xian-Sheng (aka Mr Creative) drops from the flies on a skiff to present a sound and light show that accompanies 'your puppets for the evening, my creatures, even my zombies since they have no life but what I allow them.' Sounding a gong to theatrical effect he gets the five characters to introduce themselves, then uses a rapid-fire 'word association' quiz to elicit single-word or short-phrase responses that reveal their key characteristics. Such prompts as 'Authority!', 'Work!', 'Time!', 'Love!', 'Clothing!', 'Town', 'Country!', 'Media!', 'Food', 'Drugs!', 'War!', 'The search for identity!', 'Mottos!' are interspersed with projected images of Christ crucified and the Buddha, and differentiating snatches of music.[29]

The 'exemplary gavottes' combine biographical material about Mervyn and Nina Wicks, who have been married for twenty-five years, illustrated by slides, with duologue interactions that characterise them as fire and water, doomed to extinguish each other. Then 'the Now generation'—Ken, Toby and Blanche—is further revealed. These five characters are virtually identical to Max and Sandra Tully, Hector, Ben and Kuni. Ch'ien operates throughout as narrator, provocateur and interlocutor to facilitate the revealing of character and story elements that, along with large tracts of dialogue and monologue, echo *Zero Inn*.[30] It is Ch'ien who articulates the Eastern view in commenting on the state of the planet:

> My creatures are at loggerheads. They have reached an impasse. More and more is better and better has guided the West for three centuries; it will soon turn the planet into one vast, sleazy, putrefying slum. More and more with less and less is palliative . . . but not enough to turn Poluto back to garden. Here, whatever he may do, is Merv's world in 2001 AD.
>
> SLIDE: *Ruins, chaos.*
>
> SOUND: *Funereal music.*
>
> The young are good-hearted and decent, and their instincts are sound. They make love, not war. They believe in old-fashioned things like sweat and the dignity of labour: simple work for simple minds; a limited and honourable fruitfulness. Give them their heads, let the generation loose their ancient bonds to the past and, if poverty is now endemic, it will soon be total. Here is the world that Ken and Toby and a few million more of like mind, would inaugurate.
>
> SLIDE: *Ruins, chaos.*
>
> SOUND: *Funereal music.*[31]

Although this consciousness of the threat to the planet through the pollution brought on by the imperatives of progress was very contemporary—popularised in the West through the likes of the Beatles' association with the Maharishi Mahesh Yogi—it is worth noting the first *New Zealand Whole Earth Catalogue* was yet to be published (it first appeared in 1972). It must also be noted that, as in the early counter-culture movements, Mason anoints only the male characters with the power to initiate change, even though female demigods have claimed supernatural powers from the beginning of mythologised time.

> While the West fragments the gorgeous East—I know my Wordsworth—into commodity, goods and services, its image a pile of groceries, the East can shake the West awake to the great way and the great power. Note in what ordinary habitations the supernatural chooses to abide! (*Gong*) At a time of impasse, and in the threat of wholesale dereliction, I am empowered to offer you a further option. (*Gong*)[32]

The hippy trio are not yet into the *Book of Changes*, so it is the medium Ch'ien who uses the *I Ching* and 'chance' as a way to bypass the logic which 'has failed you' in the quest for 'harmony and restoration'. The typescript ends with Merv and Ken making their first throws. It is not clear whether this is Mason's intended ending. Although it is possible, given he called it a one-act play, it would be unusual for him to leave a play so open-ended.

Given the *The Chance of a Lifetime* typescript is clearly dated 1971, it is tempting to speculate as to why Mason felt compelled to rework *Zero Inn*, following its publication by the New Zealand Theatre Federation in December 1970. Was it because the regional professional theatres were resistant to picking up a play that had been premiered by an amateur society? Or was it the trend towards more alternative theatre forms that made Mason revise his 'well-made play'?

There is no record of *The Chance of a Lifetime* ever being produced and, forty-something years on, the themes and arguments are presented much more provocatively and compellingly in *Zero Inn*. While alternative theatrical forms have their place and have produced some remarkable theatre, it is hard to beat the stimulating richness that can be gained by placing credible characters with significant pasts in present situations that conflict with their future wants, needs and desires. The way Mason writes them, such plays compel our willing suspension of disbelief, add up to much more than the sum of their parts and ensure the audience is anything but passive as they, too, wrestle with the issues raised.

CHAPTER FIFTEEN

A CLANDESTINE LIFE AND A SHOCKING DIAGNOSIS

Letters to Mike / *Four Healing Dialogues*

Throughout the remainder of the 1970s Bruce Mason focussed mostly on touring his solo plays: *The End of the Golden Weather*, *To Russia, with Love* (also coupled with his translation of Vercors' *The Waters of Silence* in *Men of Soul*), *Not Christmas, but Guy Fawkes* and *Courting Blackbird*. His development of *Courting Blackbird* from prose to solo performance piece stands as the only script he wrote for live theatre in that decade.

In the context of his abiding enquiry into what it is to be a man in New Zealand, it is necessary to note at this point that Bruce Mason was fundamentally gay at a time when male homosexuality was illegal, and remained what Lord Alfred Douglas so eloquently called in his 1894 poem 'Two Loves', 'the love that dare not speak its name.' Mason was married and had fathered three children whom he loved unconditionally. His wife, Diana, to whom he was devoted, was aware and generously accepting of his clandestine life. His children only discovered the full extent of his secret life when letters he had written from 1976 were given to Victoria University of Wellington's JC Beaglehole Room by their recipient: Mason's sometime lover, long-time valued friend and confidant, Michael Ross (an academic at Massey University in Palmerston North at the time).[1] It was because of his relationship with Mason that Ross chose to write his MA thesis about gay men married to women (*Adaptation and Adjustment of Married Homosexual Males*, Victoria University of Wellington, 1975) and Mason took a keen and supportive interest in its progress.[2]

When Mason played Schroeder in a Downstage production of *You're A Good Man Charlie Brown*, (in late 1975) he developed a close (but platonic) relationship with a member of the company. Its persistence eventually upset Diana, precipitating a 'stinking row', then two days of deep discussion with her. Mason described the outcome in a letter to Mike Ross:

> When I asked her how she would react to my going off from time to time with someone for a few days, she said, 'All right. Go off when you feel like it; do your own thing. Just don't rub my face in it, that's all. Do nothing to arouse gossip about me or the kids, or anything that might reach your mother. Apart from that, feel free.'
>
> I felt lighter in spirits than for years, kissed her passionately and with the deepest respect. I told her that in those few words she had restored my self-respect and even made a man of me, if that doesn't sound paradoxical, and later that night, was able to prove it.[3]

Within some forty-four missives posted to Palmerston North in the first twenty-one weeks of 1976, Mason characterised his sexuality and love for Ross as follows:

> I am very volatile sexually . . . any time, any place. The paradox is that despite this, my life is on the whole very contained and, within conventional contexts, almost chaste.[4]

> My love for you is strong, powerful and above all, male.[5]

> Our meeting on Friday seemed the most luminous and beautiful we have ever had. I really adore you; my whole soul and body rise to you with the deepest love.[6]

Mason also wrote of his desire to meet men while on tour with his solo shows, and he expressed sincere joy when Ross found love, at last, in a committed relationship. The most recurring topic, however, is Mason's long-term and sometimes troublesome relationship with a man he referred to as V, which he interrogated in what he called 'the Chronicle', written in the form of a Socratic dialogue and sent to Ross. In 1976 news broke that Mason predicted was 'bound to snowball into a vast and earth-shaking scandal'. A Labour politician, Gerald O'Brien, had been charged with molesting two young men whom he had invited back for a drink at his Christchurch motel room. Mason shared his reaction with Ross, who was expecting to leave for a position in Australia:

> [This] leads me to suggest that [the Chronicle] is more important than ever, but also that its first edition will have to be anonymous, again curiously following the history of *Lolita* which was first published anonymously in Paris. When the storm of its publication has died, I will sign it, by which time I may well be into my sixties and D's professional career will be almost at an end . . . It may be that I will have to change my mind about this, but this is how it seems at the moment.
>
> God, what a nasty little community we live in! How mortally scared of itself! You can imagine the pious editorials that will be written, the more-in-sorrow-than-in-anger bromides that will be emitted! You are wise to leave it, and yet, I love it, and have to live and work in it.[7]

A few days later, regarding the political scandal, he wrote:

> There is still some possibility that, in that nastiest of New Zealand cities, it was some kind of jack-up. Did I tell you that Diana said, referring to this, that if I had been the unnamed man, she would have no recourse but to resign and leave the country? . . . It made me realise how tenuous a public character is, and by what frail threads it is tethered, and how ready some are to cut them and send the balloon of reputation into the stratosphere.[8]

The charges against O'Brien were thrown out at depositions but his political career was destroyed nevertheless. As for the 'V Chronicles', Mason asked Mike Ross to return the manuscript uncopied, and it is assumed he destroyed it.[9] What remains, however, amid the material Ross deposited in the JC Beaglehole Room, is a script called *Four Healing Dialogues*, which is clearly based on Mason's relationship with V. No writer is credited on the title page and it is formatted as a teleplay, albeit without proper scene headings and with verbal, visual and even olfactory elements that suggest actual production was never envisaged. The script tells the story of K, a writer who engages in

a series of increasingly therapeutic dialogues with four iterations of Aubrey McFate, named after a force of destiny personified as Lolita's classmate in the infamous novel by Nabokov: Mason's 'idol and god in literary matters'.

Mason's McFate is first objectified in K's consciousness as a filthy old man, then as Dr A McFate MD (Chicago), then as Sir Aubrey McFate PhD, crystallographer and lastly as Able Seaman McFate A, RN, a caulker. The dialogues clearly reference actual events that are mentioned in the letters, and the last date in the script is December 1972.

When the 'filthy old' version of Aubrey McFate visits K in his study, '*an overpowering stench fills the room.*' This stage direction alone, challenging for any performance medium, offers proof that Mason only expected this piece to play out on the page. K is clearly

A pensive Diana Mason (1970s).

upset that his young lover, who is eventually identified as V and is thirty years younger than K, has used his gift of money to finance a second visit to Auckland in the last few weeks, without telling him. McFate's reference to 'Your wife, your kids, the twenty-seven year old marriage' coincides with the Masons' marriage of twenty-seven years in 1972. McFate also pours scorn on 'that slushy, soupy, slimy Socratic Dialogue. Socratic! Poor Socrates! How do you think your wife would like to read that?'[10]

The session with Dr A McFate MD (Chicago) in his psychiatrist's consulting room, is called 'resentment therapy'. K claims he has no gripes despite McFate's pointing out, 'He'll read your letters, accept your tributes, and your gifts, with only the tiniest qualms. But from him to you? Nothing. Absolutely nothing.' When a large blank screen '*springs into light*' with an image of V '*dressed, in a manner of speaking—he is naked—as a male whore in* Fellini Satyricon, *wild hair bound with a fillet, face garishly made up, eyes like black beads and as expressionless, obscenely smiling, cock stiff and gently throbbing*', K shouts obscenities at him, the least of which is 'cock-teaser!'. K admits his chief gripe is over that 'awful week-end [in] a motel, where I was expected to stay alone, for two whole days, in a town where I knew not one solitary living soul.' McFate suggests K precipitated it 'by pushing at him, and giving him the excuse he needed to opt out of the whole bit.' Agreeing with K that he was probably 'on, or wanted to be, or was about to be, with someone else,' McFate adds, 'He wanted to be free . . . Oh, he felt guilt and disgust about it . . . And he just couldn't tell you the truth.'[11]

The other 'chief gripe' of K is that V 'came out in scruples like a crop of pimples. He had the insufferable nerve to set up as an ardent spokesman on the sanctity of my twenty-seven-year-old marriage. Yet I'd told him many times how, at my most involved and intimate with him, my marriage had also flowered; that because I loved him, I could love her more, and radiated benevolence on everybody. And I saw him turn before my eyes from the angel I loved to a supercilious, mocking little devil.' The therapy is completed by K throwing custard pies at the screen image of V. A flashback to the motel sees V begging forgiveness and receiving it from K. Then we hear of K's heartache over weeks of waiting for the post 'like a lovesick turtle. Anything, anything! A card, a line, a tiny memento: anything!' But nothing, for weeks.[12]

In Dialogue Three, Aubrey McFate the crystallographer explains V to K by using a DNA double helix diagram to represent his life:

> 'You will see two alternating strands, one black, one red. The black ribbon, labelled [V's actual initials], is his normal outer life: the world of his name, given to him by his parents, school, university, social relationships, how he stands in relation to others, and largely determined by others. The red strand is his inner life, and I have labelled it V, in deference to you, since only you and he know of [V's] existence, and after all, he was your joint creation.'

McFate notes the young man was 'born and nurtured in a prosperous and meanly respectable provincial town' with its 'life-denying' and 'rigidly prescribed' patterns. 'But only children lead secret lives, and you will note in the diagram how widely spaced are his inner and outer worlds. In most people the strands are plaited, if the red ribbon exists at all; you would not force a pin between them. But in his case, and I might add, yours, they are as widely spaced as it is possible to be, this side of schizophrenia.'[13]

There is an evocation of a blissful tryst over one day in August 1972, 'And who can blame us for that?' asks K. 'Who's blaming you?' McFate replies. 'As the *I Ching* encouragingly says: No Blame. That day was augured, pre-figured, the most perfect that perhaps either of you have ever passed. There was no will in it, no forcing, no conflict of any kind and bliss was its fruit.' McFate offers epigrams: 'Bliss repeated,/ Is bliss defeated'; 'Bliss entreated,/ Is bliss defeated'. Another encounter in September leads K to say, 'Bliss that's marred,/ Is bliss that's scarred.' It gets worse in December 1972. Noting 'bliss' and 'to be blest' derive from the same root, McFate concludes that 'none can ask for, nor seek bliss; it must arrive, unsought, unheralded. It is God's smile, but it cannot be turned on for you.' He explains how V has enabled K, 'through suffering, to unravel the whole skein of desire; to know that love and bliss can never be merely the collision of two self-infatuated images' and concludes, 'the emblem of your whole life can be the red ribbon of bliss.' When K asks if that means he does not have to give V up, McFate replies, 'These are no longer the terms of your contract. There is no holding, no relinquishing. Only the miracle of your life-long affection. Which, if I may say so, is better than a poke in the eye with a burnt stick.'[14]

Another transformation relocates K to a beach for Dialogue Four, with Able Seaman McFate A, RN, who is caulking an upturned boat with oakum and hemp. He tells K his impending voyage will be 'a ride into the ocean of Being, on the good ship, Existence' and that the threads and wisps of hemp are 'gleanings and droppings from your past. Wisps of memory . . . You ride on them, but you don't see them. Your past is not behind you, but underneath you. Just where it should be; keeps you buoyant; keeps you afloat.' When K asks if he must go alone, McFate replies, 'Laddie: we come alone, we go alone. To be a man, you've got to be alone.' The final image sees K rowing into the glare of the morning sun and dissolving into its light: '*There is nothing left but silence and holy radiance.*'[15]

Given the way he fictionalised his early and young adult life in *The End of the Golden Weather, Not Christmas, but Guy Fawkes* and *Courting Blackbird*, we can only wonder how Mason might have dramatised the gay dimension of his adult life had he felt at liberty to do so. Mason also wrote, in his letters to Ross, of a relationship with a young Christchurch man (C) which, it may be deduced, dated from when he took *Not Christmas, but Guy Fawkes* to the Christchurch Arts Festival in March 1976 (at which time he undertook to return and perform all his solo works in August). One night in mid-June Mason arrived home to discover two 'disastrous' things had happened:

> One, that [C] had written my address on a letter so illegibly that Diana thought it was for her and opened it, to find a fairly typically 'obscene' letter from [C], plus crude graffito, and second, this anonymous letter from Christchurch; addressed to her: 'Do you know that your husband is an old, lecherous pansy, well known all over NZ for it. At present he has a great love affair with a 22 year old boy [name and address stated]. The whole of Christchurch is laughing about you, so you better come

> down in August, and watch the performance.'
>
> I need hardly tell you what trauma this occasioned. The maddening thing was that, in looking after Diana's diabolically demanding and difficult mother for three days, we had become very close, and the time we spend alone together yesterday, was sheer bliss, doing simple things: on the golf course in Wairakei, making silly jokes in the car, and generally revelling in each other's company. This last night was hell, with neither of us able to sleep . . . Diana said she might throw up at the end of [C]'s letter, and that she will never forget the words 'old lecherous pansy', and nor, for that matter, will I.
>
> . . . I had to tell Diana at least the bare bones of our story. I think we will survive this, as we have survived so much else, but when I think back over the years: there has been so little with which she could reproach me.[16]

About a week later, he wrote:

> Diana made me weep once last night, when she thanked me for being so sweet to her over the years; I have several times had to be understanding on her behalf. This was no great effort, since what was necessary for her had to be, at the time. But it moved me very much that she should, in these circumstances, offer me this tribute. I might add that at no point during the last week have I said 'after all, I have been charitable to you' not wanting to push that barrow at all, so that when her tribute came it was the more moving to me.[17]

Here, Mason is referring to Diana's own occasional recourse to taking a lover.[18] The next day he wrote:

> I have thought over what I proposed yesterday—that you should meet my wife—and were you staying longer than July 4, I would have pursued it . . . because I would like Diana to meet my dearest friend, and prove to her through him that I could have a marvellous gay friend, who did not flounce or caper or carry on, one capable of the most auspicious integrity of mind and soul. Well, sometimes, perhaps, but I think not now.[19]

After seeing and reviewing a modern reworking of Euripides' *The Bacchae*, called *The Forbidden Women*, Mason told Mike Ross how and why he enjoyed it, and added:

> If V represents an incarnation of Eros at his best and most winning, then [C] is a mischievous wholly irresponsible version of Dionysus. Yet what we had together was totally innocent, so utterly harmless and invigorating. To Diana, it is infirmity, my Achilles heel; what I cannot tell her is that it is the core of my life, a shining pillar of holy fire (and make what you like of that, as phallic imagery).

He mentioned having to deal with receiving more 'nonsense' from C, and wrote:

> So much in the gay world is inextricably and ineluctably violent and seedy; it was this that so shattered Diana when she read [C]'s awful letter: no hint of grace or refinement. I cannot tell her that all this is part of it: Dionysus is bawdy and by conventional standards, obscene. It is all part of reverence; it can be in its way, holy. I think one has to accept in the gay world there is a much wider 'spread' of affection and feeling; society puts no strings on such relationships, and they feed themselves, in a way: each cannibalises the other. Is it all, I have often asked myself, simply narcissism at its most extreme? Narcissus: narcosis—the root words are linked; the self drugged by its image. And then I think of you, and know this cannot be true.[20]

In his last letter before Ross left for Melbourne, Mason concluded:

> . . . let me say that you are not only the most humane person I know, but also the most intelligent.[21]

Two years later Mason wrote from Whanganui, where he was performing his solos, to tell Mike Ross he had acquired:

> a mild Bell's Palsy on the first night of a recent season of *Courting Blackbird* and *Golden Weather* in Christchurch. I discovered that I could

> not smile on one side, nor wink but I did get through my performances okay with splendid reviews . . . It seems to be slightly worse here, in that I find 'f's particularly awkward . . .

Following the Whanganui season it suddenly became much worse:

> to the point where I could give no performance at all, fluffing badly on the plosives, my cheek inflating for 'p's and 'b's as if I were a Murano glass-blower, and on 'f's and 'v's incomprehensible. Diana now became alarmed, saying that this was like no Bell's Palsy in her experience, and said as much to my neurologist . . . He called in a side-kick who confirmed it was a Bell's P of, admittedly, unusual character but that both had known cases like it, which in due course, recovered.

Unable to perform, he accepted an engagement with The Company Theatre in Tauranga to direct *Suitcases* (a double bill of *Virtuous Circle* and *The Evening Paper*) in August 1978. While he was away Diana expressed further disquiet to the neurologist, who 'more or less told her to stick to obstetrics, which she knew about, and keep off neurology, which was not her field'.[22]

Late in August Mason reported:

> My Bell's Palsy is still unchanged and it now becomes really worrying because I am receiving letters of stupefying cordiality from New York from my agent there and it is all set up that I give a private performance of *Courting Blackbird* at the 44th Street Theatre on October 16. I can only hope that six weeks of sun and delight will cure it at last, but I have now had it for three full months and, as I say, it shows no sign whatever of clearing up. I have had every test known to medical science, blood perfect, x-rays show nothing, liver, spleen, heart, lungs, all great. My neurologist even said of me, stripped, that I could have posed for Michelangelo! Small comfort.

The 'sun and delight' referred to a six-week trip he and Diana took to 'Athens, Paros, Samos, Rhodes, Vienna, Nice, Burgundy, Paris, Stratford-Upon-Avon, London, New York, Moorea (Tahiti) and home', but Mason's health did not improve as hoped. Referred to 'a top London neurologist who sent us on to an equally top surgeon', Mason was at last told he had a malignant growth in the parotid gland. The surgeon 'wanted to remove it himself but courteously said that, as NZ surgeons were among the world's best, I might as well have it done at home.' In New York, where he was quite unable to audition or perform as planned, another specialist confirmed malignancy and suggested he be operated on there. 'Offered only a fifty-fifty chance of success, with medical bills astronomical—two weeks in hospital, at least $5,000.00, without the surgeon's fee—I opted to go home at once.' But they broke their journey in Tahiti, where he and Diana had 'three blissful days in Moorea snorkelling, swimming, riding bikes around the exquisite island . . .'[23]

Wellington's 'best surgeon' confirmed the cancer, painful tests were endured—'I felt like Gulliver, supine, while Lilliputians pole-vaulted on his jaw'—and Mason was booked in for a parotidectomy in Auckland, on 21 November. 'It took five and a half hours. I surface briefly in the recovery room to be told by the surgeon—I did not remember this until five days later—that the facial nerve could not be saved, but that he had split the masseter muscle, the one that works the jaw, into two, pulling one section forward towards the mouth promising to restore my smile. This it has not done, but has at least given me reasonably intelligible speech, except for some hissing on s, and still some popping on p, b, f and v.' After expressing gratitude that 'a disaster like this has the effect of removing all that is puny in one's life', Mason added, 'My wry disclaimer to people meeting me, post-op, is to say, "I'm not just a pretty face, you know!"'[24]

While his live performing career was now curtailed, Mason remained able to write—and he did.

CHAPTER SIXTEEN

THUS DO A FEW WOMEN

Blood of the Lamb

'Eliza and Henry Doolittle Higginson' are compelled to reveal their true identities and secret pasts when their daughter, Victoria, returns suddenly from Australia to marry her fiancé.

In his preface to *Blood of the Lamb* Mason reveals we have Elric Hooper, artistic director of The Court Theatre, to thank for the existence of what would be his final stage play. In November 1979 Hooper commissioned Mason to write a play to open The Court Theatre's new studio theatre in March 1980. Most of the actors in his company were cast in the forthcoming productions of Shakespeare's *Hamlet* and Tom Stoppard's *Rosencrantz and Guildenstern Are Dead*, scheduled to play on the main stage in repertoire. Since there were only two female characters, Gertrude and Ophelia, three women on the payroll were left without roles: Elizabeth Moody and Judie Douglass, in their forties, and Susan Curnow, aged twenty-one.[1]

The provisos for the commission were that it would use these three actresses and not be set in a room, because at a recent writers' conference Mervyn Thompson had railed against well-made plays set in rooms. But Mason's outdoor setting might as well be a living room, being '*an elegant walled garden with citrus trees in tubs, flowering shrubs, two large urns of massed flowers, symmetrically placed. Double doors lead to the house, dimly visible and sumptuous: the rump of a grand piano (where Mozart presides), large artefacts and objets d'art chosen with taste and care. Outside, a swing sofa, cane chairs, small table.*'[2] There is even a telephone in the garden (although this could also be set just inside).

Mason confesses that he was appalled at the prospect of not being able to include a man. After a couple of false starts and still bereft of an idea by mid-January, he recalled hearing 'of a Lesbian couple with a child, and that the mother of the child still dressed as a man.' The way Diana told it to the director and cast of an amateur production in 2005, it was she who casually mentioned to Bruce that she had delivered a lesbian couple's baby and when they left the maternity ward, one was dressed as a man. 'This was all I knew but it was enough,' Mason adds: 'at last I had a situation of tension between two mature women and a young one.' He also found an unexpected ally in American author Marilyn French, whose book *The Women's Room* had recently engrossed his wife and daughters. 'This wise, tender and compassionate work suggested to me that—thirty-four years of marriage notwithstanding—women had needs and options I had never considered. Such considerations I have reverently attempted in *Blood of the Lamb*.'[3]

While it may be so that the women in his earlier plays have been cast in traditional roles, they are strongly drawn in realistic terms and there is an implicit socio-political consciousness at play in depicting their lots in life, even where the male-dominant status quo is reinstated. At first glance *Blood of the Lamb* could be seen as more of the same, with 'Henry' and 'Eliza' adopting active male and passive female roles. However as it plays out, their backstories and the ways they manage the present situation do arise from the different world view Mason has exposed himself to and brought to his imagining. As with his depictions of Māori he does not purport to represent all lesbians or even typical lesbians here, but this couple in particular whose adoption of male/female roles is entirely credible.

In declaring the play 'is now offered for production anywhere in the world,' Mason stipulates there is to be 'no transposition of theme or setting into another country (implying that, say, English audiences lack the ability to project themselves imaginatively into the South Pacific).' Recalling how *Birds in the Wilderness* might have been picked up from the showcase season at London's Lyric Theatre if Mason had been prepared to relocate it to Northern Ireland, which 'would have made mincemeat, not to say nonsense, of my theme', Mason insists *Blood of the Lamb* must travel 'true to label'—just as Henry travels as Gladys when overseas—or not at all. In presenting his 'two précieuses, pedantic, clerkly Eliza and wild-lungeing [sic] bawdy Henry, as New Zealand archetypes', he refers, presumably, to Moliere's one-act satire *Les Précieuses Ridicules*, which caricatures the witty and educated intellectual ladies who met in seventeenth-century Parisian salons to indulge in lively conversations and word games.

> The tribulations implied by the title come from life in New Zealand's 'green, indiff'rent land' but then, so do their victories. Nor do actresses abroad need to struggle towards a coarse Kiwi patois: my ladies speak standard English. Victoria's speech, though, has accreted adhesions and abrasions from her five years in Australia, and will not be authentic without them. If these stern provisos are faithfully observed, *Blood of the Lamb* may take any stage with my blessing.[4]

The play's full title is *Blood of the Lamb or Così Fan Poche, A Three Part Invention in homage to WA Mozart and GB Shaw*. The main title relates to a graphically described story Henry tells of how she, as Gladys, lost her virginity and became pregnant to a Gisborne-born, Christ College-educated, Drury farm manager who interrupted what would have been a consensual act of seduction to slaughter an injured lamb, then bathed in its blood before taking his now appalled bride-to-be by force.[5] It also refers to the cleansing power of revelation:

> These are they which came out of great tribulation, and have washed their robes and made them white in the blood of the Lamb.—the Revelation of St. John the Divine, 14.

Così Fan Poche (thus do a few women) is a variation on Mozart's *Così Fan Tutte* (thus do all women). Shaw's *Pygmalion*—which in turn draws its title from 'The Story of Pygmalion and the Statue' in Ovid's *Metamorphoses* and involves the idea of women being 'made over'—is referenced in how the two older women reinvented themselves as Henry Higginson and Eliza Doolittle Higginson by virtue of becoming market gardeners. Victoria's insistence on understanding why and how the pair she calls her parents metamorphosed from Gladys Mary Talbot and Jennifer Louise Adams into Henry and Eliza drives the play's core action. While there are two acts, each with two scenes, the action is continuous. Each scene commences with an action replay of the last beat of the previous scene.

The credibility of Victoria's growing up unaware her transvestite 'father' is a woman may seem problematical if the play is seen as naturalistic, but such devices have been common in theatre through the centuries, not least in Shakespeare's plays (where initially it was men who played women masquerading as men) and in opera, which is constantly referenced throughout the play. There are also many actual historical precedents, including New Zealand-connected Harry Crawford, born Eugenia Falleni (whose story inspired the play *Eugenia* by Lorae Parry, Victoria University Press, 1996), and Amy Bock, also known as Percy Redwood (dramatised as *In Confidence: Dialogues with Amy Bock* by Fiona Farrell).[6] Besides, Victoria went to boarding school from the age of six, was only home for the holidays and did not bring friends home. It was when school was over for good that she saw Henry stripped to the waist in a remote part of 'the acreage'. Aghast at the idea that her father—or is he her stepfather?—was a hermaphrodite 'freak', she took off to Australia without explanation.[7] Although it is conceded there were 'raised eyebrows, furtive sniggers,' in the district, no one ever asked if Mr Higginson was 'in *fact* a man. Who's going to ask that? In this country? No one.'[8] Henry stands in the crossover realm where, as a woman she would be considered butch and as a man he would be seen as effeminate. Within the play, Henry's camp theatricality may be seen, in part, as a defence against the fear that revealing the truth will alienate Victoria from them forever. The stakes are high as the stories are told to explain how the present came to pass, which brings true dramatic energy to the play. Mason's love of eloquence is fully realised as the stories unfold, mostly through Henry who, in refusing to confirm she is 'a raving bloody butch dyke,' adds, 'rave, I don't. Never have. Cascades of eloquence? That I grant you.'[9]

The status and nature of Gladys/Henry and Jenny/Eliza's lesbianism is gradually revealed, echoing the growing of their own awareness. They saw their affection for each other at boarding school, from age thirteen, as normal. Inseparable, they spent their holidays together or 'wrote the stickiest letters since glue was invented' but it was 'totally innocent. Puppy love . . . What else do you expect, in the gynaeceum?' While at university, where they studied classics together, both winning prizes, Gladys was living at home, Jenny was in a hostel, and they saw each other every day. But Gladys saw marriage to Rodney Kirkland as inevitable destiny and had no problem with heterosexual sex until what she anticipated would be her consensual loss of virginity turned into rape, preceded by the slaughter of the wounded lamb: a savage induction into 'the ways of Kirklees'. She was too exhausted to resist his further 'love-making'—'it didn't hurt quite so much; in fact I rather enjoyed it'—but knew her life had changed forever: 'He had taught me, in one horrific, blood-dripping image, what men are, what my country is, what history was—a bloody charnel-house—and I wanted no part of it, ever.'[10]

Gladys' subsequent sexual preference arose, therefore, from a rejection of men and all they stood for, as life partners especially. In contrast there is no suggestion Jenny has had any heterosexual encounters, and it may be assumed she is lesbian. Although she accepted her role as chief bridesmaid to Gladys without question, it was Jenny who, after they had escaped to Gisborne, saved Gladys from a drunken and furious Rodney's further assault by shouting that he could not marry her because she and Gladys were lovers. 'I still don't know why I said it,' she tells Victoria: 'it wasn't true; I scarcely knew the word Lesbian.' But it literally made Rodney sick and he staggered off. And soon after, at Maungatokerau, inland from Tologa Bay, they found white water flowing down a sheer cliff, 'three basins, each filling the next', the lowest at their feet. They tore off their clothes, sank to their necks, 'reached for each other, embraced, and wept, wept, wept, [vowed] never to harm, much less kill, anything that lived and breathed . . . swore undying love [and] there, on the grass, above that magical spring . . . became lovers.'[11]

Questioned about how faithful they have been, Henry does admits to the 'odd excursion' abroad, and given it is earlier mentioned that she travels 'true to label' as Gladys,[12] and had 'rather enjoyed it' with Rodney,[13] it is reasonable to deduce her extracurricular encounters had been heterosexual. (Mason uses feminine pronouns for Henry in his stage directions so they are maintained here.) While ever-faithful Eliza is incontrovertibly lesbian, Henry is probably bisexual; the flipside of a married man who has occasional homosexual encounters (a scenario Mason never visited in his plays although it was central to his own life). Having scoffed at the conventional nature of their unequal relationship—'Just like any straight marriage! Dad has a bit on the side, mum swallows her tears and smiles bravely into the sink!'—Victoria wants to know how they make love. She represents the limits of heterosexual understanding by quoting Scheherazade's phrase (from *The Thousand and One Nights*) about two young girl lovers, who 'had two bodies and not a single clarinet to play.' It is Henry who counters with *The Book of Common Prayer*'s 'Solemnisation of Matrimony':

> You don't have to understand it, Victoria: just accept it. It's a human option, a—(*reads from the Service*): 'natural affection, implanted'—for all I know—'by God'. (*She closes the book.*) As our divine and darling Wolfgang Amadeus might have said, 'Così Fan Poche'. Thus do a *few* ladies. And not so damn few, either.[14]

Victoria is robustly heterosexual. When Henry denigrates the most notorious military leaders of history as 'erectile tissue,' Victoria cries, 'But that's the part I like!'[15] Despite spending so much time away from home, she emulates both her mother's eloquence and her pragmatic approach to resolving big issues. For example, in order to accommodate Amilcare's desire for the Nuptial Mass she 'couldn't care less' about, she has undergone 'a satisfactory course of instruction in the [Roman Catholic] Faith', even though she calls it 'hot air baloney'.[16] So beneath her strong-willed, no-nonsense 'Aussie sheila' persona, she—like her other mother-figure, Eliza—is prepared to compromise for love.

Victoria's maternal grandparents (parents of Gladys/Henry) are glimpsed sufficiently to offer meaningful contrasts with the later generations. Hugh Talbot, a leading Auckland barrister, 'was a frantic, rip-roaring old tomcat, always out on the tiles.' His wife Ruth was the 'daughter of a rich Waikato cattle baron'. Gladys, their only child, was only five when Ruth died, officially of angina, but Henry thinks it was of grief. 'I barely remember her. Just a sad, frail little wraith, a melancholy tendril that waves in my mind.'[17] But it was Ruth's money that paid for her husband's 'wicked ways' and gave Gladys the trust fund, payable on her twenty-first birthday, that allowed Henry and Eliza to buy their market garden: 'By 1959, it had accumulated to nearly nineteen thousand pounds, a tidy sum, then.'[18]

Jenny/Eliza's father was, and probably still is, a Hamilton accountant and her mother is never mentioned. She has neither seen nor heard from, or of, her parents or five brothers 'for donkey's years', apart from about three years ago when her eldest brother, Harold, came into the shop to order a corsage: 'I knew him instantly and a big, fat, prosperous slob he was too. I put on dark glasses, kept my eyes down, mumbled away in a glottal Kiwi bleat. He didn't recognise me, I'll swear.'[19] To consolidate this familial estrangement, the actress playing Eliza would have to make up a private backstory for her character, probably to do with running away from ignorance, intolerance, persistent questions about boyfriends, who she would marry and when.

Mason's most searing critique of the Kiwi male is reserved for the 'landed gentry' Kirklands and their sense of entitlement: Victoria's biological father, Rodney, and her paternal grandfather, George. Gladys' first impression of Rodney was that he was 'good-looking, twenty-six, randy as a buck rat and thirsting for a wife', having screwed his way around the world on a 'Cork's Tour'—'short for corkscrew. A screw in every port . . . That man was Priapus incarnate . . . He could have been a national monument, like the Pohutu geyser, tirelessly erupting every hour on the hour.' With her father's blessing, Rodney would take Gladys for drives in his 'spanking new Jaguar', strip her to the waist, clamp his mouth to her breasts 'like a giant suckling baby.' Although she 'relieved his tension' she would not let him 'rifle her chaste treasure'—she 'stuffed it full of tampax'—so 'one day, Rodney, man of few words and those basic, said "Fuck this love-talk; let's get married".'[20] This, followed by the 'blood of the lamb' episode, the initiation into 'the ways of Kirklees', the drunken pursuit to Gisborne to violently retrieve his fleeing bride and his vomiting at discovering she was a lesbian, must qualify as New Zealand literature's most vivid characterisation of a farming family's 'heir apparent'.

Mason captures the generational depth of their value system by having Rodney's mother Sybil—by Eliza's account—ring the Gisborne hotel to give Gladys her blessing and get 'walloped' by

George for her trouble. And the network of patriarchal power is confirmed when the 'tomcat barrister' Hugh Talbot rings to abuse his daughter 'in a hideous, roaring eruption of filthy words' only to have a stroke, albeit mild, in the process.[21]

Eliza explains to a puzzled Victoria that she calls Henry 'he' because, 'Henry's Henry. I never think of him as anything else. He wears the pants as you might say'. And when Victoria points out Mozart was a man, she exclaims, 'But we don't hate all men!' and Henry adds, 'They have their uses, as you've been discovering, Victoria. It's Caesar we hate.' Eliza includes Hannibal, Genghis Khan, Napoleon, Hitler and Stalin in the group Henry calls 'Wreckers. Destroyers. Man as erectile tissue.' Henry responds to Victoria's liking that part with, 'Then, bully for you, but there's a place for it: keep it there.'[22] Anyone who participated, or became embroiled in, casual or formal debates about feminism in the 1970s will recognise the validity of this exchange.

Two Māori men in particular are profiled as part of the Pokorua Pā community on the foothills of the Raukūmaras where, in 1959, Gladys and Jenny took refuge in the guise of 'a married couple who had suffered some nameless sorrow.' Mohi Tutanga was the young man they found spread-eagled on the tray of his truck at Tologa Bay amid the apples, carrots, swedes, turnips and kūmara that he was there to sell. In response to Victoria's derision: 'Enter the Noble Savage. Despised and rejected by the Pakeha world, they found shelter with our brown brothers, simple children of nature. Pause for a puke', Henry is quick to tell her 'the Maori world, if you don't know it already, is a male chauvinist pigsty.' But Mohi, who called them 'dollies' and was a 'hound dog' with 'roving hands, that had to be slapped down' became a compassionate conspirator once he had 'just about bust a gut' at being 'wised up' about the nature of their relationship. Eliza explains it was Mohi who found Gladys a 'shapeless old tweed suit, the colour of porridge [that] gave him an elephant crutch [and] there was a horrible little polka-dot blue tie' that clipped on, before presenting them to Hakaraia, 'the kaumatua . . . nearly eighty, white bearded, almost blind . . . Covered with moko [he] lived in a kind of grubby pomp, with women to attend to his every need, and an imperious old bastard he was too.'[23]

Their new home is described as: 'A community of about twenty families, all related [and] almost self-supporting: they lived entirely off the land. Sold pigs and vegetables and fruit to pay for what they needed. Not much: clothing, kids' schooling.' The young couple were blissfully happy there, learning the rudiments of market gardening and introducing flowers as a cash crop too, which led to their adopting the Eliza and Henry names. When the returns on sales improved, 'the kaumatua composed a waiata in our honour; we were celebrated on the marae in song and dance.' Loose shirts and baggy pants allowed Henry to conceal the pregnancy for nearly eight months, but when she fainted between two rows of corn and could work no more, 'People had begun to stare, whisper, giggle, particularly the kids. They would tag him, call out "tanewahine!"—man-woman—and rush off in stitches.' When old Hakaraia was told, 'the Heavens fell in. If at Kirklees, we had betrayed class, family, home and decency, at Pokorua, we had betrayed the universe! We were monstrosities, convulsions of nature.' Although Mohi spoke up for the couple at the huge marae meeting, from which they were excluded, the kaumātua—who felt 'we had defiled the mana of the entire pa; through us the whole hapu was in a state of mortal sin'—decreed they must be banished. Even when Gladys/Henry went into premature labour, before they could be driven to the Tologa Bay Cottage Hospital, she was too tapu to be touched by the old ruahine (midwife), who issued instructions to Eliza.[24]

This picture of a late 1950s Māori community on the East Coast differs significantly from the happy-go-lucky and somewhat dissolute lifestyle at early 1950s Tamatea, implied by a starry-eyed Reverend Athol Sedgwick in *The Pohutukawa Tree*. In contrast to the matriarchy of Aroha Mataira, however, the patriarchal misogyny of Werihe Paku is clearly apparent in *Awatea*, set in the early 1960s. While all three communities predate the cultural shifts that came with television, a decade or so separates Mason's writings of the two earlier plays. There is another decade between his revision of *Awatea* and writing *Blood of the Lamb*, so his own maturing perception of the realities of Māori culture may in part account for the differences. By 1980, the social and political drives towards more publicly apparent equality for women and Māori became quite challenging for some;

individual behaviour and use of language could be challenged to the point where fear of being culturally insensitive or politically incorrect inhibited some people. While the arts and artists came in for their fair share of criticism, Mason was never one to pussyfoot around such minefields. He shocks his audiences into challenging themselves by articulating opposing views through characters who are true to themselves. His pleasure in paradox is also evident in the way Henry and Eliza reveal Victoria was named in honour of the queen who refused to outlaw lesbians 'on the grounds that no woman could do anything so disgusting'. And Henry does concede that Victoria's survival, under the rudimentary circumstances of her birth, was partly due to Rodney's 'good genes'.[25]

Echoing *The Pohutukawa Tree* and *The End of the Golden Weather* is Mason's recurring critique of the impact of colonisation on the New Zealand landscape. This is probably the closest Mason gets to an editorial voice, and here the polemic is delivered through Henry's description of Kirklees:

> Rolling dale on dale of the crispest and freshest green; the huge, slowly moving white carpet, here and there a rogue strand of black, of the thousands upon thousands of sheep. A century before, these were the tribal lands of the Ngati-Kahungunu and the Rongowhakaata, dense with jungle-thick bush and throbbing, I don't doubt, with omen and portent. And now? Not a single native tree, not a scrap of bush, not a fern, not a flower; no trace whatever of a people who had lived and fought and loved and died here for over five hundred years. In one century, the Kirklands had turned it into Yorkshire which, but for the brilliant light, it might well have been. We arrived at a little copse of English trees by a stream, ludicrously—God, how ludicrously!—landscaped to look like *The Hay Wain* by John Constable, even to the tumble-down cottage and a plaster horse between the shafts.[26]

Setting the rape of Gladys within this context echoes the taking by force of the land itself and the defiling of Māori culture.

The place of religion is also a recurring theme for Mason, and here there are interesting comparisons to be made with the Old Testament versus New Testament battle of wits in *Hongi*, the shattering disillusionment Johnny and Aroha experience in *The Pohutukawa Tree* and the more comic confrontation the boy has with his faith in *The End of the Golden Weather*. Gladys and Jenny went to Diocesan School for Girls in Auckland, an Anglican boarding school, but as Henry and Eliza they are no longer church-goers, arguably because the rejection of their lesbianism by the Pokorua community kaumātua back in the late 1950s was seen as 'a mortal sin'. Nevertheless they sent Victoria to another Anglican boarding school, Craighead Diocesan School for Girls in Timaru, where she received a prize in Divinity in 1974. However, she never went to church other than at school. Despite her insincere embrace of the Catholic Church to please Amilcare, she sees the prospect of being given away by her mother masquerading as her father as a 'squalid farce', is unimpressed by Henry's asking 'is the Church so averse to dressing up?', and threatens to 'spill the rancid beans' to Father Mulcahy.[27]

Even after she has heard the whole story, and despite empathising with them over many recollected moments, Victoria remains upset that she was unwittingly cast in their farce: 'a hostage to your lifestyle'. Here Mason executes the classic device of making all seem lost before the miracle of resolution is achieved. When Henry concedes they got it all wrong and counsels Victoria to go with Ham, 'without a backward look. Ka mutu. E finita la commedia' (meaning: the end; the farce is finished), it seems intolerance has won the day. But Victoria is asking for authenticity:

VICTORIA: *(after a long pause)* Mother.

ELIZA*'s eyes flick towards* VICTORIA *in surprise*; HENRY *does not move.*

VICTORIA: *(slightly louder)* Mother.

HENRY *slowly turns and looks at her.* VICTORIA *comes up to her slowly.* HENRY *and* ELIZA *look at each other carefully, then collapse in an embrace.*

Victoria wants the wedding to go ahead as planned: 'It's just that we can't go through that charade in church. That would be more than parody; nearer blasphemy. And it's not necessary! Now that I know, why pretend?' Henry can wear an elegant trouser suit and 'be *mother* of the bride!' Because no one considers the possibility of a bride's mother giving her daughter away, Victoria suggests Henry's Italian tutor, Alessandro Scotti, should do the honours: 'It would be a compliment to Ham and his brother, to you and, for that matter, me.' It is Eliza who misses out in this arrangement, so there is subtextual pathos in her observation: 'You realise we're at the end of an era, Henry?'

The denouement lets Eliza acknowledge this country still allows 'the fresh start; the new life' and declare it is good they have been forced to change: 'Diamonds are made under the highest pressure, they tell me.' She is delighted to learn Victoria will stand up for herself in the marriage, and observes that her stroppiness makes her their daughter. Eliza gets Victoria to agree that parents are 'those that feed and clothe, nurse and nourish, read stories, sing songs and hold your hand in the dark.' As she settles into completing work on the veil, she asks if Victoria would still have left them if they had gradually revealed the truth of their lifestyle and what led up to it, as they'd intended, over the few weeks after she'd left school.[28]

VICTORIA: (*after a brief reflection*) I think so. Yes, I couldn't have handled it then. I'd still have found it . . . yucky.
ELIZA: And now? Still yucky?
VICTORIA: (*with sudden affection*) No . . . Eliza.
ELIZA: (*parodying the moronic drawl of the notorious television commercial for 'Ajax'*) 'Was yucky: now, not'. (*In normal voice*) Well, I guess that's the most we can expect from this time and clime.

Resolution achieved, Mason creates a pleasing dramatic 'book-end' by bringing Henry back on '*in the full rig and fig of Father of the Bride: grey topper, cutaway coat, striped pants, pearl-grey waistcoat, cravat, pearl pin.*' It is the last hurrah for her male drag, expressed in a hyper-tragic parody of Pagliacci—she plays six bars on her oboe—'before the dread dominion of the trouser suit' claims her. All three dance and join in singing 'a welcoming paean! Vittoria ed Amilcare', which is a garbled version of 'Non più andrai' from *Le Nozze di Figaro*, reprised from

'Father of the bride'—Elizabeth Moody (Henry) and Judie Douglass (Eliza) in *Blood of the Lamb*. Court Theatre, directed by Elric Hooper, designed by Simon Alison (March 1980).

their Act 1, Scene 1 greeting of Victoria, to which they march off.[29]

As with all his plays, in claiming the playwright's advantage of putting differing views in the mouths of his characters rather than revealing and expounding his own, Mason has once more reflected the 'form and pressure' of the age and left his audience with plenty to ponder. While he began by exploring what it is to be a man in New Zealand, he ends by exploring the state and status of women; of same sex couples in particular. It is tempting to see Mason's own secret homosexuality reflected in this play's concerns and to sense a poignant resonance in Victoria's call to live an authentic life.

Although *Blood of the Lamb* should be produced true to its time, the 1980s, its core themes remain relevant. Whatever is regarded as 'old thinking' by later generations will always be history worth remembering, lest it be repeated. Despite being contained in a single set, in linear time, and within one afternoon, the story that unfolds is epic, both in terms of these particular characters and the wider social histories their stories reveal. While Mason ensures there is plenty of drama in the present action to complement the dynamics inherent in the past events, the story material could well be developed as a feature film, or tele-feature, that brings the past into present action, filtered through subjective memory to allow for moments of operatic hyperbole. But Mason's brief was to write a play for three women, so that's what he did, trusting his audience's imaginations would create the other characters and paint the rich pictures his script evokes. *Blood of the Lamb* is a classic case of creative constraint producing a theatrical gem: a diamond 'made under the highest pressure.'[30]

CHAPTER SEVENTEEN

PARTING SHOTS

Two Sketches and Four Teleplays

Bruce Mason did not go gently through the last year of his life. His 'rage against the dying of the light'[1] took the form of prolific writing: accepting commissions to write two revue sketches for Wellington Repertory and complete four teleplays for Television New Zealand (TVNZ).

Mason was conferred with an Honorary Doctorate in Literature by Victoria University of Wellington in 1977, the year before he was diagnosed with cancer of the jaw. In the 1980 New Year Honours, while he was feverishly writing *Blood of the Lamb* for The Court Theatre, the Crown made him a Commander of the Civil Division of the Most Excellent Order of the British Empire (CBE). Given his critiques of Britain's impact on the New Zealand landscape, he would doubtless have preferred Companion of the New Zealand Order of Merit (CNZM), but New Zealand would not establish its own award system until 1996.

In an audiotape sent to his friend Mike Ross in 1981, Mason spoke of plans to write two new plays. *King, Queen, Jack* would dramatise a collision between a scruffy Māori youth, a has-been English actor and a recently widowed lady called Augusta Briggs. This might have had its genesis in Mason's relationship with C in Christchurch. The other play, unnamed, was to be about Labour politician and potential party leader Colin Moyle. In 1977 Prime Minister Robert Muldoon had, under parliamentary privilege, accused Moyle of being questioned by police on suspicion of homosexual activities. No charges were laid, but Moyle resigned (making way for David Lange to enter parliament in the by-election). There is no evidence either play was drafted so we can only guess how Mason might have treated those stories, but his sharing the ideas with Ross suggests he was at least contemplating new plays with gay male characters and themes.[2]

It was also in 1981 that Mason painstakingly recorded his solo shows for the NZBC Radio, holding up the right side of his cancer-compromised face to aid articulation. It is fair to assume it was being confronted with his mortality that drove him to accept the challenges of the revue sketch and teleplay commissions, in 1982. While this book has focused on his stage plays, these final works are surveyed because they offer an insight into 'where he was at' in what became the last year of his life.

'Madame Bluebottle', a sketch dedicated to the Wellington Repertory Theatre's 'honourable Fergus Dick, whose inspired idea it was' relocates Puccini's *Madama Butterfly* plot to Wellington: the Japanese Embassy and a brothel called The Purple Oyster (a variation on Wellington's best-known covert brothel, The Purple Onion). Outrageous stereotypes decree the 'Engrish' spoken by the Japanese Ambassador and 'Rootenanat' Guchi Yamaguchi of the Imperial Japanese Navy is 'atlocious'. The brothel Madame, for whom Guchi has fallen, has 'abjured her rife of sin' and taken a pseudo-Japanese name: Cha Cha Face. She performs a tea ceremony using chunky New Zealand Railway cups. Puccini's *Madama Butterfly* music is used throughout and 'Un bel di, vedremo' is parodied to convey the torment of this particular wife awaiting the return of her long-gone husband.

Another sketch, 'Darling: You Were Wonderful!', unpacks the fragile ego of a leading actress with a subtly savage yet compassionate accuracy It is set in Sybil's dressing room immediately after her opening performance in *The Queen Must Die*: a fictitious play set during the Spanish Inquisition at the time of the equally fictitious Pope Sylvester X (and apparently foisted on its director, Fergus Dick, by Wellington Repertory). Derek's fawning attempts to praise her are wilfully misconstrued by Sybil as admiration for everyone else and denigration of her performance. Such is the skill of Mason's psychologically insightful writing that despite her appalling self-centeredness, there is pathos in her inevitable self-inflicted isolation and loneliness.

Although television was not his preferred medium, Mason had adapted *The Evening Paper* for the launch of television drama in 1965. In the 1970s he had written a number of episodes of the long-running series *Close to Home* and scripted a six-part documentary series called *Hello Goodbye* (1975), which drew on studio and stock

footage to profile recent popular music. NZ On Screen records that the four teleplays TVNZ commissioned were on a theme of Mason's own choosing: the importance of tolerance, which is especially poignant in light of his inability to dramatise the gay subculture of which he was a part. Although Mason makes no mention of the binding theme in his notes to the scripts, tolerance versus intolerance can be perceived as the generator of dramatic energy within the very different scenarios. Three of the four teleplays were produced in Dunedin by John Anderson, who also directed two of them. They were broadcast in 1983, the year after Mason's death.

There is little indication Mason had fully embraced the visual language values Ian Mune had attempted to impress upon him as they adapted *The End of the Golden Weather* for the big screen. The film premiered in 1991, so Mason did not live to see it. Although

The Governor General, Sir David Beattie, presents Bruce Mason with his CBE (1980). They had grown up together in Takapuna. SUE HIRST tele-movies like Mike Walker's *Kingi's Story* (1981) thrived on the power of the picture and emotional subtext, Mason's scripts remained steadfastly dialogue-driven; a quality that renders his best stage plays rich and dynamic, but can sound overblown on screen, especially given the naturalistic acting style TVNZ required in those days. They were not ready to embrace the heightened 'reality and non-naturalism' being pioneered in television drama by British playwright Dennis Potter (his ground-breaking *Pennies From Heaven* was made by BBC TV in 1978, although his richly eloquent *The Singing Detective* was not produced until 1986).

Nevertheless, Mason's critical enquiries continued into what it is to be a man, a woman, in a close relationship, in a family and in a New Zealand that is socially and morally repressed, and therefore hypocritical. Implicit in his critiques is the plea for tolerance. Given he had focused on Māori in his five *Healing Arch* plays, then decided, in 1968, to leave the ground he had 'turned over' to the impressive array of new Māori writers,[3] this quartet of teleplays may be seen as his parting shot across the stern of Pākehā New Zealand.

Daphne and Chloe

The name of the longest of Mason's quartet of teleplays, *Daphne and Chloe* (one hour), is a twist on the Greek classic *Daphnis and Chloe*, in which the titular boy and girl are abandoned, raised as shepherds and learn the truth about love the hard way.

That the author, Longus, lived on Lesbos may be relevant to Mason's choice of title. Although the original story—which is also the basis of a one-act operetta by Offenbach and a ballet by Ravel choreographed by Fokine—does not relate to lesbianism, it is one of the areas of intolerance Mason addresses here, possibly drawing subtextual parallels with his own experience of being gay.

Classical music lover and advertising account manager Edith Barnes (forty), and hobby wood-whittler and accountant Daphne Stringer (a little older), live in adjoining beachfront units. Together they swim each morning, drive to work, lunch and dine, and attend concerts. Edith is also learning Italian in anticipation of a trip they plan to take to the home of opera (echoing James in *Swan Song* and Henry in *Blood of the Lamb*). Both women work for the advertising company Willoughby and Weems, 'House of your Dreams' (as with *Zero Inn*, Mason draws on his own work experience). When twenty-two-year-old Kevin McDermott, the new 'rouseabout', starts work as Edith's assistant, he cannot believe the elegant Edith is really forty. Bernie, the office predator who has failed to 'score' with her, dares Kevin to try his luck.

But a sincere relationship develops with Edith awakening Kevin to an appreciation of Ravel, Shostakovich, Brahms, et al, and the wonders of the Italian language, culminating in their making love (with the '*utmost delicacy*').[4] Although there is no clear evidence that Daphne and Edith have had a sexual relationship, Daphne feels deeply betrayed and bitter at losing companionship with her closest friend. Edith is fully aware her relationship with Kevin will probably end badly for her, but it is ten years since George, the great love of her life, died in a tragic accident and she needs this. Despite Kevin's resistance to Bernie's crass probing over whether he scored—'Mind your own damn' business!'[5]—Bernie gleefully feeds the gaggle of gossips who make up the typing pool. It is he who has come up with the gag about 'our two Lebanese friends, Daphne and Chloe,' not that there is any indication anyone is classically educated enough to get the joke. His quaint use of 'Lebanese' for lesbian is probably also a joke, although the implication is that some of the other characters don't know the difference.

The arrival at Willoughby and Weems of young Susan, also to be mentored in copywriting by Edith, turns Kevin's head and, inevitably, a relationship blossoms between them. Having predicted her idyll with Kevin could not last, Edith attempts to be sanguine about Kevin's new girlfriend, but is shattered by a harsh dressing-down from Susan in which she refers to Kevin as Edith's gigolo, claims 'the whole place is busting its sides' about their affair (echoing the anonymous assertion about Mason's affairs with C), and reveals the 'Daphne and Chloe' nicknames.[6] That evening, Daphne finds Edith unconscious on her apartment floor, presumably from an overdose, and calls an ambulance. When Daphne manoeuvres for Kevin to lose his job and he goes, taking Susan with him, the companionship between Daphne and Edith resumes.

Given Mason's more open representation of lesbianism in *Blood of the Lamb or Cosi Fan Poche*—'Thus do a few ladies. And not so damn' few, either.'[7]—written less than two years before, we have to suppose he acquiesced to the more conservative limitations of public television by simply implying Daphne and Edith's relationship here. In both cases it is fair to note that while one partner is fundamentally lesbian (or may be, in the case of Daphne), the other was originally straight and then turned to lesbianism through either disaffection with brutal men (Henry) or grief and loneliness (Edith). Until Edith met the classical-music-and-nature-loving George, however, Edith was also bored by New Zealand men: 'All that crudeness and mateship. All that blind rage. "God's Own Country!" Spare me.'[8] In *Blood of the Lamb*, when Victoria tries to understand how the physical relationship between her mother/father (Henry) and nurturing mother (Eliza) works, Henry refers to the solemnisation of matrimony by replying, 'It's a human option, a—(*reads from the Service*): "natural affection, implanted"—for all I know—"by God".'[9] So when Kevin observes that the way Daphne and Edith share their lives is 'full of interest but it's hardly a full life, is it?'[10], we cannot assume he speaks for Mason.

Intolerance towards older women taking younger men as their lovers (to which Daphne is as vehemently opposed as Susan), and of close relationships between women, be they intimate or not, is also critiqued by Mason. As depicted in the television production, Daphne has a single bed and Edith has a double, however it is never indicated that the women share the double. Even though lesbianism was not illegal, as male homosexuality was at the time, it seems TVNZ believed its viewers could not tolerate it, which effectively demolished Mason's plea for tolerance. As Eliza puts it in *Blood of the Lamb*: 'The world acts as if it didn't exist, because it won't consider it.'[11] Given gay male relationships and bisexual men are conspicuous by their absence in Mason's work, it is worth wondering whether he hoped we would extrapolate from these two plays in confronting our intolerance of all same sex relationships. If so, he is arguably putting intolerance of his own affairs with much younger men up for scrutiny as well.

The Garlick Thrust

In *The Garlick Thrust* (originally submitted as *The Game and the Rules*) Mason returns to the viewpoint of a twelve-year-old boy. The small farming community where it is set (somewhere between Hamilton in the Waikato and the Waioeka River in the Bay of Plenty) in the winter of 1981, is a far cry, however, from *The End of the Golden Weather*'s Te Parenga c.1933–1934. A parallel could be drawn between 'The Night of the Riots' and the 'civil war' raging over the Springbok rugby tour, with anti-apartheid demonstrators taking direct action to disrupt the games. But young rugby-loving Geoff Garlick's 'Cinderella' status in a dysfunctional farming family makes him significantly different from the earlier boy (also named Geoff in the film version of *The End of the Golden Weather*). In his author's note, Mason simply states, 'The purpose of this play is to show an area of stability in a chaotic domestic situation, with which a child is heroically coping.'[12]

The first we see of Geoff is at school on a Friday afternoon. He has stayed back to align his teacher and rugby coach, Mr Griffiths, to the 'emergency thrust' strategy he has devised as Mountford Normal's secret weapon in the shield match against Merrick Intermediate. The game is to be played the following morning, the same day the All Blacks versus Springboks test is scheduled to be played in Hamilton. It is Mr Griffiths who dubs Geoff's move 'The Garlick Thrust.'[13]

At home, as always after school, Geoff is obliged to look after his baby nephew Bubby, whose mother Louise (Geoff's sister) works in a factory. While illegally on the Domestic Purposes Benefit (DPB), Louise pays most of it to Mrs Jesson who looks after Bubby during the day, gives farmer Bert his lunch, and prepares the evening meal. Louise has to do this because such domestic tedium made her 'take it out on Bubby'.[14] The older brothers, Roy and Neville, work at the mill and also expect to be paid for any work on the farm. They all treat Geoff as their domestic servant and he has a clear sense of the order required to avoid total chaos (for example, ensuring there is beer in the fridge; telling Louise to leave money for Mrs Jesson so that she does not get reported). It emerges that their mother (Bert's wife) ran away with a passing carnival two years ago, about the same time Louise got pregnant.

Also there for the night is Louise's current boyfriend, Derek, whose car will take her and her older brothers to the big game in Hamilton, where they plan to 'knock the shit out of' the protesters.[15] They will be leaving early and Bert is determined to go fishing up the Waioeka, a two-hour drive away, before the sun gets to his favourite pool. He has no interest in seeing the test—'Knuckle, punch up, knocking shit: what's that do for the game?'[16]—and Geoff agrees. Everyone assumes Geoff will look after Bubby; Mrs Jesson cannot as she is going to Taupo for the weekend.

The next morning, after he has juggled feeding Bubby with preparing a huge fried breakfast for his siblings and Derek, and waved them off to Hamilton, Geoff pins a note to Bubby's pyjamas and, just as his father's alarm goes off, escapes to hitch-hike to school. As Geoff meets with his team and Mr Griffiths to go over their strategy, Bert is obliged to bond with his grandson. The shield match gets under way—and Bert arrives with Bubby. At half time, with his team down by a penalty, Geoff is surprised to find his dad there and not angry. Bert claims it was Bubby who insisted they go to watch Geoff play and Bubby who said getting angry 'was a waste of time'.[17] The second half gets under way, and at the strategic moment 'the Garlick Thrust' is unleashed and Geoff scores the winning try.

The bonding of Geoff with his father as they take Bubby fishing, despite knowing the sun is too high and they won't catch anything, is intercut with actual footage of the anti-tour demonstrations and ensuing violence at Rugby Park in Hamilton. Contemplating his son Geoff and grandson Bubby—the next generations—moves Bert to sudden laughter followed by equally sudden tears, which touches Geoff deeply. Credits roll over their embrace.

The Garlick Thrust is probably the teleplay where Mason succeeds most in giving action and visual language a role in counterpoint to the dialogue, and in the produced version director John Anderson enhances that quality (for example, in the sequence where Geoff runs, in slow-motion, towards his house, lost in a rugby-playing reverie with his school bag as the ball). Script editor Christopher Hampson has also made judicious dialogue cuts to keep the action moving and has rendered the text less flowery in parts (for example, Roy Garlick no longer calls his father 'Pater', 'Pater mine', 'Daddy' and 'Daddy dear').[18]

It is tempting to seek some level of allegory in this work, but while one could perhaps see Geoff's 'Cinderella' status in the Garlick household as similar to a black South African house servant, the metaphor does not hold throughout the drama. The moral thrust is more along the lines of the need to treat each other with respect, domestically and at a national level.

Do Not Go Gentle

Taking its title from the well-known Dylan Thomas poem, the first thing to note about *Do Not Go Gentle* is that its central character, Charlie Jameson, is dying of cancer in his sixty-first year, just as Mason was when he wrote it. After serving with the Air Force in WWII (Mason served in the Navy), Charlie became a travelling salesman, which tempts us to see this half-hour teleplay as Mason's brief Kiwi rejoinder to Arthur Miller's *Death of a Salesman*. While there maybe something heartfelt in the way Mason depicts the loss of 'the Kiwi dream', and he may have drawn on his personal experience of touring solo and having clandestine sexual encounters in lonely motels, it would be wrong to see the raging Charlie, his long-suffering wife, Dora, or their children as in any way autobiographical. As with *Swan Song*, it is uptight and mean-spirited New Zealand he is characterising here, albeit with the boozing and fornicating Kiwi male as its counterpoint.

Charlie is on his deathbed. George Gibbs and Fred Murphy, his mates down at the jetty, which he can see from his window if he strains to sit up, describe Charlie as 'a two G man: girls and grog.' But it's too late to even give him a drink what with Dora on constant guard. While they concede 'Hatchet-face', as they call her, has had it hard with Charlie—'Ah, poor old trout. Poor old bugger. Never right for each other.'—they hatch a plan to get him some grog by cunning and stealth.[19] This becomes the driving quest of the background action.

Dora is a strict Baptist and their now adult children, Derek and Mary, have followed her into the church, leaving Charlie scornful of their intolerance for the creature comforts he holds dear. Dora has suffered his infidelities on the road in silence and openly disapproved of his love of alcohol. Now, as she tells the Reverend Symonds, she knows her duty: 'To see my husband into a Christian grave, at peace with God.'[20] But Charlie is staunchly resistant.

Alone with Dora, it emerges they met at a post-war dance in Paeroa (as did Hingawaru and Miriam in *Hand on the Rail*, and Smithson and Isobel in *Swan Song*). She was lonely and grateful for the attention he, so smart in his Air Force blues, paid her. Now she regards their 'quickie in the tussock grass' as 'squalid; shaming', but, as he recalls it, she was 'ablaze with joy', and he felt full of potential 'to Kingdom Come'. Thinking she was pregnant, she told her parents. Her father insisted they marry, 'so I was hooked,' says Charlie. 'Potential? Down the plughole. And you weren't pregnant at all. False alarm: irregular. Old trick.' Mutually disillusioned, he found solace with 'girls' on the road and she turned to the Church. Now he wants to know, 'What's it all been about, Dora? We come from nowhere, go back to nowhere. My epitaph if you're thinking of one: "He got nowhere fast".'[21]

Edited out of the broadcast version is a remarkable sequence that offers a vivid summary of the difference between men and women. The popular and valid feminist rhetoric of the 1970s is given to Dora. As she plumps up Charlie's pillows while he tells her to smother him and get it over with, he realises he has an erection. He throws the sheets and blankets off and exclaims at this (off-screen) 'wonder of nature.'

DORA: You're incorrigible. Hopeless.

CHARLIE: But aren't you amazed? Don't you say, filthy old beast, right enough, but vitality unquenchable, or some such memorable phrase? On his last legs, he could still get his third leg up. That can be my epitaph, Dora dear. I trust you to have it engraved, send it out by the gross, on gilt-edged cards. 'He was on his last legs, he still–'

Furious, DORA *pulls up the bedclothes.*

DORA: Oh, shut up! You're just like a dirty little dog, cocking that idiotic third leg of yours at the universe. You men. You infants! You think that makes you lords of creation? A few inches of engorged flesh: that makes you kings and emperors? Oh, I know it all; I worked it out years ago.

You fight wars to flash it around, whatever the politicians say. Twenty years, twenty five, and there's a whole generation of you without memories, steaming. Where' the war? No war. Right: let's have one, Korea, Vietnam: what's it matter? Anywhere will do . . . And the same goes for that idiotic game of yours, yes, that Rugby nonsense: a lot of grown men in rut, kicking an egg. Havoc, chaos, that's what your sex stands for. Oh, I've known it all my life.

CHARLIE: Then what does yours stand for? This I must know.

DORA: Harmony, I hope–

CHARLIE: Cracked chords, more like–

DORA: Order, proportion. Men and women? Basic. Creation: that stuff. And then God sets me down beside you, an imbecile child, a cowardly, drunken oaf. My lot? Chaos and discord. And that's the world, it seems to me. A grubby union between potential goddesses and dirty little dogs. Do you wonder I found religion?[22]

How ironic that the moral rectitude of public television should have caused this scene to be cut. Apart from the richness of the debate, it shows Dora to be a much stronger adversary and maintains Mason's dramaturgical strategy of endowing both sides with strong arguments.

Charlie tells the Reverend Symonds he wants 'No service, no choir, no mealy mouthed carry-on.' He wants to be buried at sea from George Gibbs' launch. Showing tolerance for human frailty, the minister agrees to get Dora out of the way so the mates can come and see him, with the longed-for Scotch. In response to Symonds suggesting it is not too late to receive the 'Mercy of God', Charlie retorts: 'Stuff his Mercy! I want his apology . . . [for] this caper, this run-around, this rigmarole. This life He's supposed to have called me into. All simmering with joy.'[23]

When Derek and Mary finally get in to see him, Charlie tells them he feels he was tricked into marriage and paternity and, since they grew up and joined their mother as 'paid up members of the mealy mouthed brigade', they are total strangers to him. He feels Mary has judged him all her life, and asks her if she blames him for her existence. But she replies, 'You gave us life!' Derek asks his father what he wanted.

CHARLIE: Of life? How grandiose can one get? All right. In one word. Glory. I came into this world for Glory, nothing less. (*Sings softly . . .*) 'Some talk of Alexander and some of Hercules . . .'[24] I was Alexander! I was Hercules! War hero. Young in a young country, brimming with fertility. Fresh start, old shackles loose. And what does my young country offer me? The road, with a case of samples. Glory. Oh, glory Hallelujah! Do you know all that can be said of it, this green and pleasant land of ours? It's resounding epitaph? They had good dentists . . . And why? Because we've turned Glory into marshmallow. That's why. (*He struggles to sit up; they help him . . .*) Kids: do you know what's killing me, really killing me? Littleness. Born big, I've been gnawed away by the rats and mice of littleness. Born too big for my boots, I've been cut down to bootie size.[25]

It is very tempting to hear Mason's own voice in this, given what we now know of the magnificent plays he wrote that were ignored by his country's top theatres. It may also be seen as a variation on Philip's 'angry young man' rant in *The Evening Paper*: 'You could have had Paradise here, the Just City! And what have you done? Mucked it. Turned freedom into safety tickets.'[26]

At last, with the tolerant collusion of the Reverend Symonds, Derek and Mary, and George and Fred bring the tipple to the bedside, secreted in a Raro orange juice can, and confirm all is arranged for his burial at sea. Thus Charlie departs 'into that good night' as '*all dissolves into a clear white light.*'[27]

Rise and Shine

The unproduced *Rise and Shine* also confronts approaching death and, like *Swan Song*, focuses on the relationship between an old dying man (called James in both cases) and a much younger woman who has left her controlling husband. Other writers will recognise this syndrome of rebirthing character and story elements that were stillborn in unproduced works. Originally submitted to TVNZ in treatment form as *The Commode*, then *Decline and Fall*, the full script is dated May–June 1982. *Rise and Shine* stands as Mason's final work and, given its small cast and relatively contained geography, mostly in the home of James and Kitty Tyndall and in Marcia Stone's place next door, it could easily be adapted to the stage for a cast of three senior actors and a younger couple in their twenties.

Ex-barrister James Tyndall, KC, QC, CBE (he didn't want the bench) is seventy-six, wheelchair-bound, dying of muscular dystrophy and eloquently cantankerous. His seventy-two-year-old wife, Kitty Tyndall, is so stressed at having to be his nurse that she caps the demeaning task of emptying and cleaning his chamber pot by planting it on his head then curtseying '*with ironical savagery*' and performing mock obeisance before collapsing in a fit of guilt: 'James: forgive me. Sometimes, it's all too much.'[28] She is about to take a weekend off to visit their daughter Thelma and the grandchildren. Neighbour Marcia (sixty-nine), an excellent pianist, will care for him (having done it all before with her large and incapacitated husband George, now deceased). James' putting down of Marcia's incessant piano-playing next door, which will doubtless impede her hearing the bell with which he is supposed to summon her, provokes Kitty to call him a 'selfish, cantankerous old bugger.'[29] When he waxes lyrical about 'bell, book and candle. For excommunication. For extinction', she exclaims: 'My God, the relief it's going to be! To be free of that tongue! Even for a week-end! Love, honour and cherish: that's what I promised. Not listening to a life time of dreary double talk.'[30] Mason may well be satirising his love of eloquence and his own expertise at it here.

When Kitty pops in next door for a final briefing, and a sherry to celebrate her freedom, Marcia claims to 'love that English voice!',[31]even if it does belong to a tyrant. With James, after Kitty has departed, Marcia thrills at such words as 'tintinnabulate' as he reminds her of 'the Byzantine arrangements between me and my commode'.[32] He is settling down to read Edward Gibbon's *Decline and Fall of the Roman Empire* when the taxi returns with Marcia's daughter Bobbie (twenty-five). Next door, Marcia is impatient with her daughter's uncontrollable weeping and, on discovering she has left her husband Dennis and six-month-old son Lancie (with a doting neighbour), she informs Bobbie it is most inconvenient and that her promise to look after Mr Tyndall must come first.[33] In a surprising twist, Bobbie, after gazing at '*the sternly magnificent grandee*', runs to his wheelchair, kneels, puts her head on his lap—rendering James' face '*alive with wonder and disbelief*'—and asks him to help her. She then surprises her mother even more by offering to look after him for the weekend.[34] But Mason tantalises us by not yet revealing the cause of this behaviour.

Wine with lunch has made Marcia '*euphoric and garrulous with it*', leading her to speak—in a pastiche of James' eloquence, riddled with misplaced metaphors—of how marriage and motherhood diverted her from being a concert pianist to becoming 'the unchallenged doyenne of Auckland's music teachers' while raising three hefty sons who have all become engineers, 'dispersed all over the planet'. Bobbie her 'sweet afterthought', is a singer and the only one of her children who turned out to be musical. Marcia dozes off before she can get James to bed for his scheduled sleep, so Bobbie will attend to what he calls the 'odious, not to say odoriferous, chores', which she brushes off by likening it to caring for her child: 'A young baby: a helpless old man? Opposite ends of the life spectrum.'[35]

A post-nap chat between James and Bobbie reveals she has left her ambitious accountant husband Dennis, the self-made son of a railway worker, because he treats her like a chattel, allows her no friends and stops her singing 'because it's an activity he can't share' (Bobbie studied at the Melbourne Conservatorium and 'could have had a fair career'). Dennis also 'wacked Lancie, for filling his pants twice one evening: at six months old!' Worst of all, he binds her breasts: 'He's into the boyish look,' not because he is gay, 'I would have known by now. Because he can't stand women looking like women. They've got to be chums or they challenge male supremacy.' Then to prove to James they are not bound now, she bares her breasts '*her back to the camera . . . with the utmost grace and delicacy.*'[36]

That night, in her living room, Marcia plays Debussy on the piano, while James and Bobbie hold hands, then Bobbie sings 'Caro Mio Ben' by Giuseppe Giordani. Later, having put James to bed, Bobbie tells her baffled mother she loves him: 'It was love at first sight.'[37] Marcia's attempts to get Bobbie to talk about her marriage and contact Dennis are thwarted by the tinkle of James' bell. When he tells Bobbie he had hoped she would come and kiss him goodnight, she says, 'I'll do more than that', '*strips off all her clothes [and] climbs into bed with him.*' Again Mason calls for '*supreme taste and delicacy*'.[38] It is not a sexual encounter—James is impotent—just a snuggling closeness. Meanwhile, in the early hours of the morning, Marcia phones Dennis.

With breakfast over, James declares that eloquence and chivalry are 'twin orbs of the soul.' Prompted by Bobbie he summaries his life, from 'articled clerk, in a good Birmingham firm' from where he would cycle to Stratford every weekend to see Sir Frank Benson as Macbeth and Antony, through a world war and a general strike that together 'killed chivalry, stone dead. What use eloquence, in chaos and cacophony?' He therefore emigrated to New Zealand, where he hoped to at least find 'that innocence of heart, from which chivalry and eloquence can arise.' Instead he found 'a green, unpleasant land. Sour in spirit. With stunted lives and stunted minds.' He married 'an agreeable girl, now a complaining shrew, though I can hardly blame her', and fathered 'three dull children, to whom I can't converse; I never see them and don't want to. As for eloquence, I learnt to thunder away in Court, for fair rewards.'[39] Again, it cannot be said Mason is reflecting his own family life but rather characterising aspects of middle-class New Zealand.

The arrival of Dennis leads to an aggressive confrontation with Bobbie before James convinces her to leave them to talk in private. On hearing that Bobbie slept with James the night before, 'All night long . . . For warmth. For sheer, simple human warmth', Dennis calls him a 'disgusting, dirty old man', whereupon James slaps him hard on both cheeks. James judges Dennis' explanations for his treatment of Bobbie as 'medieval' at first, and then 'Old Testament!' He tells Dennis to 'write your own chivalric code. Act on it.' When Bobbie returns Dennis concedes he is 'a bit' chastened: 'The old sod's made me think.' Alone for a moment with Bobbie, James explains he dealt with Dennis as a 'good deed' to atone for 'five years of spite and contumely' towards his long-suffering wife. 'Now, I can die serene.'[40] And die he does, as Bobbie and Dennis leave to 'work out their salvation. For better, for worse,' as Marcia puts it. She finds James and takes the returning Kitty in her arms. Together they contemplate his serene face, as 'Caro Mio Ben' accompanies the closing credits.[41]

There is an echo of Charlie's rage, in *Do Not Go Gentle*, against the 'littleness' that was imposed on him, in James' judgement of New Zealand as 'a green, unpleasant land. Sour in spirit. With stunted lives and stunted minds.' It is fair to assume both characters channel more than a dram of Mason's personal feeling, given the depth and breadth of the plays he would leave behind and the scant attention that was paid to them by professional theatres during his too-short lifetime.

EPILOGUE:
A PROPHET IN HIS OWN LAND?

Bruce Mason died in Wellington on the last day of 1982, aged sixty-one. His teleplays *Daphne and Chloe*, *The Garlick Thrust* and *Do Not Go Gentle*, as well as the *Kaleidoscope* arts programme featuring Mason, all went to air the following year. When *Kaleidoscope* interviewer Helen Paske asked him what the point of theatre was, the ailing Mason answered:

> It contributes enlightenment. It contributes coherence. It lays a kind of grid on the disorder of the world and out of this, makes sense. That's what it's about. It makes sense and it also makes beauty. There's nothing more exhilarating than a great performance in theatre—nothing; nothing in this world is more exhilarating, except possibly a great performer in opera but you can get the same frisson from a great actor too—and we've got some very good actors.

He revealed that although he had worked for twenty-five years on the assumption that theatre could have a role in changing society, he was no longer sure the arts could do that. When asked why, he replied:

> I don't know, it's just that the great historical events of the past years have neither been prevented nor accelerated, I think, by anything artistic. I still would like to think that the theatre is important; that one's life can be infinitesimally changed by seeing things. And from time to time you see a fine performance in a fine play . . . You go out of the theatre a slightly different person from when you went in. So cautious optimism is how I feel about it now.[1]

In the same *Kaleidoscope* feature, this observation from Ralph McAllister lends weight to the idea that Mason was expressing his own disillusionment through his characters:

> He had a great belief in his own abilities and don't get me wrong if I call him one of the most arrogant people I've ever met. I think arrogance is a sadly underestimated virtue. We have it when we're young but we tend to lose it as we get older. Bruce had to fight so much for recognition in his own field, he had, perhaps, the appearance of arrogance ... to my mind the determination an artist must have if he is going to succeed. He had to fight so many battles for himself and for us in what then, and possibly now, is a fairly mean-spirited community.[2]

Reflecting Mason's fondness for quoting scripture in his plays, the observation 'that a prophet has no honour in his own country' (John 4:44) may well be applied to him. It was not until nearly two years after Mason's death that Downstage Theatre mounted New Zealand's first fully professional production of *The Pohutukawa Tree*. Another twenty-five years elapsed before the next professional production was staged by Auckland Theatre Company. Its box office success—their most popular classical production ever—led to their producing an ensemble version of *The End of the Golden Weather* two years later, then *Awatea* the following year: thirty-eight years after its second professional production. At the time of writing, however, the 1974 stage versions of *The Hand on the Rail*, *Swan Song* and *Hongi* remain professionally unproduced, as do *The Light Enlarging / Virtuous Circle* (1963) and *Zero Inn* (1970). Of his other full-length plays, neither *Birds in the Wilderness* (1959) nor *Blood of the Lamb* (1980) have been produced professionally beyond their premiere seasons. And his eminently adaptable teleplay *Rise and Shine* (1982) remains unproduced in any form.

Bruce Mason was a playwright by vocation. His natural response to the world he experienced and observed was to write a play or sketch about it. Theatre was his chosen medium and in that form he achieved distinction in both senses of the term: excellence and the identification—through critique and celebration—of what differentiates New Zealand and New Zealanders. Of course the world was not obliged to take any notice let alone go to the trouble of producing his work. But the primary purpose of theatre remains, as Shakespeare's Hamlet so eloquently puts it: 'to hold as 'twere the mirror up to nature: to show virtue her feature, scorn her own image, and the very age and body of the time his form and pressure.'[3] Mason certainly did just that, but over a period when most of the professional theatres that arose around him preferred to skim the cream of new British and American theatre and stage their contemporary plays and classics along with those translated from Russia and Norway. While the audiences who were attracted to such fare felt the role of theatre was to bring other cultures to them, those who stayed away regarded much of the theatre on offer as elitist and pretentious. This was a far cry from the way the original Old Vic Theatre attracted 'the poor' because—as Mason had recognised and appreciated—their liking for theatre arose from its relevance to them.

When the tide did turn in the favour of home-grown work, and social comedies by the likes of Joseph Musaphia and Roger Hall made home-grown theatre popular again, Mason's plays remained unproduced. He was seen as either too serious in embracing the big themes so readily accepted from overseas playwrights, or politically incorrect as a Pākehā writer of Māori-themed plays, or too middle-class by those preferring the more overtly political works of such excellent playwrights as Mervyn Thompson (invariably directed by himself), Renée and Dean Parker. He was also seen as 'yesterday's man' by those who preferred to nurture 'emerging talent'.

Ironically perhaps, given the plays Mason's reputation was built on, it is new Māori and Pasifika playwrights who are better served through such initiatives as Taki Rua Productions, Tawata Productions and Pacific Underground. It is simply not part of their kaupapa to produce plays that have come from elsewhere.

Their distinctive cultural differences and their own discrete languages are an advantage because unless they tell their stories in their own voices, they will not be heard at all, whereas plays originating from other English-speaking countries can delude Pākehā audiences into believing their lives are being reflected. Our major arts festivals also seem to have supported Māori and Pasifika productions on the premise that their greater cultural distinction renders them more exotic to audiences both at home (oxymoronically) and internationally.

In celebrating the recognition Mason's major plays are now beginning to get, in Auckland at least, we can only wonder what the effect might have been on his career and subsequent output if he had seen each one produced professionally within a year or two of their being written. And what might the flow-on effect have been, in encouraging our best creative writers to consider theatre as their preferred mode of expression? It still remains difficult to see how or why a writer who is mature enough to have something to say, and who hopes to make a living sufficient to sustain a family life and own a home, would choose playwriting as a career in New Zealand. Too many of our Pākehā-led professional theatres have simply not been hungry enough for home-grown plays, or proactive enough to ensure development commensurate with the initial nurturing received by the international plays and playwrights they usually prefer to produce. Acting as 'cover bands' for other people's cultures will never meet the primary needs of our society.

A couple of years after he emigrated from England, aged nineteen, Roger Hall was enthralled by seeing Bruce Mason perform *The End of the Golden Weather*: 'It was not only the best night I'd had in the theatre in New Zealand, it was one of the best nights I'd had in a theatre anywhere.'[4] Hall went on to become New Zealand's most prolific and commercially successful playwright, by reflecting us back to ourselves. Greg McGee (who noted in his memoir that his school, Waitaki Boys' High, had produced English playwright JC Sherriff's *Journey's End* rather than *The Pohutukawa Tree*)[5] sparked a new wave of interest in Kiwi theatre with *Foreskin's Lament* (1980), and, since Mason's death, a large number of extremely proficient playwrights have emerged. A few have enjoyed multiple productions of their plays around the country; more see each new play produced once, then relegated to 'the freezer' from which it may or may not be exhumed and resuscitated someday. Many promising young playwrights soon realise this is not conducive to their moving beyond student-style living conditions. Some have turned to writing, storylining or even directing for *Shortland Street*, New Zealand's daily television soap opera since 1992. Very few scriptwriters make a consistent living writing longer-form television drama.

Some have a crack at film in the hope of a breakthrough (which may well require them to move offshore, lose their distinctive voice and assume the American position in the hope of sustaining a career). There are even playwrights who argue they have grown up on *Sesame Street*, that American culture is ingrained in their psyches and who have written pseudo-American plays and musicals in the forlorn hope their plays will attract wider audiences (a twenty-first-century equivalent of Mason's early and quickly abandoned attempts to become a playwright by pretending to be English). Most of the dedicated New Zealand playwrights who, like Mason, persist in pursuing what they feel in their bones as their true vocation do so alongside work that produces a more secure income, have 'breadwinner' partners whose more secure careers allow them the freedom to take that risk, or continue to live frugal lives, foregoing the option of having a family and one day owning their own home.

At the time of writing, Playmarket—New Zealand's only playwrights' agency, advisory service and bookshop—supports a culturally diverse assortment of established and emerging playwrights through a range of development programmes, support initiatives, competitions and annual awards. These include the Bruce Mason Playwriting Award, established in 1983, to recognise early success in the career of the winning playwright and to encourage their continued exploration of the theatre medium; the Adam NZ Play Award (formerly the Playmarket New Play Award, established in 2008), for an unproduced play, which attracts up to 120 entries each year; and the Playmarket Award, inaugurated in 2012, for a significant body of work developed over decades. However, few mainstream directors are willing to read through the vast back-catalogue accumulated by Playmarket and discover its undoubted wealth. The majority of better-funded professional theatre companies do not have fulltime resources dedicated to reading new New Zealand plays, let alone seeing them developed to production fitness like the pre-processed plays they source from overseas. Auckland Theatre Company's Literary unit offers a number of initiatives to develop New Zealand playwrights and their work but although many excellent plays have evolved this way, a significant number remain unproduced.

Sparked largely by the creativity of graduates of drama schools and university theatre studies, the twenty-first century has seen a marked increase in devised theatre by actor-director-designer-composer cooperatives, who may or may not see the playwright's skill as relevant. Some suffer from 'premature performance syndrome', present a display of performance skills and design-led production values to little greater purpose, add up to less than the sum of their parts and/or remain performer-specific with no prospect of a post-premiere afterlife. The best devised works are those that take what has been conceived within the excitement and passion (or possibly the struggle) of the workshop process, then gestate it from a playwright's perspective, within a zone of deep and private contemplation.

Building on Bruce Mason's solution for making a living from his vocation with *The End of the Golden Weather*, it is fair to say New Zealand leads the world in the production of solo shows. The task Toi Whakaari: NZ Drama School routinely sets its students (to devise and present a twenty-minute solo piece) has led to many pieces being developed into hour-long Fringe shows with varying results. The most notable success story in this regard is New Zealand-raised Malaysian-born Indian Jacob Rajan, whose *Krishnan's Dairy* (1997) laid the foundation for an impressive body of further works. Co-written with director Justin Lewis, produced by their Indian Ink Theatre Company and performed by Rajan (usually with an onstage musician and sometimes with other performers), their highly original plays have allowed their creators to sustain relatively healthy careers.

Overall, however, the current climate tends to favour young Kiwi theatre-makers whose 'voice' is consistently heard in Fringe festivals throughout the country and in our leading venues for independent co-op productions, such as BATS Theatre in Wellington and The Basement Theatre in Auckland. But what of those who may evolve into more mature, experienced, wise, insightful and skilled playwrights, more likely to craft works that resonate more deeply and remain in the repertoire for generations to come?

What New Zealand lacks and needs, if its playwrights are to find their voices on our stages and sustain them, is a playwrights' theatre. This need not necessarily be a 'bricks-and-mortar' venue. It could be

---

Bruce Mason plays bridge on holiday (1970s).

a development and production entity that works with existing venues and co-producers around the country to feed us a free-ranging diet of organic, home-grown plays both new and from the back-catalogue's 'freezer'. That said, a concentrated powerhouse of activity, focused fulltime on bringing playwrights together with directors, actors, designers and technicians to realise their work in the dimensions for which it was conceived, is a consummation devoutly to be wished. As in any civilised country, central government has a crucial role to play in investing 'seed funding' to sustain our cultural health and wealth. In a March 1956 postscript to his final letter to Dr John Pocock, in their quest for 'a theatre we can take seriously, for which . . . our own playwrights will feel confident in writing plays of high import', Bruce Mason put it this way:

> I understand from a recent *Observer* article by Kenneth Tynan that the liveliest theatres in Europe are those of East and West Berlin, both heavily subsidised by the state. Without such subsidies . . . every company is at the mercy of what some people would call free competition, but which Tynan does not hesitate to give the name economic dictatorship, which, by submitting every play to a plebiscite, effectively prevents the generation of those large emotions, and the free working of the imagination, which properly the theatre exists to serve.[6]

Until most of the plays fully produced by our professional theatres are home-grown and some, at least, reach beyond populist comedy to explore pressing themes; until all sectors of our increasingly diverse society are represented in those works; until directors see reading untried scripts and being the first in the world to bring plays from the page to the stage as their most important role; until our best writers see being a playwright as a credible career option; and until we export, as well as import, world-class plays, New Zealand theatre cannot claim to be a culturally mature and truly creative participant in the global theatre scene. Given our identity—our sense of distinction in both its meanings (excellence and points of difference)—has evolved through primary produce, sporting prowess, adventuring skills, ingenuity, innovation, creativity and cultural self-expression, it stands to reason our theatres' primary role is to reflect and exemplify that.

If Mason's plays had all been produced professionally in his lifetime and remained in the repertoire for each new generation, who knows what impact they would have made on New Zealand theatre practice. The more global our society is, the more essential it is for us to appreciate and value what gives Aotearoa New Zealand distinction. It is the culturally specific that speaks across time to the universe. Bruce Mason understood and exemplified this abiding truth.

John Smythe, August 2015

NOTES AND REFERENCES

Foreword

1 Personal conversation with John Smythe, August 2007.

Prologue

1 Bruce Mason. *New Zealand Drama: A parade of forms and a history*. New Zealand University Press, 1973. p.43.

2 Bruce Mason to Dr John Pocock. 'I'. 3 May 1955. *Theatre in Danger: a Correspondence.* St Paul's Book Arcade. 1957. p.21.

1 The State of the Home-grown Play pre-1953

1 Howard McNaughton. 'Drama', *The Oxford History of New Zealand Literature in English* 2nd edition, ed. Terry Sturm. Oxford University Press, 1998. pp.322–323.

2 AH McLintock (ed.). *Encyclopedia of New Zealand* vol. 3. RE Owen Government Printer, 1966, pp.490–491; Peter Downes. *Shadows on the Stage: Theatre in New Zealand—the first 70 years.* John McIndoe Ltd, 1975. p.55.

3 McNaughton, *The Oxford History . . .*, p.324. Referencing *New Zealand Herald*, 9 April 1870, p.5; *Daily Southern Cross*, 9 April 1870.

4 Ibid., *Daily Southern Cross.*

5 Ibid., referencing *New Zealand Herald.*

6 Ibid.

7 Peter Harcourt. *Fantasy and Folly: The Lost World of New Zealand Musicals 1880–1940.* Steele Roberts, 2002. pp.15–16.

8 Herbert Bowen Bridge, the son of Colonel Cyprian Bridge of the 58th Regiment, was born in Kororareka in 1849 and was the great grandfather of this author: John Bowen Smythe.

9 Harcourt, *Fantasy and Folly*. p.36–38.

10 McNaughton, *The Oxford History . . .*, p.328. Referencing Christchurch *Press*, 11 January 1890, p.5

11 Adrian Kiernander. 'Introduction' in *The Land of the Moa* by George Leitch. Victoria University Press, 1990. pp.9–16.

12 McNaughton, *The Oxford History . . .*, p.329.

13 Kiernander, p.58.

14 Ibid., pp.44–45.

15 Downes, summarised.

16 John Thomson. *New Zealand Drama: An illustrated history 1930–1980*, Oxford University Press, 1984. p.6.

17 The Currency Press. '*The Time is Not Right Yet* by Louis Esson'. Accessed 03/09/15. http://www.currency.com.au/product_detail.aspx?productid=1785&ReturnUrl=/search.aspx?q=Esson: 'Louis Esson (1879–1943) . . . pursued the idea of Australian folk drama on the model of the Abbey Theatre in Dublin. Esson met WB Yeats and JM Synge while travelling, and both advised him, against his inclination, to stick to Australian subjects. Esson worked to establish a nationalist drama in which themes of working-class urban and bush life would become the basis for great international artistic achievements. After a second overseas trip (1916–1921) he founded the Pioneer Players with Hilda Bull (his second wife), Vance Palmer and others. The amateur company strove to bring Australian plays to the public and Esson struggled to supply most of its repertoire in 1922–1923.

Its last production was Esson's *The Bride of Gospel Place* in 1926. *The Time Is Not Yet Ripe* (1912), a political comedy, is his best known work.'

18 McNaughton, *The Oxford History . . .*, pp.331–332.

19 Louis Esson's 1912 play *The Time Is Not Yet Ripe* was directed by this author in Melbourne in 1972.

20 Peter Harcourt. *A Dramatic Appearance: New Zealand Theatre 1920–1970.* Methuen, 1978. pp.46–48.

21 Ibid., p.45.

22 Ibid., p.46; Thomson, p.22; McNaughton, p.336.

23 Bruce Mason in *Landfall,* 1956, qtd. in Harcourt, *A Dramatic Appearance*. p.51.

24 Harcourt, *A Dramatic Appearance*, p.83.

25 Thomson, pp.42–43.

26 Sebastian Black, 'What kind of a society can develop under corrugated iron?: Glimpses of New Zealand history in New Zealand plays'. *Australian Drama Studies* 3.1. October 1984. pp.33–52.

27 Claude Evans. *Overtime.* The Pegasus Press, 1955. p.16

28 Black, p.34.

29 Stella Jones. *The Tree.* Whitcombe and Tombs Ltd, 1960, p.9; p.18.

30 Thomson, pp.11–13.

31 Ibid., Victor S Lloyd. 'Foreword' to *Seven One-act Plays.* Radio Publishing Company of New Zealand, 1933. p.7.

32 Sue Dunlop. *The Role of Women in the Culture and Context of a Developing New Zealand Theatre: 1920–1950.* Victoria University of Wellington: MA thesis. p.77, p.84; p.56.

33 Ibid., pp.138–139; *Rabbits* in Llyod, *Seven One-act Plays*, pp.121–132.

34 Ibid., Epilogue, p.174.

35 McNaughton, *The Oxford History . . .*, pp.339–340.

36 Ibid., p.340.

37 Thomson, p.34.

2 Emerging from the Flaxbush

1 Mason family records and folklore, some possibly apocryphal. Supplied by Belinda Robinson. April 2015.

2 David Dowling. 'Mason, Bruce Edward George 1921—1982'. *Dictionary of New Zealand Biography (DNZB)*, updated 22 June 2007. URL: http://www.teara.govt.nz/en/biographies/5m37/1

3 Bruce Mason. 'Narcissus Observed' in *Bruce Mason Solo.* Price Milburn with Victoria University Press, 1981. p.87. (Based on Mason's essay 'Beginnings', *Landfall* 20, June 1966, pp.143–149.)

4 Ibid., 'Narcissus Observed', pp.88–90; 'Limp Bananas', p.104.

5 Ibid., 'Narcissus Observed', pp.90–91; Dowling, *DNZB.*

6 Ibid., 'Narcissus Observed', p.92.

7 Ibid., pp.93–94.

8 Dowling, *DNZB*; *Evening Post*, Volume CXXVII, Issue 87, 10 October 1939, p.16; Volume CXXIX, Issue 142, 17 June 1940, p.12; Mason to Pocock. Letter two, 3 May 1955. pp.15–16.

9 Bruce Mason. 'Variation I: Bo Baron and the Impressionable Young' in *Bruce Mason Solo*, . pp.152–153.

10 Mason to Pocock, Letter two, pp.15-16; Sonja Davies, *Bread and Roses*, Penguin Books, 1988, pp.38–39; Bill Sheat in email exchange with this author, 3 September 2009.

11 Ibid., Mason to Pocock, *Theatre in Danger*; *Evening Post*, Volume CXXIV, Issue 45, 21 August 1942, p.6; Issue 90, 13 October 1942 from Dowling, *DNZB*. p.2. http://www.playmarket.org.nz/playwrights/bruce-mason

12 Mason to Pocock, Letter two, pp.15–17.

13 Ibid., p.17.

14 Ibid., pp.41–42; Bruce Mason, 'Foreword' (April 1979) to *Birds in the Wilderness.* Typescript, held by Playmarket, 1958, 1968. p.i.

15 Mason to Pocock, *Theatre in Danger*, p.19.

16 Ibid., p.21.

17 Diana Dekker. Obituary of Dr Diana Mason. *Dominion Post*, 7 June 2007.

18 Ibid.; Dowling, *DNZB*; James Bertram. *Flight of the Phoenix: Critical notes on New Zealand writers*: Victoria University Press, 1985. p.60.

19 Ibid., Dowling.

20 Don and Jan Farr (ed.). 'Theatre Personalities' No. 6: Bruce Mason. *New Zealand Stage*. Vol. 1 No. 7, August 1967. p.8.

21 Bruce Mason. 'Note to the second edition' in *The End of the Golden Weather*. Victoria University Press, 1970. p.9.

22 Mason to Pocock. Letter six, March 1956. p.91.

23 Ibid., Letter two, May 1955. p.21.

24 Told to this author by Sir Tyrone Guthrie in Melbourne, 1970, when Guthrie directed a Melbourne Theatre Company production of *All's Well that Ends Well* and the author was his dramaturg.

25 Mason, 'Impressions of the Theatre in the Soviet Union' in *Bruce Mason Solo*, pp.215–217.

26 Witnessed and recorded by this author at a 1976 television conference in Edinburgh.

27 Bruce Mason. *Kaleidoscope* interview, TVNZ. Recorded 1982, screened 1983. Clip 3, 01:34–03:24 http://www.nzonscreen.com/title/kaleidoscope---bruce-mason-1983

28 Dowling, *DNZB*.

29 'Theatre Personalities', No. 6: Bruce Mason. pp.8–9.

30 John Smythe. *Downstage Upfront: The first 40 years of New Zealand's longest running professional theatre*. Wellington: Victoria University Press, 2004. pp.63–82.

31 Farr, p.9.

32 Mason, *New Zealand Drama*, pp.45–47.

3 Self-reflection from Page to Stage
Not Christmas, but Guy Fawkes; Courting Blackbird

1 Bruce Mason. 'Author's Note' in *Bruce Mason Solo*. p.229.

2 Ibid., 'Narcissus Observed', pp.94–95.

3 Ibid., 'Et in Arcadia Ego . . .', pp.96–99.

4 Ibid., pp.99–103.

5 Ibid., 'Limp Bananas: An occult farce', pp.104–106.

6 Ibid., 'The Conch Shell', pp.120–133.

7 Ibid., pp.133–135.

8 Ibid., pp.135–137.

9 Ibid., 'Author's Note' in *Not Christmas, but Guy Fawkes*, p.229.

10 Ibid., 'Author's Note' in *Courting Blackbird*. p.230; 'Theme: Progenitors', p.147; 'Coda', p.190.

11 Ibid., 'Theme: Progenitors', pp.141–148.

12 Ibid., 'Variation I: Bo Baron and the Impressionable Young', p.149.

13 Ibid., p.150–152.

14 Ibid., pp.152–159.

15 Ibid., 'Variation II: Bo Baron and the Bourgeoisie', pp.160–167.

16 Ibid., 'Author's note', p.230.

17 Ibid., 'Variation III: Bo Baron, Love and Marriage', pp.168–173.

18 Sonja Davies. *Bread and Roses: Sonja Davies, her story*. Penguin Books, 1988. pp.38–40.

19 Stephen Hamilton. *A Radical Tradition: A history of the Victoria University of Wellington Students' Association 1899-1999*. Victoria University Students Association in association with Steele Roberts, 2002. p.95.

20 Mason, 'Variation IV: Bo Baron and Higher Education' in *Courting Blackbird*, pp.174–175.
21 Ibid., pp.175–180.
22 Ibid., pp.181–182.
23 Ibid., 'Variation V: Bo Baron and the War for Civilisation'. pp.183–185.
24 Ibid., 'Variation VI: Bo Baron and the Ineffable Light'. p.186–187.
25 Ibid., pp.188–190.
26 Davies, p.40.
27 Mason, 'Author's Note' in *Courting Blackbird*, pp.230–231.

4 Short and Satirical

Pause; The Bonds of Love; The Evening Paper; The Licensed Victualler; The Verdict; A Case in Point; Wit's End; We Don't Want Your Sort Here

1 ADM. Review, *Critic*. Otago University Student's Association (OUSA), 8 June 1944. p.6.
2 Catherine Cross. Correspondence, *Critic*. OUSA, 26 June 1944. p.2.
3 'Wellington's Unity Theatre', *Landfall* 9, 1955. p.159.
4 Rachel Barrowman. *A Popular Vision: The arts and the left in New Zealand 1930–1950*. Victoria University Press, 1991. p.219.
5 Bruce Mason. 'Founder-producer of Unity Theatre Dies in London'. *Dominion*, 18 November 1975. p.4, qtd. in Barrowman, p.173.
6 John Braty. 'Still Life with Chip Frier'. Viewed at http://www.tate.org.uk/servlet/ViewWork?workid=1452. Updated 2010; Wikipedia article. 'Kitchen Sink Realism'. https://en.wikipedia.org/wiki/Kitchen_sink_realism. Updated 17 August 2015.
7 John Russell Taylor. *The Penguin Dictionary of the Theatre*. Penguin Books, 1966. p.146.
8 Bruce Mason. *The Bonds of Love*. Typescript, held by Playmarket. 1955. p.1–5.
9 Ibid., p.5–9.
10 Ibid., p.13–14.
11 Ibid., pp.16–19.
12 Mason to Pocock. *Theatre in Danger*. p.21.
13 Bruce Mason, *The Evening Paper*. Typescript, held by Playmarket, 1953/1964. p.1.
14 Ibid., pp.18–33.
15 Ibid., pp.36–40.
16 Trisha Dunleavy. *Ourselves in Primetime: A history of New Zealand television drama*. Auckland University Press, 2005. p.21.
17 National Film Unit director Hugh Macdonald used the same Sibelius symphony for his 1970 three-screen spectacular *This Is New Zealand*, to accompany soaring aerial shots of the alps and other landscapes.
18 Mason, *The Evening Paper*, pp.47–61.
19 Ibid., pp.62–75.
20 Ibid., pp.76–85.
21 Mason, *New Zealand Drama*, pp.45–47.
22 Mason, *The Licensed Victualler*. Typescript, held by Playmarket, June 1954. p.2, p.4.
23 Ibid., pp.1–4.
24 Ibid., pp.5–11.
25 Ibid., pp.11–14.
26 Mason to Pocock, *Theatre in Danger*, p.63.
27 Bruce Mason. *The Verdict*. Typescript, held by Playmarket, 1955. pp.5–7.
28 Ibid., pp.7–17.
29 Ibid., p.17.

30 Ibid.,

31 Ibid., pp.18–22.

32 Sarah Gaitanos. *Nola Millar: A theatrical life*. Victoria University Press, 2006. p.177.

33 'Capital Punishment in New Zealand'. URL: http://www.nzhistory.net.nz/culture/the-death-penalty (Ministry for Culture and Heritage), updated 5 August 2014.

34 Bruce Mason. *A Case in Point*. Typescript, held by Playmarket, 1954. pp.1–6.

35 Ibid., pp.6-8.

36 Ibid., pp.9-11.

37 *Wit's End* programme, held by Bill Sheat. December 1956.

38 Bruce Mason. *Every Kind of Weather*, ed. David Dowling. Reed Methuen, 1986. pp.23–26.

39 Bruce Mason. 'Herself Surprised' from *We Don't Want Your Sort Here*. Paul's Book Arcade, 1963. pp.57–63.

40 Mason, *Kaleidoscope* interview, Clip 4, 01:30.

41 Bruce Mason. 'Author's Note' in *We Don't Want Your Sort Here*, p.44.

42 Ibid., 'The English Tongue' in *We Don't Want Your Sort Here*. pp.32–35.

43 Ibid., 'Author's Note', p.6.

44 Ibid., 'A Gastronomic Tour of God's Own Country', pp.11–13.

45 Ibid., 'Summer Lament', pp.14–15.

46 Ibid., 'A Matter of Taste', pp.16–18.

47 Ibid., 'Good Neighbour Policy', pp.19–20.

48 Ibid., 'The National Song', pp.21–23.

49 Ibid., 'A Cure for Delinquency', pp.24–26.

50 Ibid., 'An Angry Young Man Needs a Cause', pp.27–28.

51 Ibid., 'La Belle Dame sans Merci', pp.29–31.

52 Ibid., 'An Ordinary Man', pp.36–38.

53 Ibid., 'Press Conference', pp.39–42.

54 Ibid., 'The Mad Hatter's Gin Party', pp.45–56.

55 Ibid., 'Author's Note', p.64.

56 Ibid., 'Look Back in Anger', pp.65–66.

57 Ibid., 'Waiting for Godot', pp.66–67.

5 Blood and Bone Exhumed
The Pohutukawa Tree

1 Mason, *Kaleidoscope* interview, Clip 3, 01:34–03:24.

2 Bruce Mason. *The Pohutukawa Tree*. Price Milburn, 1960. p.19.

3 Mason, *The Pohutukawa Tree*, p.5; 'Letters to the Editor'. *Te Ao Hou*. No. 20. November 1957. p.58.

4 Mason, *The Pohutukawa Tree*, pp.5–6.

5 Bruce Mason. 'The Maori as Artist'. *Te Ao Hou*. No. 31. June 1960.

6 The other two were The Southern Comedy Players and the Community Arts Service (CAS).

7 Bruce Mason. '*The Pohutukawa Tree* in Wales'. *Te Ao Hou*. No. 34. March 1961.

8 Bruce Mason. 'Note to the second edition' in *The Healing Arch: Five plays on Māori themes*. Victoria University Press, 1987. p.279.

9 Although t-shirts were US Navy issue in WWII, they only became a popular fashion item after Marlon Brandon wore one in *A Streetcar Named Desire* (on stage 1947; on film 1951). It was James Dean who popularised the t-shirt-and-jeans combination in *Rebel Without a Cause* (1955).

10 Mason. *The Pohutukawa Tree*, p.29.

11 Ibid., p.9.

12 Ibid., p.7.

13 Ibid., p.52.

14 Ibid., p.74.
15 Ibid., p.90; p.95.
16 Ibid., p.23.
17 Ibid., p.24.
18 Ibid., p.43.
19 Ibid., p.97.
20 Ibid., p.79.
21 Ibid., p.83.
22 Ibid., pp.94–95.
23 Ibid., p.79.
24 Ibid., p.47.
25 Ibid., p.93.
26 Ibid., p.86.
27 Ibid., p.93 ('those nagging things that are so important to us . . .').
28 Ibid., p.102.
29 Mason, 'Note to the second edition' in *The Healing Arch,* p.278.
30 Mason, *Kaleidoscope* interview, Clip 3, 11:55.
31 Mason, *The Pohutukawa Tree*; 'Note to the second edition'. *The Healing Arch*. p.279.
32 Mason, *Kaleidoscope* interview, Clip 4, 03:30–04:03.
33 McNaughton, *The Oxford History . . .*, pp.341-342; Thomson, p.32.
34 Auckland Theatre Company media release, 24 September 2009.

6 How Do We Nest Post-war?
Birds in the Wilderness

1 Bruce Mason. *Birds in the Wilderness.* Typescript, held at Playmarket. p.i.
2 Ibid., pp.i–iv.
3 Ibid., pp.v–vii.
4 Ibid., pp.vii–viii.
5 Bruce Mason. 'Preface' to *Blood of the Lamb*. Price Milburn with Victoria University Press, 1981. p.9.
6 Mason, *Birds in the Wilderness,* p.viii.
7 Davies, pp.37–40.
8 Mason, *Courting Blackbird* in *Bruce Mason Solos,* p.147, p.149.
9 Mason, *Birds in the Wilderness,* p.13.
10 Ibid., pp.21–23.
11 Ibid., p.26.
12 Ibid., pp.60–61.
13 Howard McNaughton. 'The Plays of Bruce Mason'. *Landfall.* No. 106. June 1973. p.130.
14 Mason, 'Foreword' to *Birds in the Wilderness,* p.x.
15 Ibid., pp.4–5.
16 Ibid., p.77.
17 Ibid., pp.39–40.
18 Ibid., p.46.
19 Ibid., p.121.
20 Ibid., pp.87–88.
21 Ibid., pp.136–137.
22 Ibid., p.132.
23 Ibid.
24 Mason, 'Foreword' to *Birds in the Wilderness,* p.ix.

7 Remembrance of Innocence Lost
The End of the Golden Weather

1 By 'producing', Mason probably means what we now call 'directing'.

2 Bruce Mason. 'Note to the second edition' in *The End of the Golden Weather*. Victoria University Press, 1970. p.8.

3 Mason qtd in Dowling (ed.), *Every Kind of Weather*. p.97.

4 Mason, 'Note to the second edition' in *Golden Weather*. p.9.

5 Ibid., p.10.

6 Ibid., p.12. Mason qtd in Dowling (ed.), *Every Kind of Weather*, p.97, referencing John Mulgan. *Man Alone*. Selwyn and Blount, 1939.

7 Mason, *Golden Weather*, p.31.

8 Ibid., p.66, pp.68–70 (although in his final broadcast Mason changed this description of Mrs A to 'A big middle-aged woman. . .').

9 Mason, *The Pohutukawa Tree*, pp.43–44.

10 Mason, *Golden Weather*, pp.38–39, pp.46–48.

11 Mason, *The Pohutukawa Tree*, pp.43–44.

12 Mason, *Golden Weather*, p.38.

13 'Luis Firpo'. Wikipedia article. http://en.wikipedia.org/wiki/Luis_Firpo. Accessed 30 December 2009.

14 Mason, *Golden Weather*, p.56.

15 Ibid., p.82.

16 Ibid., 'Note to the second edition' in *Golden Weather*. p.17.

17 Mason, *Golden Weather*, p.80.

18 Ibid., p.82.

19 Ibid., pp.86–87.

20 Ibid., p.87.

21 Ibid., p.88.

22 Ibid., p.91.

23 Ibid., pp.92–93.

24 Ibid., pp.94–95.

25 Mason, 'Note to the second edition' in *Golden Weather*, p.10.

26 Mason qtd in Dowling (ed.), *Every Kind of Weather*, pp.96–97.

27 Ibid., p.294.

28 Mason, 'Note to the second edition' in *Golden Weather*. pp.24–27.

29 'Bruce Mason'. Playmarket. http://www.playmarket.org.nz/about_profiles.php?id=111&l=M Accessed 3 September 2015; Murray Lynch. 'Director's Notes' in programme for the Auckland Theatre Company production of The *End of the Golden Weather* at the Maidment Theatre, September 2011.

30 Ian Mune. *Mune: an autobiography*. Craig Potton Publishing, 2010. p.218, p.224.

31 John Smythe. Review: *The End of the Golden Weather* at Ilott Theatre, Wellington. 25 May 2007. http://www.theatreview.org.nz/reviews/review.php?id=789

8 The Quest for Liberty: Mother versus Daughter
The Light Enlarging / Virtuous Circle

1 Bruce Mason. 'Note' to *Virtuous Circle* typescript. Completed following its premiere in 1978, held at Playmarket, 17 August 1984.

2 Bruce Mason. Letter to Michael Ross: Item 2008.41. Victoria University of Wellington Library, JC Beaglehole Room. 18 March 1980.

3 Bruce Mason, *Virtuous Circle*, p.20.
4 Ibid., p.27.
5 Ibid., p.40.
6 Ibid., p.45.
7 Ibid., p.46.
8 Ibid., p.53.
9 Ibid., p.56.
10 Ibid., pp.1–12.
11 Ibid., pp.12–19.
12 Ibid., pp.20–37.
13 Ibid., p.47.
14 Ibid., pp.49–50.
15 Ibid., pp.53–54.
16 Ibid., pp.51–61.
17 Ibid., 'Author's Note'.

9 Confronting Political and Artistic Suppression
To Russia, with Love

1 Diana Mason, told to this author in casual conversation.
2 Bruce Mason. 'Author's Note' in *To Russia, with Love* in *Bruce Mason Solo*. pp.213.
3 Smythe, *Downstage Upfront*, pp.461–462.
4 Bruce Mason. *The Dominion*, 5 September 1968. Reprinted in *Bruce Mason Solo*. pp.222–223.
5 Ibid.
6 Ibid., pp.221–224.
7 Ibid., pp.224–225.
8 Ibid., pp.225–228.
9 Mason, 'Author's Note' in *To Russia with Love*. p.214.
10 Mason, *To Russia with Love*, pp.57–60.
11 Ibid., pp.60–65.
12 Ibid., pp.67–71.
13 Ibid., pp.72–76.
14 Ibid., pp.76–81.
15 Ibid., pp.81–83.
16 Mason, *Kaleidoscope* interview, Clip 3, 09:40–11:21.
17 Ibid., Clip 4, 01:30–02:10.

10 Shining Light Where Truth Lies
Awatea

1 Mason, 'Foreword' to *Awatea* in *The Healing Arch*, p.287.
2 Ibid., pp.287–288.
3 Ibid., p.288.
4 Ibid., pp.288–289.
5 Ibid., p.289; 'Preface' in *The Hand on the Rail* in *The Healing Arch*. p.279.
6 Ibid., pp.289–290.
7 Mason, *Awatea* in *The Healing Arch*. p.247.

8 Ibid., p.256.
9 Ngā Taonga Sound & Vision. This author in email exchange with Gavin McGinley. June 2006.
10 Mason, 'Foreword' to *Awatea*, pp.290–291.
11 Bill Sheat in telephone conversation with John Smythe. 4 August 2003; Advertisement in *Act.* Vol. 2, No. 2. Winter 1968. p.32.
12 Dick Johnstone. Downstage Theatre Oral History Project. OHC 111–29, 130.
13 Mason, 'Foreword' to *Awatea*, p.290, pp.293–294.
14 Ibid., pp.291–293.
15 Ibid., p.295.
16 Ibid.
17 Ibid., 'Note to the Second Edition' in *Awatea*. pp.296–298; Jack Shallcrass. Review of *Awatea*. *Act.* Vol. 3, No. 1. Autumn 1969. p.17.
18 Mason, *Awatea*, p.217.
19 Mason, *The Pohutukawa Tree*, p.92.
20 Mason, *Awatea*. p.230.
21 Ibid., p.237.
22 Ibid., p.240.
23 Ibid., p.244.
24 Ibid., p.246.
25 Ibid., p.256.
26 Ibid., p.259.
27 Mason, *The Pohutukawa Tree*. pp.92–93.
28 Mason, *Awatea*, pp.212–213.
29 Ibid., p.216.
30 Ibid., p.236.
31 Ibid., p.264.
32 Ibid., p.251.
33 Ibid., pp.264–270.
34 Ibid., pp.271–273.
35 Ibid., pp.274–275.

11 Generations at Risk of Losing Their Grip
The Hand on the Rail

1 Ngā Taonga Sound & Vision. This author in email exchange with Gavin McGinley. 2010.
2 Mason, 'Preface' to *The Hand on the Rail* in *The Healing Arch*. p.280.
3 Mason, 'Note to the second edition' in *Awatea*, p.296.
4 Ibid.
5 Mason, 'Preface' to *The Hand on the Rail* in *The Healing Arch*, p.280.
6 Ibid., p.281.
7 Ibid., p.130.
8 Ibid., pp.129–132.
9 Ibid., pp.137–138.
10 Ibid., pp.138–140.
11 Ibid., pp.140–141
12 Ibid., pp.141–144.
13 Ibid., pp.140–141 (identical to 1974 typescript except that in the last line, 'Team spirit? All for one, one for all?', hand-written, presumably in anticipation of the *Healing Arch* publication).

14 Ibid., pp.142–144.

15 Ibid., pp.148–151.

16 Ibid., pp.152–154.

17 Ibid., pp.154–155.

18 Ibid., pp.152–154 (in his Note to *The Hand on the Rail*, 'The Tangi', p.282, Mason offers the words to the waiata, by Pahu, along with his own translation, somewhat more colloquial than that given by Sir Apirana Ngata and Dr Pei te Hurinui Jones in their celebrated collection *Ngā Mōteatea*).

19 Ibid., p.157 (presumably this is where Mason means 'Po! Po!—a lullaby' by Enoka te Pakura, offered in the Appendix pp.284–286, to be used).

20 Ibid., pp.158–159.

21 Don Brash. 'Orewa Speech'. Scoop.co.nz. http://www.scoop.co.nz/stories/PA0401/S00220.htm Accessed 19/10/2015.

12 An Operatic Rage against the Dying of the Light
Swan Song

1 Mason, 'Note' to *Swan Song* in *The Healing Arch,* p.286.

2 Ibid., *Swan Song*. p.203.

3 Ngā Taonga Sound & Vision. This author in email exchange with Gavin McGinley. 2010.

4 Mason, *Swan Song*. p.167.

5 Ibid., p.170.

6 Ibid., pp.174–177.

7 Ibid., pp.182–187.

8 Ibid., pp.187–191.

9 Ibid., pp.191–193.

10 Ibid., pp.194–204.

11 Ibid., pp.205–208.

13 A Chief, a King, Some Gods and Muskets
Hongi

1 Ngā Taonga Sound & Vision. This author in email exchange with Gavin McGinley. 2010.

2 Mason, 'Note' to *Hongi* in *The Healing Arch*. pp.277–278.

3 Ibid., p.278.

4 Mason, *Hongi,* pp.9–13.

5 Ibid., pp.14–18.

6 Ibid., pp.18–21.

7 Mason, 'Note' to *Hongi*, p.277.

8 Ibid., *Hongi*, pp.21–24

9 Ibid., pp.24–26.

10 Ibid., pp.26–30.

11 Ibid., pp.30–33.

12 Ibid., pp.33–37.

13 Ibid., p.37.

14 Ibid., pp.37–40.

15 Mason, *Kaleidoscope* interview, Clip 4, 03:25–04:40.

14 When Drop-outs Drop In
Zero Inn / The Chance of a Lifetime

1 'Bruce Mason'. Playmarket website. http://www.playmarket.org.nz/playwrights/bruce-mason
2 David Dowling. 'Mason, Bruce Edward George 1921—1982' *DNZB*. Updated 22 June 2007. http://www.teara.govt.nz/en/biographies/5m37/1
3 Bruce Mason. *Zero Inn*. PDF of the 1970 Canterbury Area of the NZ Theatre Federation publication, held by Playmarket. p.5.
4 Ibid., pp.6–9.
5 Ibid., p.13.
6 Ibid., pp.6–7; pp.39–40.
7 Mason, 'Preface' to *Blood of the Lamb*, p.8.
8 Mason, *Zero Inn*. pp.76–77.
9 Ibid., p.17–18.
10 Ibid., pp.17–26.
11 Ibid., pp.30–37.
12 Ibid., pp.55–59.
13 Ibid., p.21.
14 Ibid., pp.14–30.
15 Ibid., pp.37–38.
16 Ibid., p.54.
17 Ibid., pp.76–78.
18 Ibid., pp.38–41.
19 Ibid., pp.41–44.
20 Ibid., pp.46–50.
21 Ibid., pp.50–53.
22 Ibid., p.25; pp.62–64.
23 Ibid., pp.65–72.
24 Ibid., pp.72–83.
25 Ibid., pp.83–87.
26 Ibid., pp.87–89.
27 Ibid., pp.91–96.
28 David Dowling, ed. Roger Robinson and Nelson Wattie. *The Oxford Companion to New Zealand Literature*. Oxford: Oxford University Press, 1998; 'The Cherry Orchard—Bruce Mason.' Playmarket website. http://www.playmarket.org.nz/bookshop/products/cherry-orchard
29 Bruce Mason. *The Chance of a Lifetime*. Typescript, held by Playmarket, 1971. pp.1–7.
30 Ibid., pp.7–42.
31 Ibid., p.42.
32 Ibid., p.43.

15 A Clandestine Life and a Shocking Diagnosis
Letters to Mike / *Four Healing Dialogues*

1 Michael Ross went on to pursue an international career and eventually be appointed Professor in the Department of Family Medicine and Community Health at a university in the USA.
2 This author in email exchange with Dr MW Ross, May 2015. The thesis was subsequently published as a book: Ross, MW *The Married Homosexual Man: A Psychological Study*. Routledge and Kegan Paul, 1983 (a title of its time in that it presupposes all marriage is heterosexual).

3 Bruce Mason. Letters to Michael Ross: Item 2008.41. Victoria University of Wellington Library, JC Beaglehole Room. 2 February 1976.
4 Ibid., 21 January 1976.
5 Ibid., 16 February 1976.
6 Ibid., 5 April 1976.
7 Ibid., 17 June 1976
8 Ibid., 21 June 1976.
9 This author in email exchange with Dr MW Ross. 1–2 May 2015.
10 Bruce Mason. *Four Healing Dialogues*: Item 2008.41. Typescript, held by Victoria University of Wellington Library, JC Beaglehole Room. pp.2–3;11–12.
11 Ibid., pp.4–6.
12 Ibid., pp.6–9.
13 Ibid., pp.10–12.
14 Ibid., pp.12–16.
15 Ibid., pp.16–18.
16 Mason, Letters to Michael Ross, 15 June 1976.
17 Ibid., 21 June 1976.
18 This author in conversation with Belinda Robinson (nee Mason). May 2015.
19 Mason, Letters to Michael Ross, 22 June 1976.
20 Ibid., 25 June 1976.
21 Ibid., 2 July 1976.
22 Ibid., 5 July; 9 November 1978.
23 Ibid., 28 August; 9 November 1978.
24 Ibid., 13 December 1978.

16 Thus Do a Few Women
Blood of the Lamb

1 Bruce Mason, 'Preface' to *Blood of the Lamb*, p.7, p.10.
2 Mason, *Blood of the Lamb*. pp.13.
3 Mason, 'Preface' to *Blood of the Lamb*, pp.7–8.
4 Ibid., pp.8–9.
5 Mason, *Blood of the Lamb*. pp.62–63.
6 Other examples include: Joan of Arc; Pope Joan; British Army surgeon James Barry (1792–1795, born Margaret Ann Bulkley); English WWI war reporter Denis Smith (born Dorothy Lawrence, died 1964); American jazz pianist Billy Tipton (1914–1989, born Dorothy Lucille Tipton).
7 Mason, *Blood of the Lamb*. pp.42–43.
8 Ibid., p.70.
9 Ibid., p.49.
10 Ibid., pp.52–64.
11 Ibid., pp.74–78.
12 Ibid., p.70.
13 Ibid., p.64.
14 Ibid., pp.77–78.
15 Ibid., p.71.
16 Ibid., p.25.
17 Ibid., p.52.
18 Ibid., p.90.
19 Ibid., p.53.

20 Ibid., pp.56–57.
21 Ibid., p.75.
22 Ibid., p.71.
23 Ibid., pp.81–84.
24 Ibid., pp.83–88.
25 Ibid., pp.88–89.
26 Ibid., p.62.
27 Ibid., pp.48–51.
28 Ibid., pp.91–93.
29 Ibid., pp.94–97.
30 Ibid., p.94.

17 Parting Shots
Two Sketches and Four Teleplays

1 Dylan Thomas. 'Do Not Go Gentle into That Good Night'in *Collected Poems: Dylan Thomas*. New York: New Directions Publishing, 1971.
2 Bruce Mason. Audio tape to Michael Ross. 1981. Held at the Victoria University of Wellington Library, JC Beaglehole Room. Reported to this author by Belinda Robinson, May 2015.
3 Mason, *Kaleidoscope* interview, Clip 4, 03:45.
4 Bruce Mason. *Daphne and Chloe*. Typescript, held at the Victoria University of Wellington Library, JC Beaglehole Room, and by Playmarket. p.40.
5 Ibid., p.42.
6 Ibid., pp.53–57.
7 Mason, *Blood of the Lamb*, p.78.
8 Mason, *Daphne and Chloe*, p.37.
9 Mason, *Blood of the Lamb*, p.78.
10 Mason, *Daphne and Chloe*, p.40.
11 Mason, *Blood of the Lamb*, p.70.
12 Bruce Mason. 'Author's Note' (originally included in the submitted treatment) to *The Garlick Thrust*. Typescript, held at the Victoria University of Wellington Library, JC Beaglehole Room, and by Playmarket. Undated.
13 Ibid., p.3.
14 Ibid., p.10.
15 Ibid., pp.17–18.
16 Ibid.
17 Ibid., p.34.
18 Ibid., Scenes 15, 16.
19 Bruce Mason. *Do Not Go Gentle*. Typescript, held at the Victoria University of Wellington Library, JC Beaglehole Room, and by Playmarket. pp.1–3.
20 Ibid., p.5.
21 Ibid., pp.11–18.
22 Ibid., pp.18–20.
23 Ibid., pp.20–24.
24 The opening line of 'The British Grenadiers', a traditional British and Commonwealth military marching song.
25 Mason, *Do Not Go Gentle*, pp.30–31
26 Mason, *The Evening Paper*, p.80.
27 Mason, *Do Not Go Gentle*, p.35.

28 Bruce Mason. *Rise and Shine*. Typescript, held at the Victoria University of Wellington Library, JC Beaglehole Room, and by Playmarket. p.2.

29 Ibid., p.3.

30 Ibid., p.4.

31 Ibid., p.7.

32 Ibid., p.12.

33 Ibid., pp.16–18.

34 Ibid., p.20.

35 Ibid., pp.21–24

36 Ibid., pp.24–28.

37 Ibid., p.32.

38 Ibid., p.33–34.

39 Ibid., pp.34–36.

40 Ibid., pp.37–48.

41 Ibid., pp.49–50.

Epilogue

1 Mason, *Kaleidoscope* interview, Clip 4, 04:50–06:07.

2 Ralph McAllister. *Kaleidoscope* interview. Clip 2, 08:20–09:07.

3 William Shakespeare. *Hamlet* in *The Arden Shakespeare.* Routledge, 1992. Act 3, scene 2. ll.21–24.

4 Roger Hall. *Bums on Seats*. Viking, 1998. p.57.

5 Greg McGee. *Tall Tales (Some True)*. Penguin NZ, 2008. p.11.

6 Mason to Pocock, Letter six, pp.103–104.

SYNOPSES

PAUSE (1944)

Young Joe returns from the Great War disillusioned until his wife, Ethel, revives his spirits with optimism about starting a family and helping to shape the 'new order'. Twenty years later they remain childless and their life is mundane. Joe stuns Ethel with the news he has enlisted again, for WWII, claiming he can only attain peace in the turmoil of war.

COURTING BLACKBIRD: A Theme and Variations in the Baroque Style (1952/1976)

Mason's narrator flirts with Marxism under the charismatic influence of Bo Baron, extradited to New Zealand by his English–Jewish parents. The variations cover Bo Baron and 'the Impressionable Young', 'the Bourgeoisie', 'Love and Marriage', 'Higher Education', 'the War for Civilisation' and 'the Ineffable Light'. Semi-autobiographical, *Courting Blackbird* claims artistic license to depart from reality in some key respects.

THE BONDS OF LOVE (1953)

Culture clash and sex-role conditioning cause conflict in the relationships between English sisters Sally and Edna and their unsophisticated Kiwi men, George and Bert. Their lives are squalid compared with the paradise advertised by New Zealand House in London. Resolution is achieved through awkward compromise.

THE EVENING PAPER (1953)

The mundane routine of family life for Ernest and Elfrida Branson and their adult daughter Winsome is upset by the arrival, from England, of Elfrida's cousin once removed. Philip Dalton is a 'born again Kiwi'. Winsome becomes as enamoured of Philip as he is with New Zealand but he rejects her advances. The Branson parents resist, then reject his attempts to awaken them to the wonders of their land.

THE LICENSED VICTUALLER (1954)

This short operatic farce pits the Temperance Division of the Hikitene Women's Guild against those who would like their local victualler to be licensed to sell alcohol. The perceived social evils and values of alcohol are entertainingly debated.

NOT CHRISTMAS, BUT GUY FAWKES (1955/1958/1966/1973)

Mason's raconteur sends up his own pretensions and hubris in sequences entitled 'Narcissus Observed', 'Et in Arcadia Ego', 'Limp Bananas' and 'The Conch Shell'. The recounted experiences are more autobiographical than *The End of the Golden Weather* and *Courting Blackbird* despite their poetic and theatrical flourishes.

THE VERDICT (1955)

Two couples at a winter resort pass judgement on a recent murder trial, unaware one of the key players is listening. When she confronts them, their own fallibilities, moral shortcomings and hypocrisies are exposed. (Inspired by the Parker–Hume murder case.)

THE POHUTUKAWA TREE (1955)

Aroha Mataira lives with her children Queenie (seventeen) and Johnny (eighteen) on the last acre of Ngāti Raukura land, adjacent to the Atkinsons' citrus orchard where they work. Embracing Christianity has allowed Aroha to reconcile her ancestor Whetumārama's spirited defence of Te Parenga with its steady loss, 'slice by slice', to Pākehā progress in the decades since. Johnny has a secret passion for Robin Hood, comics and alcohol, and loves riding and caring for Sylvia Atkinson's horse. Queenie develops a liking for Roy McDowell and sex. When Sylvia marries and settles into Hawkes Bay society, along with her horse, and Roy refuses to marry the pregnant Queenie, Johnny desecrates the church. Aroha's shame, loss of faith and inevitable loss of that last acre cause her to will herself to death.

A CASE IN POINT: An argument on the necessity of hanging children (1957)

At the Suffolk County Assizes in 1833, eleven-year-old Ned is on trial for stealing thirteen pullet eggs. The farmer just wants to frighten the boy by bringing the charge. The defence lawyer argues cogently and pleads for mercy, but the judge needs to make an example as a deterrent. It is justice that is on trial. (Written to support the campaign for the abolition of capital punishment.)

BIRDS IN THE WILDERNESS (1958)

In February 1957, after three years of marriage, librarian Juliet (twenty-eight) and public servant Bernie Bascombe (thirty-three) have moved out of a rooming house and into a ramshackle old place which used to be a corset factory. Now pregnant, Juliet envisages nuclear family bliss but Bernie has advertised rooms for rent to immigrants arriving on the *Captain Cook*, which also brings entrepreneurial Jacko Sternberg, an ex-Navy buddy of Bernie's from their war service in the North Sea. Along with an ageing Hungarian couple who lost their children in the revolution, and a Canadian ex-British Empire Wrestling Champion with his mute 'secretary' from Te Kuiti, they set up Woodenit, making furniture and other wooden goods, despite their lack of expertise. While Juliet grows from hating the intrusion to loving this odd collection of people, Bernie comes to loathe the enterprise. Reality and pragmatism prevail, leaving the audience to consider the values by which we live and work.

THE END OF THE GOLDEN WEATHER (1959)

A solo narrator (unnamed) recalls how the 'golden weather' of his boyhood, and that of the nation, was lost. He tells the story in a scene-setting prologue and then in two acts of three parts each.

'Sunday at Te Parenga' reveals a rich array of characters on the beach, including 'thin-as-a-spoon' Firpo in training, a biceps-bulging Empire wrestling champion, and Sergeant Robinson, policing moral standards of dress. In the evening a houseful of guests play charades and are treated to the boy's father's hilarious comic skit.

In 'The Night of the Riots' the boy recalls how he became aware of the Depression and witnessed Te Parenga's futile attempt to stage a demonstration, where Sergeant Robinson just did his job and men felt robbed of all power and pride. This was the end of the nation's golden weather.

'Christmas at Te Parenga' puts pressure on the children to behave and sees the boy's aesthetic sensibilities confronted by Kiwi crassness when his attempt to present a concert of music, dance, drama and historical tableaux is upstaged by his little brother and greeted with hilarity by the family friends. But when he sees it from his brother's point of view, his own humanity deepens.

'The Made Man' details the boy's relationship with the mentally disturbed Firpo. Exploring round the rocks and up a green staircase, the boy first discovers Firpo at the abandoned bach to which he has been relegated by the ageing Atkinsons. His declaring he would never laugh at Firpo renders him Firpo's friend. But on the beach Firpo is the unwitting butt of insidious ridicule and only the boy's mother shows some sense of compassion.

Firpo becomes a cause for the boy. When the local lads use him to set up an athletic challenge, the boy goes to great lengths to help Firpo win, including buying him meat, only to find he is a vegetarian. His attempt to pray for Firpo is drowned out by a choir practice and shouting at them to 'shut up!' gets him into further trouble.

Everyone turns out for the big race and for a moment it looks as though Firpo could have a chance, but inevitably he fails. The boy's efforts to help him back up the steps are rewarded with frightening hostility from Firpo. When the holidays are almost over, the boy discovers Firpo had become violent and the Atkinsons put him in 'the nuthouse', asserting that he would be happy there. The boy now knows 'summer is quite at an end.'

THE LIGHT ENLARGING / VIRTUOUS CIRCLE (1963)

After twenty-two years of happy marriage, Barbara Everiss is planning to run away from her small-town home with itinerant Irish tenor Kevin Hogan. Despite having no complaints about her accountant husband John, who epitomises safety and security, and is a good lover, she wants to expand her experience of life. Kevin's desire to settle down is simply ignored by Barbara. But John's return from Auckland with their single but four-month pregnant daughter, Miranda, complicates things. The role of mothers and expectations of daughters are thoroughly canvassed and Barbara remains determined to make a break until she discovers Kevin and Miranda have decided to pair up and shack up, 'up the coast'. Thus the status quo for Barbara and John is resumed by default. But Barbara's suitcase remains packed.

TO RUSSIA, WITH LOVE (1965/68)

Three character studies set in Moscow embody the state of Soviet Russia (based on Mason's visit in 1958 and responding to events in 1968).

American oil magnate Eugene B Timms tape-records his impressions of Russia before heading off to the Bolshoi Ballet with his interpreter.

Young American tourist Irving David Jr, who raises money by surreptitiously selling back-copies of *Time* magazine to Russians, tries to sell Solzhenitsyn's *The First Circle* to Dmitiri Doroshenko, who invites him to his room (in a poorer part of town).

Dmitri hosts Irving in his room. His passion for literature and freedom of expression emerges as they drink vodka. Secrets are revealed. But Irving's naïvety leads to Dmitri's inevitable downfall.

AWATEA (1965/1974)

The high expectations placed on 'Dr Matt' by his father, Werihe Paku, and the Omoana community come to a head as the truth is revealed.

Outside the cliff-top house of old, blind Werihe Paku, in remote Omoana, hāngī food is being prepared for the New Year's hui to celebrate the annual visit of his generous and all-healing son, 'Dr Matt', the pride of the district. But Matt who, has written a weekly letter for thirteen years and hosted this hui for seven, has not been heard from for a month. At last the postmistress, Emma Gilhooly, brings a letter. Matt is on his way and the hui will proceed. The local policeman, Sergeant Jameson, and Detective Inspector Brett from Auckland, arrive and tell Gilhooly that Matt is in trouble. It emerges

Matt is not a doctor and never has been. He has been a freezing worker but a workplace accident has left him unable to earn. In order to maintain the illusion of wealth, he has robbed a safe, assaulted a night watchman and stolen a car (usually he hires one). Fearing this news will kill the old man, Gilhooly persuades the policemen to play along with the usual deception. Brett will pose as a doctor from Australia, about to take Matt to Sydney for a year-long course.

After a long wait for Matt and Brett to arrive, the hui proceeds with formal Māori greetings then hāngī kai. Werihe shows off Matt's graduation robes and the bundle of his detailed letters about his patients to Brett, and then reveals how he lost his sight and Matt became his light, his awatea. Matt, alone with Brett, tells his side of the story, expresses his disillusionment and challenges the patronising attitudes of Pākehā.

A fortnight later Gilhooly brings two letters which Jameson intercepts. Brett's letter reports that Matt has a nine-month prison sentence and Gilhooly insists that the truth would kill Werihe and that only Matt can ever tell him. Matt has written briefly to his father of his supposed doings in Sydney. Werihe smells a rat and finally forces the truth from Gilhooly. He is devastated and furious but does not die from it. He wants Matt's letters destroyed, but she realises Matt is a gifted a writer and could therefore turn them into books. Their closeness, as surrogate family, emerges as Werihe dictates his next letter to Matt, not revealing they know but leaving the way open for his son to tell the truth at last.

THE HAND ON THE RAIL (1965/1974)

'Ko wai koe? Ko wai tō tūpuna? Kei hea tō kāinga?'
Who are you? Who are your forbears? Where is your home?

These questions haunt both Hingawaru Karani and his estranged son Rangi, who took off from Matakaiti to Auckland ten years ago and is now wanted by police following a fatal brawl.

Married to Miriam, who sees Māori ways as past and irrelevant, Hingiwaru has tried to assimilate as they work the 'punk land', which was bought from his tribe by her father, in 'Matakait'. While their two daughters have married happily into Pākehā worlds, Rangi is perceived as a 'hori' in the city where (revealed by flashbacks, facilitated by Detective Inspector Brett's interviews) he has raged against Pākehā values and hypocrisy. At the funeral of his victim, Rangi sees his father and takes off. Hingawaru visits the young woman who has just had Rangi's baby and is giving it up for adoption. By the time she realises where Rangi has gone, he has drowned himself. Hingawaru adopts the child and takes it back to Matakaiti, where Miriam sees the whole sorry cycle starting again.

SWAN SONG (1965/1974)

Kura Smithson brings her terminally ill Māori father, James Smithson, to Tiromoana on the last leg of a whistle-stop tour of scenic treasures: a daughter's gift to her dying father. Drug-assisted flashbacks reveal that Kura's mother, Isobel, was ambitious for James to become a diplomat and then prime minister. Thanks to his war service, however, he discovered opera—and an Italian opera singer—in Rome. Back home, he left the Foreign Service and joined a road gang.

Also at Tirimoana, soprano Jenny Lucas is running away—with her mother—from her controlling husband but a persistent Dr Lucas, who is a psychiatrist, catches up with them. Jenny's concert in the hotel lounge attracts Smithson down from his deathbed, and he gets her to take him back upstairs while Kura and Dr Lucas commiserate. Smithson dies happily and operatically; Kura and Lucas drive off together; Jenny takes the bus with her mum, leaving the women who run the hotel to observe, 'There's nowt so queer as folk.'

HONGI (1968/1974)

England, June 1820: Thomas Kendall takes Hongi Hika to meet His Britannic Majesty George IV. Hongi, who impresses with his command of English, compares and contrasts the natures of chiefly versus kingly status; people versus the land; social systems and the law; work in mines and mills; and Old versus New Testament. In private Hongi and George speak of wives and how to rule effectively. The king gifts Hongi one inscribed musket, the means to buy more, and commissions a full suit of armour for him.

Meanwhile, back in the Bay of Islands chaos reigns in Hongi's absence. The taunts of children lead to the Cutler's mission station home being ransacked. The missionaries' hope that Hongi will return imbued with a gospel-inspired desire for peace is dashed by his arrival with 600 muskets, bought in Port Jackson with the gifts from King George IV. Cutler blames Kendall, who claims the guns will protect them. At breakfast, the self-invited rangatira demands to be called Mr King Hongi and counters Cutler with observations of England's penal system and the savagery of child labour. The sacrament of Christian communion versus the tikanga of cannibalism is also debated. Claiming his gods are greater than Cutler's, Hongi offers to protect them in exchange for more lead, powder and muskets. To his wife's dismay, Cutler concedes, to avert 'Utu. Pillage. Insult.'

As Hongi's rampaging musket wars ensue (offstage and in stylised forms), Cutler anguishes over his and Kendall's responsibility in the matter. Ten thousand die before Hongi is wounded and brought to the Cutlers. Mrs Cutler wants him condemned but Cutler sees him as 'the stuff of myth and legend.' The final battle of wits sees Hongi claim that the cycle of peace and war is the way of the world, while Cutler strives to save a boy prisoner from being killed and fed to Hongi. 'The iwi once was a rock,' says Hongi, 'but your words make it pebbles. When we knew no letters, we knew no sin.' He makes Cutler promise not to teach the boy to read, jokes about dining with Hine-nui-te-Pō and dies.

ZERO INN / THE CHANCE OF A LIFETIME (1970)

Maxwell Tully—a high-achieving, under-educated and overbearing advertising executive—has completed his dream house on the remote shores of Te Moana o Whaitiri (Thunder Lake), and installed his angry—for many reasons—wife Sandra and long-suffering mother-in-law Leila for Christmas. It's after midnight when three night visitors arrive seeking shelter. Max judges heavily pregnant Kuni, joint-offering Benjamin and *I Ching*-throwing Hector as no-good dropouts, and his values are cathartically confronted. Sandra is delighted at first, then challenged, while Leila's life is transformed. Max undergoes a surprising transformation . . . Or does he?

BLOOD OF THE LAMB (1980)

As market gardeners, 'Eliza' and 'Henry' plan their daughter's wedding amid much eloquent banter. It emerges that Victoria took off suddenly to Australia aged sixteen and has now returned to her Canterbury foothills home to marry her Italian–Australian fiancé. But first she wants to know why her birth certificate says her father is unknown and her mother is Gladys Mary Talbot. Henry reveals s/he was Gladys and is Victoria's mother.

'Henry' and 'Eliza' recall how they were inseparable at boarding school, and when Gladys became engaged to Rodney Kirkland (heir to Kirklees Station), Jenny agreed to be bridesmaid. Gladys looked forward to losing her virginity with Rodney in remote farmland, until he slaughtered a lamb with a broken leg, bathed in its blood and took his protesting fiancée by force. She swore off men.

The fiancé's imminent arrival adds urgency to completing the saga. Gladys and Jenny escaped to Gisborne. Rodney's attempt to reclaim his bride was thwarted by Jenny declaring she and Gladys were lovers. Gladys and Jenny ended up inland from Tologa Bay where they indeed became lovers.

Henry describes the next phase as farce. Posing as husband and wife, they were welcomed into an almost self-supporting Māori community on the foothills of the Raukumaras, where they learned market gardening and became Henry and Eliza. When Gladys/Henry's pregnancy became obvious, the kaumātua banished them but Victoria came early. Their progress south to their own market garden completes the saga. Forgiveness and reconciliation are achieved.

Four teleplays on the theme of intolerance

DAPHNE AND CHLOE (1982)

A challenge to intolerance of same sex couples. In the wake of her husband's untimely death, Edith has formed a relationship with Daphne, which activates the typing pool gossips at their workplace. But the arrival of attractive young Kevin turns Edith, and upsets Daphne. Then Susan arrives, attracting Kevin.

THE GARLICK THRUST (1982)

A challenge to racial intolerance and bad sportsmanship, set against the controversial 1981 Springbok tour. Rugby-mad Geoff Garlick (eleven) has invented a move his teacher dubs 'The Garlick Thrust', sure to win them the annual inter-school shield match on Saturday. But his siblings expect him to baby-sit his nephew while they head for Hamilton to beat up anti-tour protesters, and his dad just wants to go fishing. This leaves Geoff to take a stand for fair play.

DO NOT GO GENTLE (1982)

A challenge to repressive religion. Ex-travelling salesman Charlie is at home on his deathbed, an angry old man. His Baptist wife, Dora, tries to reconcile him to her god while keeping his mates and their whisky at bay. Both Charlie and Dora get to vent their true feelings about each other and the hand life has dealt them before a relatively compassionate minister gives safe passage to the mates.

RISE AND SHINE (1982)

A challenge to intolerance of physical dependency and controlling husbands. Eloquently cantankerous ex-barrister Sir James Tyndall, wheelchair bound by muscular dystrophy and eloquently cantankerous, is left by his despairing wife, Kitty, in the care of their neighbour, Marcia. When Marcia's daughter Bobbie turns up after escaping from her controlling husband, she bonds with James through classical music and opera. That night they offer each other the comfort and understanding each needs—and the next morning, James sorts the young husband out by way of atoning for his own bad behaviour. As the young ones leave, Kitty returns. She and Marcia find that James has died.

ACKNOWLEDGEMENTS

Sincere thanks to:

Creative New Zealand for initial funding.
The Mason family for preserving the texts of the many unpublished and sometimes never performed plays, and ensuring their safe passage to Playmarket.
Murray Lynch at Playmarket for his unflagging encouragement, advice and support, and Fergus Barrowman at Victoria University Press for agreeing to the co-publishing deal.
Belinda Robinson (née Mason) for her commitment to accuracy and generous support.
Dr Michael Ross for preserving Mason's correspondence and, with Belinda, allowing me to quote from it.
Sue Hirst at the Victoria University of Wellington Library's JC Beaglehole Room for making me welcome.
Helen Paske (the *Listener*) and the TVNZ *Kaleidoscope* team (when will we see its like again?) for the extended interview with Bruce Mason, and NZ On Screen for preserving it.
Bill Sheat for his depth of knowledge and willingness to share it.
Alister McDonald and Laurie Atkinson for their archival knowledge.
Bronwyn Taylor for permission to use Terence Taylor's *Awatea* photo.
Salesi Le'ota at Playmarket for his eagle eye.
Michael Smith for permission to use his Auckland Theatre Company photos.
The Whitireia New Zealand Publishing team:
Holly Hunter, Diana Russell and David Taine.
Liz Melchior for her support, patience and keeping me connected to the real world.

John Smythe, September 2015

INDEX